From Boyz To Men

By J. Alexander

The Boss Life Series

Book 1: From Boyz To Men

Book 2: Made Men

Book 3: Man Down

Published by: Boss Life Publications

From Boyz To Men ©2014 J. Alexander

Boss Life Publications
From Boyz To Men by J. Alexander

Cover Design:

Nu Class Publications
www.nuclasspub.com

Editing:

Brooke's Editing Service
Email: iambrooke2124@gmail.com

To Contact J. Alexander for appearances and book
signings:

Email: spaid850@gmail.com

Acknowledgements

First & Foremost, I must praise the higher above for all of my blessings. I am extremely thankful for the abilities to write what dwells in the mental cavity of my being, and through immeasurable diligence and determination, I am now out living societies claims and predictions that once a bad seed, always a bad seed. I have come such a long way out here in "CORRUPT CUNNUCK" a.k.a. "HOMICIDE HARTFORD," and feel (La-Z-Boy) comfy in my present standings as a man, father, son, friend, and life partner. That being said, WALKWITMEH as I tour guide you through the illicit life of Germ, Pintz, Yak and Angus---GOD BLESS My birth place Hartford Conneticut...2014. ~ J. ALEXANDER

Here we go again MOM. Love you more than you could ever fathom. You have helped complete yet another project and I'm overly appreciative for your typing. However that does not mean I hired someone else...no one knows my pen as you do mom. You are truly the umbrella in my rainstorm.

POPS, you are still my dude, no matter why, or what separates us! Until we reunite, ONE-UP!

Ms. Deanna Howard, big-sis, thanks for being a wonderful and understanding sibling over the years and also a great supporter of what I've become---a Boy To A Man. Love you Dee!

My 1st. born...Javon "Young $paid" Gray, I hold so much love and admiration towards you. I find myself looking up to you in many ways. You've made me very proud by completing high school, also by not trailing my ill-mannered *footsteps in to the drug-game; instead, you use your intelligence, wit, upbringing, and personal experiences as a voice through your muzik. Always keep it 100 with yourself...you are destined for stardom. Continue to do it "STRICTLY FOR YOUR DOUBTERS." We're going to the to kik ONE-UP!*

Awe...my rarest jewel, Secret Shanelle Gray; you have just blossomed into a 12-year-old diva. You hold a sacred place in my heart and the key has been lost in time and space; yes, I direct this towards my absence from your life. FORGIVE DADDY FOR ABANDONING YOU POOH! YOU ARE FOREVER GOING TO BE DADDY'S LILTTE GIRL! Gimme kissey...stanka butt-butt, lol.

Last but not least, my best friend, soul mate, fiancée, and lover; words cannot explain what I feel for you. 20-years Ma' 20-years..., There's no doubt in this crazy mind that there is a woman who can compare to you and I say this wholeheartedly, Mikia L. Eady! I am definitely still DRUNK-IN-LOVE even after all these years together and apart! Last stop...the ALTER! LOVE U BABE...

FRIENDS: To my brutha Swerve (Jersy860);Avenue Ave; Ahmed Gibson; Carti & Jay (mix-tape stand); Charlie-Boy; Dime(Bedrock); my brutha; Fred Sanchez; Corey Jahmal; Djuan Davis; Jinkx (Bridgeport); Marlon Lawrence; Meech80/Miz (Rochester, Ny.); Nestodagreat (N.H.); Obama(Flint); Boogie; Catman; Popeye; Trell; Rosey; Roger: My Guy Spike; Taz; Tim Robertson (thanks homey); Ty Hightower & Lil-Bit; Brandnew (Uptown/bridge); Andre Hudson (POTZ); Toby(forty-deuce); Chubb; Aj-Williamsbey; Tee-Tee & Summer; Villain (Yammy); Antony (Rig Lyfe); Natasha McIntosh; Tiff & Trell; RaeBae Roye; Ivette Vazquez; Mila Carrion; Kisha Lee & G-Money(Va.); Tammy Capri(you've done such

AWESOME design work); Kendra Mrshoney Littleton; Melissa BlackWidow Colon; Tina Mathis & Malcolm; Judy Cruz; Carlos Gray; Prina & Charlene Smith; Kashan Klien(Mi.); Jamale Nicholson(Oh.); Stackz(Pa.); Seanan Wooten; DJ QT; Jeannette Ransom-Frazier; JeaNida Luckie-Weatherall; Jeanette Lyons; Jocelyn Boffman Green; Authoress IamCrystal Alexis; Doris Barner; Lisa Tyrrell Perry-Amos; Maria Ja'Nae Vasquez; Felisha Bradshaw; Latorria Jetson; Rocky Chris Rose; Sheri Harrigan; Lashunda GaPeach Cato; Barbara Allen Labry; Kisha Green; Andrea Wheeler; Alexis Nicole; Nikia Kiki Harry; Casey Smith; Ten Smith; T. Styles; June Miller: Eyone Williams; Jason Poole; Al-Saadiq Banks; JM Benjamin: Shellz Prettypersuasion G; Author G-Five; Iam Obsession; Papaya: Lisa Muhammad; LaTanya Garry; Judy Richburg: Racquel Williams, Rayshonda King; Seana Wooten; Theresa Hodge; Tee Tee Mccune; Chocolatecream Wilson; Samantha Naturalista Pettiway; Tiffany Declouette; Toni D Futrell; Toni Doe; Yas Min; Jessica Ismile Mallett; Yahya Yehia; Amard Williams Omar; Christina Williams; Sha Cole; Andrea Ramsey; JoLicia Dewey; Nicole Johnson & Melvin Brandon; Glenda Boyd; Nikki Robinson; Kristie Fluker; Lashawn Green; Ellissa Gabrielle Keisha Medina; Marguerite Dyer-Hunt; Pamela Rhone; Shell B Brew; Kitty Katz; Lisa French; Poetic Jewelz; Recognize Ringo; Katavious Ellis; George Sherman; Latasha Hill; Calandra Nosugarcoating Shit; Marge Gary; Trinity DeKane; Diallo Skyfall Jackson; Damenia Uvonda; Quilla Thomas; Lashaeera Lee; Stephanie Wiley; Quintin Djqt Tarantino; Antinea J. Maye; Marina LadyVendetta Smith;

FAMILY: To all of my in-laws, Mary Anderson-Cooper; Reese Cooper; Cam Cooper; Renee & Eric Edmunds; Jamal & Janeeta; Deneen; Shana; Charmaine; Alexis; Auntie Viola; Auntie Vanessa & Curtis; Uncle Jr.; Pretty; Melquan, Malaysia; Charles & Michael Hite; Rick Anderson; Tyus & Aaliyah; Bunny; Bernett Anderson;

Shaun; Terry & Keisha; Debra & Bridgette Fleming; Kea Kai, Quan Ware & Baby Ava; Parnell; Dominique TheCashQueen; Antwan Smith; Meechie; Tyshaun Taylor; Pinky; Uncle Patrick, Latoya & Aaliyah Ledbetter and my second-son Tyrell "Boo" Hightower; Dum; Obama(Mi.); Christina Marie & ShootaBoy; Chris; Yolonda; Kawanna & CoCo Flow; Star; Wes; Marlon; Snail; Wiggz; Young Chris, Lou & KiKi

BOSSLIFE/MDC-FAMILY: Young $paid; Ty-Nitty "TheProducer;Tyrone "TyStylles"Davis; Quan "Riza"Ware; Marlon God's-Gift; Apollo; LateNightSnacks; Badnews Greedy-Gang; Mook; Jt Tino; Cool Patterson;

AUTHORS/PUBLISHERS: G-Street Chronicles; Nikki Urban/Diamonstonproductins; New Era Books; Cole Hart; Shiana Lesa Jones; Roy Glenn; My Favorite *Author Al-Saadiq Banks; Kenya Whiter-Black; Lisa Muhammad; Felisha Bradshaw(Grapevine Mag); Siren (for a great review); Papaya Sistah's On Lit (for a great review); Real Queenb Divas; NeNe Capri;*

This is to Mz-Robinson the greatest PUBLISHER; my inspiration. You have been such a big deal on several of my projects and having been my personal secretary (lol) when I needed some enlightening and guidance when I felt I was stuck in traffic. You continue to provide me with a platform where I now feel comfortable and confident within my writing. So without further ordo, THANKS UH BILLI, Mz-Robinson.

In final thoughts, walkwitmeh...turn the lights off and welcome to the BOSS LIFE SERIES, FROM BOYZ TO MEN... ~J. ALEXANDER~

From Boyz To Men

Book 1 of The Boss Life Series

By J. Alexander

Chapter 1

Fresh off the Porch

As the gritty life in Corrupt Cunnuck grew deadlier, so did its children. Not quite the murder Capital by way of statistics, but for a major city and being the Constitution State, Hartford, Connecticut, was becoming a giant morgue. The young had no ambition and no drive. It was solely about money and ways to get it; the easy way, ski masks or the hand-to-hand way, which brings us to today, January 15th, 2005.

$$\$\$\$\$\$$

The ninety-degree weather in the city was by far scorching. There was no breeze out what-so-ever, unless a speeding car flew by, which only helped to flare young Germ's ill-mannered temper. In just a wife-beater, UConn fitted hat and fatigue shorts, Germ patrolled the block in a pair of wheat timbs. He had been on the pavement since six o'clock this morning only to make sixty dollars thus far, and it was now ten thirty in the morning.

"Yo, I got the next two sales, too!" Germ playfully grilled his little cousins, Yak and Pintz.

They hit the pavement two to three hours after Germ, so in Germ's book all was due in his favor.

"Man...you always trying to bo guard shit, Germ. We trying to eat, too!" Yak spat, thirstily craving a piece of the action.

"Listen, little nigga, this my set-up, and I've been posted up since dawn so chill...you gonna make some fetti," Germ assured his little cousin from Florida.

Yak was a shorty, for real. He stood 5'6, brown skinned, and rocked a mouth full of gold. Being fourteen years old, he hoped to grow a few more inches to surpass his little man complex, but he was still a go-getter by all means.

Yak and Pintz had been in Connecticut for three years now, living with Germ and his pops, Uncle Marv, as everyone called him. Yak and Pintz were brothers, and Marv's nephews, from his sister, Bianca. After Bianca's tragic death through a vicious rape and strangulation case, Marv accepted his nephews with open arms, as any good uncle should.

"Fall back, Yak, the first is tomorrow, so you already know what it's hittin' for." Pintz reassured.

Just as Pintz finished preaching, they all noticed dope fiend, Twan, creeping out of the alleyway where they always kept their packs, well at least, where the brothers did. Germ was hood. He kept his eight ball cut into dime-rocks cuffed in the crevices of his ass.

Twan was inconspicuously easing his ragged body down Babcock Street. He was twenty-five-years young and already turned out on crack-rocks for two years now. Out of habit, Twan always wore a dingy white t-shirt, torn dingy khakis and a mixed– matched Nike Cortez'. Being a block runner gave him certain details and whereabouts of the hustlers' stash spots throughout the entire strip. Repeatedly, Twan would stakeout a hustler's stash after bringing a custee through, only to double back and take all he could find, but today he chose the wrong ones to fuck with. From a short distance, Twan started to pick up his pace.

Yak returned from the alleyway with an empty brown bag in his grasp and yelled, "Catch dat nigga! He got my work!"

Germ shook his head in amusement as Pintz and Yak took chase.

"I told your little ass to stay on deck...catch him yo' self," he said, full of laughter as he leaned up against a dusty Chevy Impala.

"I'm gonna do more than catch him, cuzzo," Yak replied in pursuit.

Twan had not lost it one bit, he was an All-American track-star back in high school, only to get strung out on society's poison while dealing with some trick broad he intended on marrying. However, phat-ass Pam, Twan's girl, had graduated from woollies to that glass dick right out of high school and brought Twan right along with her.

"Catch that nigga, Pintz, that's my whole pack," Yak screamed in stride, as his older brother flew past him.

Yak had not lied when complaining about his work. He had just copped a shaver (3.5 grams of crack) from Big-Meat before hitting the block, so it was imperative that they retrieve Yak's drugs, or he would be looking for a front, should Twan elude them. Twan appeared to be pulling away as he bent the corner of a blue house along Babcock Street.

"Damn!" Yak cursed, feeling they'd never catch him now.

Using the back yards to meet up with his homies, Angus happened to be hopping the fence into a yard and saw Twan bailing like he'd just killed someone, so out of instinct, he flipped him in passing.

"Fuck you running so fast for, Twan? And what's dat in your hands?" He questioned, after noticing a brown bag in his grasp similar to the ones they used to hide their work in before stuffing them into their stash spot.

Out of breath, Twan replied, "Nothing man, I ain't do nothing."

4

"Nah, mufucka, you think you slick. You done hit some of my shit wit' your fiend ass!" He spat and gave Twan a hard kick to the face and then, went for his newest toy.

By this time, Pintz and Yak had bent and was in awe, seeing that Twan was face down on the pavement being pistol-whipped by Angus, Germ's right-hand.

"Shoot dat nigga, A', he got my pack," Yak ordered, before joining the brutal assault by stomping Twan in the mid-section.

Yak noticed the plastic bag, containing his dimes, roll out of Twan's hand during the rag session. He quickly bent down and grabbed the bag off the ground and then kicked Twan repeatedly in the mouth, knocking out his teeth. They fell to the ground like miniature, broken and discolored mints. Angus was feeling antsy. There was an itch he felt that needed to be scratched. Ever since buying his new .22 Dillinger, he'd been dying to let some rounds off. Without any further thought, he aimed the ratchet at Twan's temple, ready to pull the trigger, when unexpectedly, Germ appeared, still laughing.

"Y'all little nigga's, fall back," he said.

He noticed the hot metal in Angus' grasp and could see the desire to kill in his eyes. To Germ, the entire situation had an eerie vibe to it, and naturally, he felt he had to do something before it was too late. Angus was known for being hotheaded and doing what Germ considered dumb shit.

"You too, Angus, let him ride this one out, it ain't dat serious, bruh." Germ said, smoothly.

He knew murdering Twan would have the block hotter than fish grease, and the last thing they needed was unwanted attention from Hartford's finest.

"Fuck this nigga, Germ. Dude always doing some   fuck-boy

shit, but yet, we're always fucking looking out for him." Yak said, angry.

He was right, but Germ felt to kill Twan for fifteen rocks was not only senseless, it was heartless.

"I said...chill!" Germ ordered.

For a brief moment, everyone halted, hearing Germ's commanding voice roar in the diminutive area. There was silence between them until they were interrupted by a woman's voice.

"Y'all get out my damn yard with that foolishness! I'm calling the police," Ms. Mary warned from out of her kitchen window. "Get out now you little drug dealing pieces of shi-"

Her words were silenced by the sound of what sounded like a fire cracker echoing. On the side of the building, blood oozed rapidly from the small hole in Twan's forehead. Angus had stolen the twenty-five year old man's life for fifteen measly dime rocks that wasn't even his. Angus' cold heart was bleeding profusely, which could only worsen by the minute. You see, Angus had grown up very deprived, in a dilapidated single parent home. His pops had died earlier on in his life due to being killed during a mugging. His mom was a prostitute and high strung on dope. To this day, he had never known what it was like to sit down and pray amongst family at dinnertime, had never known the feeling of opening up Christmas gifts on the 25th of December, or what it was like dress up for church on Easter Sunday and hunt eggs. For Angus, it was actually Hell-On-Earth; another boy trapped in the hood, living the street life.

Fearful of being pointed out in a police lineup for the murder of Twan, the four youngins fled the scene hastily. As Angus was kicking up dirt, he swore he would double back and put a few gold sleeping pills in the entirety of Ms. Mary's head if he was identified as the shooter.

$$$$$

The next morning, the four youngstas were on their way to Pope Park to shoot some hoops when they noticed the block was shut down. As they made their way through the yellow-taped area, the crowd of onlookers gawked at them menacingly but didn't dare to speak out. They were all too familiar with how things worked in the hood, and they knew that the best way to keep themselves from ending up like Twan was to stay quiet. Just another unsolved murder, due to the shiesty capitol's menacing street-life and drug trade.

Chapter 2

Young Lust

While Germ and the boys were shooting hoops at the court far up on the hill of the park, a group of young teens pulled into the parking lot, planning to chill and smoke a little weed. From young to old, people came in droves with their own intentions of having a good time. Although it was only eight in the morning, there were several pedestrians consuming the large park, which was separated by a two-way street. The larger of the two held a Crawfish pond, a play area for young kids and a large swimming pool. On the smaller, hilly side is where the basketball courts were and where all the illegal, ill-mannered activity went down, which is where the fellas were currently doing them.

Today Asia, Avonne, and Courtnee rode shotgun with Melodie. Melodie was well-off; being in the upper-middle class living range, or stigma society labeled and separated all races throughout America by. Melodie was of the Indian decent, 5'6", petite, with firm perky breasts. She held a small waist and tight abs but had an ass that attracted men from miles away. Melodie's hair was jet-black and when not in a French bun, she let it cascade down to her apple bottom. Melodie's parents owned a small chain of 7-Eleven's, where she worked part-time, but her future lay in the field of medicine. She wanted to become a Gynecologist.

"I done told you, Courtnee, not to light the weed in the car," Melodie said, smelling the sulfur smell from the striking match.

She had forgotten her lighter back at home.

From Boyz To Men

"My dad is gonna smell dat shit!"

"Shut up, bitch, you always crying. Yo'...damn...daddy ain't gonna smell shit! Crack open one of them air fresheners and this nice ass glass roof!" Courtnee said, unconcerned for her friend's lively-hood.

Reluctantly, Melodie retracted the translucent top on her dad's new Lincoln MKT, then accepted the finger like blunt and began inhaling deeply. Regardless of what she aspired to be in life, she always enjoyed a nice blunt with the girls.

Courtnee and Avonne were sisters; only a year apart. Courtnee was also the head of their little clique. At seventeen, she had grown nicely into her 34DD bra. Surprisingly, her waist was a 24, which helped to anchor the 32" bubble she often squeezed into a size-too-small pair of jeans. Being a red-bone made all the hood fellas lust after her like an antidote to a disease.

"Damn, bitch, all that complaining, I see your ass sucking on that green dick like a pro!"

With that, the car erupted in laughter. Goodie-two-shoes maybe, but ghetto fabulous, most definitely, which is why they kept Melodie's ass around.

"And you know it, bitch," Melodie shot back after blowing a ring of smoke into the air.

"Aye...there's Germ and his two cousins, y'all," Asia said, noticing his hood-swag anywhere.

"Yeah, that's his fine-ass, but I've got that on lock, so your best bet is to jump on one of his cousins or dat badass, Angus!" Mel said, claiming her dude.

Although she and Germ had been off and on for six months, she still felt they were an item, and was not about to let one of her

J. Alexander

girls get the chance to sample the dick.

"That's alright, cause Angus gon' be dat nigga someday, now pass the weed girl…" Asia replied in a sassy manner.

On many late nights and early mornings, Angus would fuck the dear life out of Asia's youthful goodies. She was 5'8", 130 lbs., thick, with average hood-chick looks. She once had many goals but living in Hartford's South End depleted all of her prior ambitions to get out of the hood. Now a full blossomed teenager, her dark skin and 32C, 22-28' frame catered to all of the upcoming dealers throughout Frog Hollow (south side of Hartford). Promiscuous was an understatement when labeling Asia.

"Girl…you keep on fooling with that Angus, you gonna get caught up in his grimy bullshit," Melodie warned. "Hmmph!"

Melodie backed the MKT into an empty space, and the four girls hopped out. Avonne now had the blunt, pulling on it as if it would be her last toke. She noticed Yak was staring and blushed. He had been trying to holler at her for weeks now, but she knew he was a male-whore and did not want to be bothered. She returned his lustful smirk with a roll of her eyes.

"Bitch, you know you feeling Yak!" Courtnee said, twisting her mouth up, "with his fine self."

"Hey, Pintz…" Avonne said seductively, being funny in reply to Courtnee's slick remark about Yak being fine.

"Alright now, don't get it twisted, hoe! You stick to the little nuts, and I'll juggle the big ones, boo!"

With that, Courtnee and Asia shared a high-five. Pintz was Courtnee's catch and would fuck her little sister up in a minute with the rumor of their infidelity.

From Boyz To Men

"What it do, lil' mama?" Pintz answered, wiping some sweat off his face.

They had been playing a two-on-two since arriving at the court.

"You, but my sister would kill me if I put this kitty on you!" Avonne smiled seductively, hoping to agitate Courtnee some.

"Got dat right, bitch," Courtnee cut in quickly. "So, cut your bullshit out fo' you catch a bad one."

"Ah hush, girl. Don't nobody want your sloppy seconds."

"Hmmph!"

The two evil eyed one another before Pintz broke up their little sibling rivalry.

"What's dat y'all totin' on?" Pintz asked, seeing the still white cloud hovering over Avonne's head.

"Some Reggie Miller, boy!" Avonne answered.

"Reggie Miller?" Pintz questioned.

It was obvious that he wasn't on their up north slang, and he began to feel some type of way as the girls took turns looking at each other and then him.

"Pintz, you so crazy, regular weed, you know we don't smoke those woollies you be on, fool! And nah…you can't hit this blunt with those coke-lips," Avonne made clear, her free hand glued to the curve of her hip.

Before relocating to Hartford, in Florida, they smoked weed laced with coke, but as long as a glass stem wasn't involved, they felt it was hood. So naturally, the habit stuck with him over the

1

years.

"Don't worry yourself, ma', I've got plenty woollies, ya heard?" Pintz assured her, and then chucked the ball to Germ to continue their early morning basketball game.

Together, Melodie, Asia, Avonne, and Courtnee watched and enjoyed the show. Each one routing for their young loves whenever they had the ball or was on the defensive, which made the fellas go all out. The hour had struck noon. The humidity outright bullied what slight comfort the human body previously endured. Except for Melodie, all of the girls' hair began to lose its hold, sticking to their faces. As did their tight t-shirts, from their own broken sweat, which made it difficult to hide the erectness of their tender nipples that now stuck out like knobs on a cabinet door.

"Girl, you better cover those little knobbies up!" Courtnee said, staring at Asia's breasts.

In reply, Asia said, "Germ wasn't saying that last night when he was nibbling on 'em."

Everyone laughed, including Germ. He wouldn't mind digging her young ass out, but he knew Mel would stomp a mud-hole in her, and then him. She was extremely overly protective when it came to him.

"Yeah, cover my titties up fo' I smack fiyah out you!" Angus barked, although his dick was on swole at the moment.

Just as Angus went to cross Pintz over, he heard some loud music getting closer by the second. Off instinct, he stopped and then, surveyed the area to see where the thunderous boom was coming from. As the thunderous boom unveiled its producer, a 1999 Escalade on twenty-two's swerved into an empty space taking up two spots. Knowing exactly who was behind the dark windows, Angus quickly stepped off. He did not want to be caught slipping.

See on the low, Angus stayed in some shiesty shit. Either fucking some OG's broad, stealing cars, or climbing through a dope boy's window and robbing them blind, is what provoked him to carry a strap at all times.

As M.O.P's 'Ante Up' blared loudly out of the amplified system, OG, T-Kill and his two flunkies hopped out of the truck. T-Kill was the neighborhood bully. He had been in and out of juvenile detention until he finally made it to Big Cheshire, a level-5 state correctional facility for Connecticut's most hardened criminals, murderers, and drug dealers. There he bulked up his scrawny physique into a picture-perfect, 182 lb, 6 foot brawler; a real menace to society.

T-Kill's claim to fame was to stalk and prey on the weak and take from the rich. The entire hood dreaded the likes of him. However, you had your up and comings, who could care less about him. Their motto was *'he bleed just like us'*. And right now, a few hearts were about to stand the test of this particular motto.

Looking around, T-Kill said, "What's good, ladies, fellas?"

Then he probed the crowd, searching for any sign of weakness.

"What's good?" Germ jumped out there, still bouncing the ball.

He was never pressed for some rec'.

"Now come on, Germ, that's no way to greet a fellow homey, is it?" he tried to make the situation seem light, just as he did all his other vic's before his devious ways took over.

"You right, old-head, so I suggest you give us that same

1

respect," Germ frowned and then looked around at his conglomerate to make sure T-Kill understood he was serious about his team.

T-Kill smiled, admiring Germ's young heart. Not many in the hood had the gall to oppose him. Even still, he had the mind to punish him where he stood, but he was in a good mood today. That is until he noticed Angus pop up from the back of the crowd. His demeanor quickly transitioned from sugar to shit.

As Germ stared into Pintz's eyes, his look said there was about to be some major trouble. Just three days before Angus murked Twan, he went along on a home invasion with Angus, which just so happened to be T-Kill's Grandma's house. Grandma Killinger lived all alone on Hungerford St., where T-Kill safely stored all of his cash, guns and work, which was only two houses down from Asia's. On many late nights, while peeking out of her window, she noticed T-Kill coming and going with a small bag in tow, which of course she assumed to be drugs and money.

She knew he did a little something in the hood, so she put her boo-thang, Angus, onto him, hoping for the perfect jooks. After thoughtful planning, Pintz and Angus climbed through the bathroom window of his Grandma's crib. Through a swift search of the kitchen, they stumbled upon T-Kill's stash in an old grey teakettle that sat on a wicker stand. Just as Pintz made it through the window, a shadow appeared out of the darkness holding a large skillet.

"Get out of my house, you thief," she warned, swinging the skillet with all her might, grazing Angus over the eye.

It was just enough to make him stumble. Unbalanced and somewhat coherent, he gun-butted the elderly woman until she lay unconscious.

"Come on, let's go!" he said to Pintz and then dove head first

1

through the window.

Pintz was now an accomplice to a possible homicide, all for two-ounces and $900.73 cash. The robbery wasn't much, but enough for someone to get on T-Kill's shit list. Once safely away from the scene, they split the purse down the middle and kept their caper a secret; that is up until now.

Fearing she would also catch hell behind T-Kill's tyrant ways, Asia eased her box cutter out of her bra. She knew, without a doubt, that living in close proximity to T-Kill and the fact that she was fucking with Angus, he would most definitely feel she played a role in the heist.

"There...go...that...lil'...nigga...right...right...th...th...thhe ...there..," Zoe, one of T-Kill's flunkies stuttered, as Angus walked up.

Since he was able to utter his first words, Zoe developed a speech impediment where he now found it difficult to get out a complete sentence without stuttering.

Even though T-Kill and Angus weren't standing toe-to-toe, their eyes were locked and doing a death dance. Envisioning his Granny's head bandaged up, T-Kill's chest muscles began heaving in and out, symbolizing that his tolerance and temper were rising.

"Lil' Gus, what's the word?" T-Kill questioned, a little too calmly for not only Angus' taste, but Germ's as well.

By now, Angus was locked and loaded. Before he made his way back towards the crowd, he had taken the 7-shot Dillinger off safety, which was cuffed in the lining of his shorts, concealed by his white tee.

"What's good, T-Kill," he nodded once, letting the name roll

1

J. Alexander

off his tongue sarcastically.

"I think we need to politic a bit, lil' homey," T-Kill gritted his teeth, his stare deadly.

Asia was not the biggest chick, but she was down for her crown and would carve a nigga or hoe up if they violated her camp. Nevertheless, for Angus, Asia would lie, steal, set-up, even murder a nigga, if given the opportunity. She was the true definition of a Bonnie to her Clyde.

The scene was set. The script had been written, however, this debuting film had not yet been rated. Many rumors surfaced about the midnight invasion at T-Kill's house, also the danger his Granny was facing at the time, so naturally, the hood knew the body count in Homicide Hartford was about to go up.

When T-Kill gestured that he and Angus had some personal B.I. to discuss, Germ realized then, that more than likely, Angus was the one behind the caper. What he had not known up until this point was that his own flesh and blood was also a culprit in the midnight jook. However, he was not about to let no one step to his homey. He was willing to die for Angus, and his two cousins, should the Grim Reaper call for him.

1

Chapter 3

Vengeful Karma

Indiscreetly, the crowd began to lessen. They were dispersing in fear that they would become a statistic and a victim of T-Kill's menacing ways. They knew T-Kill's reasons were undoubtedly valid, as far as his Granny, but he stayed on some bullshit, so it was just his Karma that had crept through his kitchen window that dreadful night. Only his Granny had gotten caught up in the mix of his treachery.

Germ knew how T-Kill rolled. He knew the old head kept a strap on him 24/7, but knowing his homey like a good book, Angus was also holding some heat. Germ was also glad all of the extra spectators had dispersed before shit got cooking. He was not a fan of audiences or witnesses.

"What beef you got with my peeps?" Germ asked, with a grimace.

"Whatever it is, it ain't got nothin' to do with you, youngin. But, if you don't bail now, it will!" T-Kill spat sternly, returning Germ's mug.

"You know it ain't fun, if your homey can't have none!" Germ countered, balling his fists up.

It was do or die with them. He also noticed Yak and Pintz were in similar stances, ready to get shit popping.

Tired of T-Kill's stunts, Courtnee and Avonne grabbed two empty Corona bottles and used the ground to brake them at the tips. Feeling left out, Melodie pulled out her box cutter that she kept on her for purposes such as this. Working at 7-Eleven gave her endless access to the sharp blades. T-Kill noticed the situation wasn't going the way he hoped; where it would be him, one gun and his two flunkies, Zoe and Luda, verses Angus. However, the odds grew out of nowhere, seeing that they had four chicks and four young niggas ready to die. It wasn't defeat, just the opposite, another day to plan and conquer. Only this time, his list was upgraded to eight people.

"Yo, you got dat, Angus – Germ! But this shit is far from over!" he promised, "That's on Granny!"

Zoe and Luda followed T-Kill back to the Escalade, watching their backs as they walked off. Once in the car, T-Kill felt some type of way. Never had he backed down to anyone let alone a bunch of teens.

"Yo, Gus, what's with that bullshit, homey?" Germ questioned.

He wanted some answers and now.

"You put family in danger, my dude."

"Yeah, Gus," Yak added. "You got beef with T-Kill? Cause dude too old to be pulling up on us on some other shit."

Stuck in a world of silence, Pintz was flanking Angus. Looking nervous, however, Germ was no dummy. He could see that his cousin assisted Angus in the home invasion. Pintz was family, so he could not be mad. His point was they could have at least been put on deck to the bullshit. There was nothing like going to war for unknown reason and possibly losing your life in the process.

"Man, you already know what it's hittin' for, Germ. Fuck dat lame ass nigga. He thought he was untouchable. He ain't the only cat in the hood dat know how to rob!" Angus returned excitedly.

The situation had not fazed him in the least. Since

17

conception, he had been a rumbler in his mother's womb, so this little episode with T-Kill was going down as just another test of heart and brawn.

Inside the Escalade, T-Kill was 38-hot. Unable to withstand the embarrassment of walking away from the eight youths without setting it off, as he bent a sharp left out of the parking lot, he took aim at the group, his .9mm now harmonizing a deadly concerto of whizzing hot ones.

BBlow...BBlow...BBlow...

The acoustic roar of the .9mm discharging was far louder than the firecracker pop of Angus' low caliber deuce-deuce, but it did not stop him from dumping back at the Escalade. Everyone in harm's way broke for cover in fear of that stray bullet with no name on it. The girls were screaming, only because it is what all women did in such situations. Germ, Yak and Pintz hit the pavement as the array of shells whizzed by their domes like heat seeking missiles at designated targets in the midst of a worldly war.

Even as the .22 long shells were making pinholes throughout the SUV, Zoe continued to bark out of the window, "Ye...ye...yeah mufuc – mufuckas! Ta...tak...take dat!"

"I'm gonna kill that little nigga," T-Kill boasted, as he sped away erratically, obviously nerved that his SUV was being used as target practice.

Under his breath, he said, "Somebody's got to die!"

The smoke cleared, and the danger was no more. However, they could hear the HPD's sirens blaring in the distance.

"Yo, let's get it!" Germ yelled to everyone, he wasn't trying to be the one riding in the back of H.P.D.'s pissy paddy wagon today.

Melodie, and her crew, jumped into her dad's MKT and were about to bail, but as she threw the truck into drive, a sense of concern washed over her.

Without further thought, Mel said, "Germ…hurry up, y'all get in!"

Germ, Yak, Pintz and Angus wasted no time hopping inside the SUV, cramming their sweaty bodies in the 7-passenger vehicle like sardines and rode off. After dodging the deadly rain shower, a little convo and two blunts, Melodie dropped them off on Babcock St., and then went about their B.I.

"Y'all be safe!" Asia yelled.

She was tempted to rock with Angus and his clique, but she chose to stay with her girls.

"Yo, Gus, from now on kid, put a nigga on deck whenever you pull some bullshit, ya heard? We need to know when you're out here pulling heist, so we can be on point, too. That wasn't hood back there. One of us could've gotten murked, feel me? Now, let's get high."

The two gave each other a one up (dap), and then went down in Germ's basement to get lifted.

Chapter 4

Back Then

A week later, things were back to normal for Germ and his team. The heat had died down, so it was safe to resurface and to chase that paper. It was actually safe two days prior, seeing as the homicide on Babcock Street involved a crack head. Twan's life was non-void to the community, the police and obviously, Angus. Angus swallowed his life in one quick gulp. It was just that easy to be erased from America's census status. He damn sure would not be on 2005's; being the ill shit he was involved in!

The mid-afternoon air was unforgiving. It was as if a heating blanket covered the skies, creating a crematory effect over the entire city. Even at this hour, the invisible heat was hitting hard causing the hustler's to come out their white tees. From young to old, they swarmed the blocks in wife-beaters, uptowns (AF-1's), doo rags, and fitted caps. You also had those who sported all-black flavs (shades) to beat the Indian-summer weather.

Germ and his clique had been out since the break of dawn, trying to catch the last bit of Government Assistance and EBT money they could. It was nothing to cash in on a hundred or two each worth of EBT money on the 1st through the 3rd. Unfortunately, Germ and his two cousins had to hide their ties to the hood from Uncle Marv, for Angus it was not even a thought. He would pass his off to his mom to help stock up their cupboards or use them in the Bodegas around the hood. With him, it was whatever!

Germ and his cousins also used the free food card at local Bodegas. Blunts, hoagies, snacks and of course waters, were re-cooped for the trade of crack they had given to the   neighborhood crack heads.

"Got-damn…it's hot as shit… out here!" Yak said, coming out of the alley.

He'd just caught a two for eighteen lick.

Surprisingly, with the heat at a smoldering height, money was still coming through the block non-stop. It was a new block Germ started up, so in time, he hoped to make it even better than the 'Law' (Lawrence Street) or the 'Zone' (Zion Street), which were two of the South End's most booming blocks.

"Nigga, you ain't been out them gator swamps dat long for this Cunnuck heat to be fucking with you," Germ teased.

"Yeah, nigga, we used to this lil' bruh, man up." Pintz helped with the antagonizing and a few jabs to Yak's undeveloped chest, which soon became a sparring match between the two brothers.

"Y'all nigga's always goofing off, chill dat shit out fo' we get caught slipping by the deeze's."

"Fuck you two nigga's. Florida, Connecticut, it all seems the same right about now, so fuck what y'all talking 'bout!" Yak said, walking off in search of some more sales.

He couldn't care less about what they were on, right now his mind was on money

"And pull-up those pants too, lil'-nuts!" Angus added.

Although they all let their pants sag on their asses, Yak went a step further. His shit stayed damn near under his ass cheeks.

Yak paid them no mind and kept it moving. He was thirsty and had bout two dollars and some change left on his EBT card, so he headed to the Bodega down on the Law. He was in his own little world, bopping to a Rick Ross tune in his head, and he bumped into some older cat, knocking his 40-ounce from his grip right out in front of the store.

"Damn lil' nigga...watch where the fuck you going next time!" LateNiteSnackz barked.

LateNiteSnackz was from the Law. He was twenty-eight; copper toned and kept his hair in a low Caesar full of waves. Fresh home out the Feds, he played the block heavy, trying to stack his paper back up. Other than pursuing a rapping career, word had it he was into murking nigga's for that scrilla. If the count is proper, he'd take out his own momma.

"My bad, OG!" Yak quickly apologized, hoping it would halt any trouble, being he was alone. "Damn!" he mumbled, thinking why he ran off by himself. *"Fuck!"*

"Nah, lil' nigga, forty on you!" LateNiteSnackz spat.

He knew Yak could not legally cop him another bottle, but that did not matter to him. The owner of this particular store would sell him a whole case if that scrilla was intact. Yak was grateful that LateNiteSnackz had not wild out on him, so he went inside to purchase him another 40-ounce. He first ordered a half of ham and cheese on a grinder roll, then headed to the icebox.

"Damn, what kind of beer was dude sippin'?"

Being slick, he grabbed the cheapest thing on the shelf (Black Label 11-11) and headed back to the counter. From behind the counter, the storeowner eyed Yak for a brief moment, then down the two aisles of his store for any unwanted eyes. The coast appeared to be clear, so he stuffed the 40-ounce in a brown paperbag and swiped the EBT card Yak laid on the counter. However, the total of Yak's purchases exceeded the balance on the card.

"You're short $2.30 my man," Money Ross, the owner said.

J. Alexander

"I could've told you that old-head. Here, gimme my change, too!" Yak told him, putting a crumbled up five-dollar bill on the glass top.

Money Ross laughed, "That's the problem with you young bucks, y'all forgot who paved the way for y'all to even be out here getting money! It's OG's like me that made it easy for y'all to be out here hustling." Money Ross just shook his head at the youngster.

He was right! Back in the day, all Lil' Nigga's coming up on the block, walking to and from school, also the store, got rolled on. They called it a *'Rag Session',* and it went for whomever. There were no exceptions whatsoever. God forbid a shorty happened to wear a hoodie this particular day, because he'd find himself in some deep shit with it over his head, strings pulled extra tight with no way out. On the ground, doubled over in pain, is normally where they'd end up. Shirt torn, money gone and maybe a busted lip, but they were good lessons taught, and hood manners learned. Hopefully those who planned to stick to the pavement and hug the block for that scrilla would be well-refined in all aspects the hood required, if not, they would become one of three things. One: on drugs, two: in jail or three: dead. However, snitching rode along the lines of three, so it never made its own quo status in hood-life.

Money Ross shook his head at Yak's young ignorance. He handed him his sandwich, 40-ounce and change, then said, "Aye shorty, keep your eyes peeled next time. The boy, LateNiteSnackz, ain't someone to fool wit'."

"I got this, old-head, you just keep yo eyes peeled for them under covers looking to bust ya ass for selling loosies and alcohol to minors, chump," Yak responded, with arrogance, and then broke out.

Chapter 5

Consequences

Outside, LateNiteSnackz was kicking it with his homey's Dex, Blaze, Slim and Dro when Yak stepped up with the brown bag containing the new bottle of beer.

"Here you go," he said, holding the bag out for Snackz to grab.

LateNiteSnackz snatched the bag out of Yak's grasp nearly dropping it, which would've turned matters worse. Without peeping the brand, LateNiteSnackz twisted the cap and took a mean swig, only to spit the suds straight out and into Yak's face. For Yak, the only good thing about being sprayed with the beer was that it was ice-cold – because it cooled him off.

"Oh shit," Yak mumbled.

Snackz wasted no time pulling the 40-ounce out of the bag and noticed that it wasn't his favorite kind, it was a Green-Monsta – (Private Stock).

Displaying a mean mug, LateNiteSnackz said, "Nigga...you really bought me this cheap-ass shit?"

Seeing the older cats were deep, Yak began to get nervous. Nevertheless, he wasn't buying any more suds, that was for sure. He definitely wasn't going out like that, his pockets weren't right.

"You never said which kind to get."

"Damn Snackz, you gonna let the lil' nigga spin you like dat?" Dro instigated through laughter. Being only twenty years old himself, he enjoyed a hectic confrontation here and there. "You're getting soft, homeboy!"

Snackz' stare was murderous, and Dro could feel the heat emitting off Snackz. To save face and his notoriety in the hood, Dro offered to put in some light-work for Snackz.

"Yeah, smart-mouth, get dat work!" Snackz accepted Dro's apologetic attempt by allowing him to handle the Yak.

Dro was six years Yak's senior, but about the same in weight and height, only difference was, Dro had sprouting dreads; the kind they rock down in Little Haiti, Miami. Somehow Dro eased close enough to snuff Yak. The right-cross twisted his jaw some, but Yak shook it off ASAP. Yak wasn't no slouch, it's just he hadn't thought he'd get a fair one in with all the older cats from the 'Law' on deck. He was kicking himself for not purchasing the .38 snub-nose a lick from the suburbs brought through about a week ago. He only wanted two eight-balls for it, but Yak was pressed for weight, so he missed out on swapping drugs for the ratchet.

Before Yak could get a shot off, Dro caught him with another two-piece, which this time staggered him off balance. Luckily for Yak, Avonne was bending the corner. Her mom had sent her to the bodega for some dairy products; she was preparing a German Chocolate Cake. From a distance, Avonne noticed the commotion, from all the ruckus, taking place in front of the store. She knew how LateNiteSnackz and his crimey's played, so in fear for young Yak's safety, she ran to tell Germ and the others.

Minutes later, she was explaining what was going on with their peeps.

"Yak's in trouble, y'all!"

"Who?" Pintz barked, full of concern with the mentioning of his younger brother being in some type of scuffle.

25

"LateNiteSnackz and them older nigga's fucking with him. He's fighting Dro now!"

Her voice was so intense. They knew they had to act quickly. Nothing else needed to be said, Pintz and Germ hauled ass towards the Law. Just as they hit the corner, Germ noticed that Angus was nowhere in sight.

"Oh well," he thought.

Out of spontaneity, Pintz ran through the crowd and caught Dro with a wild haymaker causing him to stumble. Once he gathered his thoughts, Dro spit some lose blood from his mouth to the ground.

"Man I'ma bout to fuck some shit up!" Dro said.

The two were now squared off like soldiers on the frontline ready to claim their victory in deadly war. This time it was Dro who was caught off-guard, and it showed, because he stood there dazed and hesitant to defend himself. Dro looked to Snackz for a sign, some encouragement of some sort, but found none, only a strange face and flailing arms.

"Don't look at me, playboy. You should've kept your mouth shut, now get to it." Snackz ordered.

With that, Dro swung wildly, catching Pintz in the eye, then hooked him in the mouth. Pintz spit-out a glob of blood, and then rushed Dro. Using his size, he flipped Dro to the ground, and that's where Dro's day went south. On the sly, Yak snatched the 40-ounce out of Snackz' hands and smashed Dro in the face, splitting him on impact. Slim was Dro's partner, so he rushed into the scuffle, but was tripped up by Germ. After getting up off the ground from Germ's direct hit to the temple, the two began going toe to toe. However, Slim started to get the best of him. His reach was just too long for the short arms of Germ. Off to the side, Snackz and Dex were in tears until they heard a series of gunshots ring out from off the roof top.

Shots in Cunnuck were common, an everyday thing, so it wasn't surprising to them, it just ceased all commotion at the moment. Germ smiled, seeing a nigga wearing a black mask aiming a strap at the crowd.

"Back the fuck up!" the masked man shouted.

No one moved.

"I said...back the fuck...up! And if I gotta say it again, we gonna need a church, a good eulogist for next weekend and a shit-load of black for your loved ones!"

The smarter ones backed away from Yak, Pintz and Germ. LateNiteSnackz was thorough, he never budged, which was expected from someone of his caliber. Instead he pulled out his strap.

"Now what, chump?" he spat, unafraid of dying.

"Nigga...this the Law, now if you lil' nigga's don't get the fuck back on Babcock where y'all belong, the only thing your folks gonna be checking for is a shit-load of flowers and family members to attend your closed casket funerals!" his tone deadly and promising.

Germ knew better, and took heed to Snackz' warning.

"Let's bounce peeps!"

Adhering to Germ's orders, he and his cousins eased out of harm's way. Hitting the corner, they heard a repetition of gunfire. The masked man had opened fire on the older cats. A true gangsta, LateNiteSnackz began bussing back, but the masked man was well covered by the brick chimney. The only danger threatening the shooters life was the pieces of tar and shingles flying by his face from the bullets ricocheting off the roof.

A gun battle ensued between Snackz and the masked man, however, the seven-shot was quickly emptied, leaving the masked man no further reason to stick around and risk losing his life or being apprehended by the authorities. He was satisfied knowing the young boys made it out of danger safely. His identity was concealed, so he wasn't worried about a snitch, or anybody else pointing him out to the cops, for that matter. Retracing his steps, he hit two roof-tops, three fences and was back with his partners laughing.

"We all need some heat!" Angus stated seriously. "It's just too much wreck coming at us right now. I gotta connect, too! What's good?"

They all knew Angus was right, things were starting to flare up in Cunnuck, and they'd need some protection of their own if they wanted to remain contenders in the hood. After agreeing with Angus' statement, he then revealed his connect to them, and that the price for some reliable weapons would be steep. Pintz also mentioned an older cat from back home in Florida that sold ratchets, and that they were cheap from what he remembered. Together, they agreed to put up some change just for some ratchets and went back to pitching. Germ suggested that they refrain from Angus' idea of wasting money and drugs on some head. His mind was strictly on moving some work and stashing some bread for their new venture! He was always the smarter one when it came down to making the right decisions for his team.

Chapter 6

Everyday Shit

T he drug traffic gradually picked up on Babcock Street. Germ and his crew were bussing all-nighters, seven days a week. It wasn't nothing for them to do at least eighteen hours out of the day hustling. They were trying to reach a goal, and sleep wasn't it. They were determined to stack some serious paper and achieve real hood status. Their young minds were groomed by rap music, and hood movies such as: Boyz in The Hood, Paid In Full, New Jack City, Streetz is Watching, Belly, Clockers and of course Blow. Those were just a few influential films that dressed them every morning. They'd taken all the films messages and adapted to them like orphans with strung-out parents, looking for that better life.

As the crew stood on the block, a late model Honda Accord pulled directly in front of them. Inside were some fiends, looking to cop some work. The driver was a young white chic. Her passengers were two black males, who appeared to be four to five years her senior, but that's how shit went down throughout America's ghettos. Young to old would get strung out early and make drugs their number one priority in life. Nothing else really mattered, other than the opportunity to get high, and Germ and his crew were going to be the proprietors for their addiction.

The driver of the Honda was young, and except for the new blemishes masking her facial features, she still held some of her natural beauty. Time would tell if, like many other druggies before her, drugs would deprive her of a promising future, or a life filled with the ups and downs associated with the lifestyle?

"Go on and cop, fool!" Marlin, the fiend in the backseat urged.

He tossed his crinkled Washington's upfront; his contribution towards their score.

"Man…you always wanna smoke, but bitch-up when it's time to cop!" Harold spoke, as he bent-down to pick-up the damp bills. "Man, this only five dollars, Marlin. You said you had seven! What we gonna get with five funky dollars?" Harold spoke through agitation.

His craving to get high had him in an angry fit.

Right now, Marlin didn't care. He craved a hit and knew his five singles would do it. He actually did have seven, but a dollar went on a new stem and the other on a new lighter. His works somehow disappeared last night after he passed out in the crack house.

"Aye, y'all gots to hurry the fuck up," Germ yelled into their window. "Get out the car, too!"

They were regulars, but still, they couldn't risk a crack head pulling off with what little work they had. Ultimately, you either hopped out to cop or took it to another block. It was the number one rule in protecting your investment.

"Gon' head, Harold, before they do some stupid shit," Marlin urged.

He just wanted to cop and go. *There couldn't be much trouble in that – could it?* He thought.

Not wanting any trouble, Harold hopped out, knowing his chances of scoring were slim to none, but their stomachs were in tight surgeon knots, and the only thing that could possibly loosen the hold at this point would be a hit of crack. Wrinkled bills in hand, Harold exited the dirty Accord in a leery state of mind, knowing how the youths around this particular hood played it when it came to short money. Immediately, Yak tried to snatch the lick.

"Yo, what's good, old head? Come in the alley!" he waved on.

Harold's eye's nearly teared, seeing the anxiousness of the youthful hustle. He followed Yak into the alley with no problem.

"Aye, young, you got it loose right?" Harold inquired, his mouth watering.

"Nah! I got dimes, fool. Now, how many you want?"

Harold inquired because there would be a greater chance of getting a bigger piece for his money if it were lose versus bagged up.

With his crew just a few feet away, Yak knew he was safe. If the Deeze's so happened to roll up, they'd signal him, or if the old head pulled a fast one, well, we all know where that would lead to, a vicious beat down. Harold reached into his pocket and retrieved the wrinkled money out and flashed them at Yak like they were crisp hundreds.

"I got five bills, nephew."

"Humph?"

Yak thought he'd heard wrong, so he spit the question at Harold once more to be sure, cause five bills in his book, meant $500.00. Had Harold made Yak's day?

"You got how much?"

Harold knew off jump what it sounded like. He also noticed how Yak's mind raced, his animation spoke for itself.

"Nah, nephew, I got five dollars!"

31

From Boyz To Men

Yak stood there for a good three, maybe four seconds, before he kicked Harold in the gut, causing him to fall flat on his ass.

"Five dollars?" he barked, now standing directly over him spit spraying as he spoke.

With every stomp Yak administered to Harold's face, he lectured him on the ethics of buying drugs in the hood.

"You...come...out...here...wit...five funky ass dollars...! I...oughta... ...slump you idiot!" His timberland boot now soaked with Harold's blood.

Hearing the commotion, Germ and Pintz ran into the alley. Angus kept his eye on the Honda. He had the right mind to saturate the Honda and it's passengers with some hot ones. However, just as he went for his ratchet, he noticed a blue and white coming down the one-way strip.

Marlin and the driver, Amanda, must've seen the cruiser as well and decided it would be best to duck dirty low, in fear of being harassed by the cops. It obviously was their day of good luck, because the cruiser blew right by them with their sirens blaring loudly, probably in route to another duress call across town.

"Whew!" Angus breathed a sigh of relief as their lights became non-existent.

"Chill, Yak!"

Pintz had to push his angered brother some, or ol' Harold would have become another statistic due to the drug trade throughout the city.

Yak finally realized he was going above and beyond by stomping Harold to the brink of death. He had drifted off to a far-off place where only violence ruled. With his senses back, he hock spit on Harold, and then, snatched the damp bills up off the ground.

Back in the front of the alleyway, Angus snatched Marlin and the young Amy Fisher double out of the dusty Honda at gun point, then ushered them into the alley. He kept the small caliber gun in Marlin's spine, just in case he posed a threat, which seemed to frighten Amanda. Although she was white and caught in some halfway kidnapping by young drug dealers, she was thoroughly turned on by Angus' actions.

In Amanda's little suburbia world, this never took place. She'd only come to experience such encounters on TV and rap videos. It was a thrill for her to venture in the trenches of Cunnuck's hoods. Every dime she came across went to crack, but today would mark her first day of being jacked, a day she would remember for the rest of her natural life.

"What the fuck happened, Yak?" Germ questioned, his eyes darting from the small pool of blood, and then back to Harold's battered body.

"Man, would you believe this fool came at me with five wet ass bills?" he admitted, as if it were a crime.

"And your stupid ass nearly stomped him to death?" Germ stated, in a questionable fashion. "Man...you stupid...for real, Yak!"

Germ eyed Angus because his ways were starting to rub off on his little cousin. And to think, their gun connect would be through in a week. He was now seeing that climbing to the top was going to be a worrisome task, especially containing his comrades.

Pintz also shook his head at his little brother. He knew Yak had basically flipped out for nothing. He was also starting to notice the change in him; too much one on one time with Angus he assumed, as well.

"Hey, what about these two?" Angus broke his silence.

"What about 'em?" Germ answered. "Serve them and let 'em bounce! Y'all niggas always drawing heat to the block, real talk, this little bullshit has to stop and stop now!" Germ ordered sternly. "For one, it's not good for business, and two, it's gonna run all of our sales away, and I ain't about losing what we started over dumb shit."

"Dis fool only got five bills and not the big one's either!" Yak boasted, catching Amanda's gaze as he spoke. "Fuck you looking at, ma?"

"Oh...nothing," Amanda responded, in a silly manner.

She was drawn by Yak's violent actions.

"Wow, this is the stuff I see on TV, for real," she mumbled.

Marlin noticed how intrigued Amanda was by the young hustla, soon after, an idea popped into his demented mind.

Leaning over towards Amanda, he whispered something into her ear, "How about it?"

Her mouth twitched some, but she never spoke, she only shrugged her shoulders.

"How 'bout my friend, here, trade off our debt?" With no shame at all, Marlin offered up Amanda's innocence for drugs.

Confused, they all looked at each other for answers. Amanda was looking good, not to worn-down from the drug's side-effects just yet, so they were easily susceptible to take them up on their offer. Angus had made his decision. He tossed three dimes to Marlin, and then told him to get his buddy and kick rocks, while they handled their business, but to come back in   forty-five minutes for the girl, and not one minute later.

Marlin accepted the rocks and scrambled with haste. He helped Harold up off the ground and went around the corner to a known crack house, where they famished the free stones. As a crack head, it wasn't in his mind to save a crumb for Amanda. He just hoped they'd provide her with her own once they were finished with their sexual pleasures.

$$$$$

Back in the alley, Yak and Angus had laced their dicks with condoms, shortly after, Amanda was on her knees sucking Yak off, while Angus back shotted her. Pintz was on the side of her with his pants halfway down being jerked off by her free hand. It was apparent she had done this before.

Angus pulled all the way out and thrust long and hard back into her wetness, causing her to choke as she deep throated Yak's hardness. However, it never broke her stride, which made him find a deep love for fellatio. Amanda moaned more than she grunted, obviously enjoying the ménage trios, surprisingly, she had cum twice so far and was still at it.

"Damn...she's like a real energizer bunny!" Germ said to himself.

He just watched. He wasn't too thrilled about fucking fiends or getting some crack head, mainly because his moms died while giving birth to him. In addition, she also contracted aids through intravenous drug use. Growing up, he'd often heard rumors about how she would perform sexual favors with drug dealers in exchange for a hit, so he never indulged in those sorts of things with druggies, knowing his mom did similar things in her days before passing. Melodie's shrimp box was good enough for him.

Satisfied with their time in Amanda's sacred pleasures, Pintz hit it from the back and got some head. Once he was done, they all dumped three dime rocks apiece into her palm.

"Damn ma', you got some good-good. Don't smoke it all up with them two fools either. You worked too hard for it." Pintz said.

"Come through whenever, too, ma."

"Trust me I won't."

She smiled and gladly accepted her payment and said she'd be back when she came across some money, even after getting the okay to stop by whenever. They were now turned out on dope head.

Chapter 7

First Step

The tiresome week was nearing its peak, and the youngins on Babcock St., made it through another week without incident. It was also to the point where all of them, including money hungry Yak, was catching enough licks to pitch in on an ounce of hard. Up until now, they were only good for either buying already bagged up dimes or a shaver (3.5 grams).

Their connect, Big-Meat, was that nigga to see for weight, and I mean, dude was extra with it. At thirty-three years of age, he stood about 5'10", and weighed a 180 lbs solid, with a bald head. It was rumored that his first meal ticket came from a jookz out in Florida, four years ago. Being from Miami, gave him a major tie to some Cubans, who dealt in large amounts of China White. Cuba, a stocky dude the shade of a Werther's Candy, had it by the trailer loads and flaunted it every chance he got. He practically ran the area Meat descended from back in Florida.

Big-Meat gained Cuba's trust in no time. For starters, Cuba would dump five to ten keys at a time on him, and being the hustla Big-Meat was, he would make them disappear like hair on a person with cancer. Cuba undoubtedly observed the potential in Big-Meat and decided he would up his ante to fifty joints per re-up, and that's when the greedy snake slithered out of its hibernation. Big-Meat was showing his true colors, as most thirsty money hungry hustlas do, when faced with the temptation of running off with their suppliers load, and the reason why our foreign counter-parts don't like our kind (Blacks) today. They truly despise us for our thieving ways, however, we move so much coke and dope that they are forced to deal with us, or they'll be sitting on boat loads of coke subject to being caught with their pants down by the authorities. After flipping the fifty joints a good three times, Big-Meat ran off and relocated to Corrupt Cunnuck – Hartford, CT., where he's been getting his share of broccoli ever since.

"Listen, once we do this, there ain't no turning back, feel meh!" Germ lectured the forum. "It's one-way, our way; da ski mask, and the hand to hand way. Anybody opposing our movement gets dealt with severely. And that goes for whomever; man, woman or child!" Germ spoke sternly.

"Shit, ain't much more to talk about, cuz, here's my two hunid!" Pintz offered.

"Mine's too," Yak added.

Angus was subtle, yet he had an angered distinction about him. He tossed his deuce at Germ without saying one word. He was low-tolerant and rarely spoke unless beef arose, a jump-off was involved, or when it came down to his scrilla. His childhood wasn't like most other children's. There was no bike riding, no playing hide and seek or climbing trees with his friends. Till this day, Angus has never played in a sandbox or experienced what it's like to play two-hand touch in the middle of the street where the oncoming traffic was deadly. In addition, he had never partaken in the art of catching bees and lightening bugs. He would just watch from the sidelines as the other kids in the neighborhood joyously did their thing, which from the way he reacts nowadays, displays that he still hasn't recovered from the cheated childhood he experienced, which had left an imprint on his young soul forever. With now two-hundred short of a stack ($1,000), the M.H.B.'s (Money Hungry Boyz) were ready to turn their swag and operation up a notch. Germ counted out $700 for the ounce, and the other yard (hundred) was going for a digital scale, which they would need to weigh up the weight they were going to buy. Until now they never had the use for a scale being they were only twerking with shavers and bagged up dimes, but now, their new plans required the use of one. Nevertheless, they have always trusted Big-Meat when dealing when copping work. However, business was business, and they intended to conduct theirs like a multimillion dollar one.

$$$$$

Across town, inside the plush confines of a platinum, Buick Lacrosse, Big-Meat and Fluff were discussing Fluff's desires to become Hip Hop's next big thing.

"Nigga, if you don't holla at Hov, better yet, holla at Soulja Boy. Ask him how he did it, because my riches ain't going towards any flop music!" Meat joked, cutting into Fluff's plans of becoming a factor in the rap scene.

Fluff was Big-Meat's right-hand. They had been down together since the south, only Fluff happened to be from Opa Lock, Florida. They touched bases in juvi, as youths, both doing time for stolen cars, and remained friends ever since. When Big-Meat took that long journey up I-95 North to CT., he sent for his crimey. Now, together, they control one-third of Hartford's crack epidemic.

"That's foul, Meat. Your boy got dat '05 swag the industry is missing!"

Fluff was just about to drop a gem on Meat, when he felt his hip vibrating from the cellular phone clipped to his belt.

"Yo, Meat, these them little money hungry niggas," Fluff said, viewing Germ's house number.

He always held onto Meat's phone. It's what sidekicks do.

"See what's good wit 'em," Meat okayed.

Answering, he said, "Yo, what's good, young Germ?"

From Boyz To Men

"I'm trying to holla at big homey. Y'all 'round?"

"Always, but get at us in a half. Where you gon' be at, kid?"

"My crib until it's time to link up."

"A'ight, one!"

"Two!" Germ smirked.

He loved to fuck with Meat's flunky, as he and his boys referred to him as. In all the hoods, the right-hand usually played the do-it role.

"It's done, only they don't know what type of time we on. In the meantime, Pintz, you wanna hit the white broad, Amanda, up?"

"For what?" his eyebrows slightly rose knowing his cuz didn't flirt with crack heads.

"Nigga, you greener than I thought. So you can get a ride down to 'Stairway to Heaven' and cop us a good diggie (digital scale). We gon' need dat," Germ replied.

Pintz flashed all thirty twos. The gold reflection was enough to tint a small compact vehicle.

"I'm 'bout to get on it now, cuz!" he replied anxiously, knowing he'd be able to get some head in the process.

While Pintz was going to handle the business with the scale, Yak decided to take a trip down to the Bodega on Lawrence St., only this time, Germ and Angus was right on his heels. They needed some baggies for later after they copped the weight from Big Meat. It was about 3:30 p.m., so the school traffic from Quirk Middle and Burns Elementary was starting to crowd Lawrence Street. Germ watched a few young cats as they spit game on the P.Y.T.'s parading around in skimpy clothing. Some smiled, and some giggled back at the hustla's sex-driven attempts to invade their forbidden body parts. The others, who kept it moving, were stuck up or just weren't into the boys lustful antics.

"Fuck you, too! You ain't that fly anyways!" One of them yelled out.

From a distance, Germ laughed. He thought it was hilarious that the shorties who hadn't given them the time of day was smart not to get involved with the likes of street dwellers.

"Go get dat, Yak," Germ instructed, referring to the zip locks they needed.

While Yak went inside the Bodega, Germ and Angus remained outside politicking. They noticed a few of their regular fiends either walking or pulling up to the hustlers; obviously copping work from the cat's on the Law, which infuriated the two.

"Yo Germ, you see this shit!?" Angus barked, heated that their sales were betraying them right in their faces.

He was definitely ready to smack fire out of one of them just to make an example. It was time the hood knew who the M.H.B's were.

"Hell, yeah! Look, dat's Pam and Twan's older sista, Nett. No wonder they ain't been through the block lately!"

Germ's blood started to boil. The veins in his slender neck began to protrude through his skin, displaying his current anger.

"Don't even sweat it, Kik', I got something for this weak ass block." Angus meant exactly what he said. "Can't nothin' stop our hustle 'cept dat pine box, bruh."

From across the street, they watched LateNiteSnackz and his pack of trained wolves watch them. Snackz now realized who it was that had taken those shots at him and his peeps a week ago. Out of spite, he shot them a wicked smile, more so at Angus. All of their mugs were hardened, which left no room for resolve nor friendship, only war; war between the 'Law' and 'Babcock Street'.

Yak finally emerged from out of the store, and from the looks at the fellas across the street, he could tell there was major tension in the air. He wanted some get-back from the last incident with them, but knew the older cats held straps at all times. He wished his big bro was there to support them right now.

Blaze, Slim, Dex and Dro took two steps towards the Bodega, but Snackz stopped them. He was being cautious and looked at the roof-tops to be sure that this wasn't some trick or set-up seeing their forward (Pintz), wasn't on the court.

"Y'all fall back. Another time, another place, trust dat!" Snackz spoke just above a whisper.

At the time, his paper was more important than playing war with the youngins from up the block.

Snackz and Germ shared a head nod, understanding that now wasn't the proper time to get it poppin'.

Not once looking behind them, the M.H.B.'s stepped off with their heads held high. Their hearts were hardened and knew the only thing in life that was promised was death, so there was no need to be cautious; at least not from this fake-ass old head and his clique.

Chapter 8

With Work Comes Play

Stairway to Heaven stocked their shelves with everything from bongs, pipes, stems, and rolling paper, to triple beam and digital scales. Today Pintz was only interested in a digital scale that was capable of weighing from at least zero to a hundred grams at a time. The owner, a burly-white male with a skin-head and several eye and body piercings, didn't mind selling Pintz the paraphernalia. It was legal in some cases, specifically in dietary aid, however, the only other problem at stake would be Pintz' lack of I.D., but like the majority of the sales that ran in and out of his lucrative establishment, they too were local under-aged dealers and users, so he'd overlook it.

Pintz copped a black rectangular-shaped digital scale and rushed back inside Amanda's Honda. Even with the dark-tinted windows rolled down, Pintz' nose was bombarded by the smell of crack. Before going inside, he gave her a dime for the ride and another for some pleasure once he returned to the car. Amanda wasted no time getting her burn on and had been smoking the entire time he was inside the store handling his business.

"Damn, ma, you ain't got just the car fogged up, but out here, too. I hope yo ass high enough."

He shook his head at how a beauty, such as herself, could sell herself to the devil so easily. Seeing that Amanda was fidgeting in her seat and looking from side to side, he was not putting his life in danger by letting her drive back to the block, looking like some crazed chicken on meth.

"Hop out, ma, I got this."

Now in the driver's seat, he took another look at her and

wondered how his mom was back in her druggie days. She also was a beauty queen in her early years before letting drugs take over her essence. *"What a waste,"* he thought.

"You're gonna end up just like my mom, girl," he mumbled, experiencing a soft spot for Amanda.

However, he knew that just like all crack-heads that indulged in the streets and drugs day-in and day-out, she would in time lose all respect and dignity for herself. Soon, Amanda would refrain from the most common things, like taking care of her personal hygiene, to losing ownership of her most prized possessions, down to any trace of humanity she had prior to marrying the glass dick. For now, time seemed to be on Amanda's side, because her weight never depleted, like most crack-heads living in the streets, nor did her beauty deteriorate. Amanda made sure she maintained employment and also an ATM card, not to mention some excellent head for those times when her account was on 'E'. And this wouldn't be the first, nor last time her Honda would be used as a taxi, crack house and safe-haven for sexual favors. Pintz raised the windows up, cut the A.C. on full blast, and then drove off in route to the strip.

A block away from Babcock St. was Putnam St. Pintz brought the Honda to a standstill under a shaded tree where he could gather some privacy. After adjusting his seat to a more comfortable position, he began receiving a royal overhaul from Amanda. She was working the head of his dick while fondling his balls.

"Ooooh…" he moaned, his neck resting awkwardly on the square-headrest.

Amanda sped up her flow, riding his length with her warm mouth.

As she nibbled under the rim of his thickhead, he grunted loudly, "Ahh…"

44

She couldn't quite make out the words he uttered, but knew he was enjoying the services she was administering to him. Studying his facial expressions caused her to use a little too much teeth.

"Damn, girl...pull dem whites back!"

"Sorry, daddy!" she complied. "Is that bettr?" she cooed, jerking the end of his shaft, licking circles around the head.

"Ummmmm..." he moaned.

Just that quick, he was back on cloud nine. The more she caressed his length, she could feel the thick veins in his penis pulsating in her mouth, alerting her that he was on the verge of explosion. Adamant about bringing him to climax, Amanda began jerking his rod as fast as she could, while sucking on his balls like two jawbreakers. Amanda considered herself a good head doctor, she knew exactly when to stop jerking and start slobbing again. No more than thirty seconds of nursing his swollen dick, did Pintz deliver a heavy load of his semen into her mouth.

"Umm...daddy, that was good!" She swallowed the last drop of sperm, while still massaging his hardness.

Funny thing about it, Pintz wasn't done. He wanted to feel the tightness of her insides. Amanda would do just about anything and anywhere for a hit of crack. She had no qualms fulfilling his request for sex. Aside from her bra and panties, Amanda was now butt-naked. In an attempt to please Pintz, Amanda took out a condom, placed it into her mouth, and seductively eased it onto his erectness. Thereafter, Amanda straddled him, pulling her bikini to one side, allowing him a clear passage inside her moist cavern.

"Ahhh...!" he grunted as she inched down his length slowly.

Seeing her damn near in the nude, he could now see that she

45

was even thicker than what she appeared to be in clothing.

"This head is thick too-def!" he concluded.

With that, he secretly named her *Mo' Body*. Caught in the moment, the two locked eyes; Pintz grunting, Amanda biting on her bottom lip. It was almost as if they were making love. Amanda began to twirling her hips at a moderate speed while Pintz was thrusting upwards with great force, driving his wedge deep into her abyss. The more he drove his thick nail into her drywall, the more pleased Amanda was that her sex game was satisfying for him. Viewing the expressions he made each time she lowered herself an inch lower onto his dick, gave Amanda some added insurance that her payment might exceed the normal ten dollars, worth of crack. In addition, to make sure that would be the case; she bucked in a circular motion embracing herself for his length and girth.

"Oooh, ooh daddy!" she moaned, loving the way he felt inside of her womb.

Seven minutes later, after he busted his nut, he made sure she got another one off, which was actually her third

"Damn boy...that was awesome," she admitted, her breathing labored.

Climbing off his lap, Amanda then threw herself into the passenger seat to put her clothes back on.

"What's good, ma? Daddy too much for ya'?" Pintz joked, feeling as if he had conquered the world.

"If you say so, boy. It's like you took a Viagra, e-pill or something, that thing of yours don't know how to go down. It's too awkward in this little ass car, that's all, but trust, I got chu! I can make you fall in love with this shit if you're not careful Pintz" she promised, rubbing her crotch as she warned.

"I feel you on the awkwardness, but me being careful, not! We definitely gonna get up another time though, I gotta meet up with my peeps. Here, take this though." He gave her two more rocks for his appreciation, hopped out, and then, walked to the block.

"Bye…Pintz," she bidded as he walked off.

Pintz pulled his hurricane fitted hat down low and kept it moving. Not wanting to be seen, hopping out of her Honda in fear of what the nosy onlookers in the vicinity would think; he just nodded his head, letting her know that he had heard every word.

Chapter 9

56 – Gramz

Pintz finally made it back to the crib and found his peeps huddled at Uncle Marv's. Down in the basement was a foosball and an electric air-hockey table. Uncle Marv kept a mini-bar fully stocked with mostly top-shelf liquors. He also kept some cheap, easily affordable liquor for times when certain individuals visited. In the far right corner sat a 42" HDTV where the Germ and the others enjoyed their XBOX 360. It was very rare that Uncle Marv spent his days and nights at home, he spent them on the job, doing over time. Uncle Marv was a stickler for work and prided himself on making a better life for the boys. However, coming home to that familiar scent of marijuana, there were many incidents where he had a sit-down with the four of them and lectured them on the do's and don'ts of getting high. Most importantly, he suggested that they not do so in the public eye, and since that day they've had a free pass to do them, as long as it was in the basement. There were no trust issues with them. He wanted them to be straightforward with him in all aspects.

"What's hood y'all?" Pintz greeted, looking at the fellas in chill mode.

"Ain't shit, just laxin' blowing this Haze," Germ replied.

"Pass dat blunt, Angus," Yak yelled, fiddling with the large XBOX controller.

He and Angus were playing 'Call of Duty III.'

"Here, lil' nigga."

After inhaling deeply, Angus passed the blunt to Yak.

"Aye P', you handle dat b.i.?" Germ asked.

"Yeah no doubt...dat and then some," he smiled.

"Lemme see dat scale," Germ said to Pintz.

"Here, catch, cuzzo. It comes with batteries, too, so we hood." Pintz added.

"That's what's up, but what took so long, nigga?" Germ said with a sly grin.

"Sheeit...ain't no shame in my game. I had to get me some head, feel meh? And she can ride the dick like a fucking bull-master," he reminisced about the session he just had with Amanda in the Honda. "Damn...dat girl can fuck and suck!"

"Sit your strung out ass down and hit dis weed fool," Yak took another pull then passed it to his big brother.

Germ shook his head, smiling. He already knew the deal, he just had to ask.

"Hurry up and hit dat, we gotta go handle this pick-up."

Pintz was ready to feel the effects of the haze and accepted the piece from Yak, taking deep tokes. Savoring the essence of its potency, he exhaled rings of smoke into the air and passed the blunt off to Angus.

"You ready, cuz?" Germ asked, he was anxious to get the work, bag it up, and flood the block.

"No doubt, let's get to it." Pintz said.

"Listen y'all, me and Pintz about to go meet up with ol' boy. I don't want them feeling spooked seeing all four of us, so we'll be right back. Ya heard?"

"No doubt. You need my strap?" Angus replied.

Germ shook his head, and answered, "Nah, we hood Kik. I trust Big Meat, he's a business man."

"Trust no man, Germ! Your pops preaches that to us all the time, so I suggest you start taking heed to his words. Money is the root to all evil, bruh."Angus posed.

He didn't care who was about business, the love of money will make any man switch up on you, even family.

"Like I said, I'm hood. We'll be right back, y'all just hol' the fort down."

Never turning his head away from the screen, Yak said, "Y'all be careful, ya heard."

Instead of going up the stairs leading into the kitchen, they chose to use the exit in the basement from the trap doors that led to the rear of their building. They did this a lot when they were sneaking in and out the house so not to wake Uncle Marv.

But before crossing the threshold to the shed doors, Germ hollered back, "Kick his ass, Gus!"

It was all playful with them. Yak would always trim niggas when they touched the joystick. He was like an expert when it came to video games.

The two walked just a few blocks from their house to Baby Park where they were supposed to meet up with Big Meat. Being this was the first time they would be making a large purchase, Germ counted the buy money three times before stuffing it back into his Russell sweat pants pocket. Experiencing the hard knock life in Corrupt Cunnuck only allowed them to sport under prided clothing, such as sweats, fatigues, wife beaters, and tee's. However, timbs and uptowns was a must.

J. Alexander

"Aye Germ, did y'all run into those older cats down on the Law?" Pintz was referring to Snackz and his homeys.

"Yeah, but dude ain't pop-off. Don't know why not, but dat young Dro nigga and Blaze seemed like they wanted some knuckle time. Just a lot of mean-mugging, dat's all, nothin' major, feel meh?"

"Sheeit, maybe old-head, Snackz, got scared not knowing who came at 'em from the roof-top!" Pintz boasted, his words causing Germ to now realize that when Snackz halted his goons and surveyed all the rooftops for a hidden shooter, he was just being precautious; smart move on his part.

Germ knew Snackz was experienced and dangerous. From here on, he wouldn't take him and his goons lightly.

"Nah, Pintz, he really thought you'd be up there ready to fly some hot air mail their way if shit popped off. Don't mix dude for no punk-slouch though, you already know LateNiteSnackz is a straight killa, and one for hire, too."

It was true, LateNiteSnackz was known for putting in that work for himself and for the right price.

"Sheeit...we might could use old head in the future, cuz," Pintz suggested.

"Fo' sure," Germ agreed.

The two were politicking as Meat's Platinum Lacrosse eased up in front of them. When the passenger window rolled down, they heard a southern drawl direct Germ to hop in the back seat.

"Hold up, lil' nigga, where you going?" Fluff barked, as Pintz tried to slide inside the vee.

"He's in on this, Big Meat, and it's only fair he knows what's

51

poppin'," Germ said in Pintz's defense.

He actually brought Pintz along hoping their Florida ties would get them a better number on the Oz.

"He's cool!" Big Meat said. "Hop in, Goldie," Big Meat okayed. "So what's up youngin'?"

"I need an onion. What's it gonna cost me?" Germ asked.

"An onion? Where you get ounce money from? Your block doesn't bang dat kind of noise, lil' nigga. Y'all niggas out there jacking custee's?" Fluff questioned seriously, he just couldn't fathom them stacking up that much doe.

And not to mention they despised jack boys, although it was how they were able to supply the city in the first place.

"You got me fucked up, fat boy. We pitch dem rocks day and night. It's either' heaven or hell on my block, and the traffic don't stop, so miss me with that fuck-boy shyt! Fuckin' flunky!" Germ verbally attacked Meat's right-hand.

Meat was laughing his ass off inside, too. He felt Fluff had it coming, being he was always trying to intimidate the young hustler's when they came around to cop.

"Fall back, Fluff, let me holla at the youngin' myself," Big-Meat ordered.

"Look...I got seven dead ones. We got business or what?" Germ was heated, his face displaying his frustration.

He wanted to murk Fluff something bad.

"I like you, Germ. Err' thang's 'bout dat scrilla wit' chu. Give the lil' nigga two of 'em."

Fluff reached into a brown bag and pulled out two square

blocks, then tossed them to Germ. His stare was evil. He didn't appreciate being played like that, especially by some lil' nigga on the block pitching dime rocks. Little did Fluff know, he was in the midst of Hartford's most feared boss to ever run the drug trade.

"Nah, Meats, I only got seven hundred. I ain't taking no fronts!" Germ made very clear.

Working for the next man wasn't part of his plan. Although it would've helped them out, but that would also open up doors for him to come through looking for his paper on some boss type shit, and that just wasn't going to happen at least not now.

"Dat's on me, youngin', now get out and get dat scrilla. Holla when you ready to re-up, ya heard," Big-Meat said, and then jumped on his jack dismissing him as if his seven hundred was nothing to his pockets. "Hurry up! I've got somewhere else to be."

"Yeah, we got other sales, chump," Fluff barked, elated to bust back on Germ for the disrespect earlier.

"You bitch ass...," Pintz started to rip Fluff a new asshole, but Germ stopped him for the sake of business and peace.

When Fluff's head snapped around; he and Germ locked eyes. They mean-mugged one another until Germ broke the tension with a head nod. It was hard not to get shit cracking, but that would hurt Germ's plans. As they were now outside of the vehicle, the passenger side window lowered where Fluff continued to stare at them with an angered face.

Germ just laughed it off and said, "We'll holla soon, fat-boy! Later Big Meat."

Germ and Pintz walked back to the crib, somewhat confused, but happy Big-Meat gave them that extra boost. Still, Germ saw right through his ploy. Big-Meat was just trying to lockdown the entire south side with his work. For now, they would use him for what it was, but only if he stayed on the up and up.

Chapter 10

Da Workshop

"Yo, pass me some more bags," Yak spat, tying the knot on the last baggie he had in front of him.

While Pintz had the duties of chopping up the work, Germ weighed the small pieces precisely. Each dime rock weighed 0.1 on the scale. Some might have been just a little heavier, but best believe they intended on getting their ten dollars per rock. Yak's job consisted of bagging them up. All Angus had to do was cut the baggies in two, that way they get more bags for their bucks. At Yak's request, Angus tossed him a handful of the baggies he had just finished cutting.

"Here you go Speedy Gonzales."

The foursome had been chopping, weighing, and bagging for the last hour.

"Here, these the last ones, Germ," Yak informed.

He had two-hundred-eighty bagged up dimes on a plate, ready to be turned into a profit.

"It's about damn time," Pintz said, he was tired of hopping, he felt like he'd worked an eight hour shift at UPS loading trucks.

Their little operation had gone down rather smoothly. The total from both ounces, amassed five-hundred-sixty rocks, which would bring in $5,600.00, but they knew with all the shorts, they would never see that. Germ grabbed a calculator and figured at $8.00 per rock, they would still rake in $4,480.00, a very marginable profit from the original $700.00 invested. The extra ounce from Big-Meat was a good look and would be used for the purchase of their artillery. Now that the hard part was over, Germ was on the phone politicking with someone very important.

"Good luck, playboy, I'll see you in a week," Germ said, ending the call.

"Yo, who was that, Germ?" Being nosy, Yak questioned.

He was young, but inquisitive about everything that went on around him.

"Melodie's cousin out of Newport News, VA. Dude has a line on some major heat. I think if we gonna reach that plateau and be able to hold our hood down, we gonna need some clean ratchets on deck." Germ preached. "So, with that free ounce Big-Meat threw us, we gotta flip dat with the quickness. It's going towards dat heat."

No one was more thrilled than Angus. He had a certain thirst for the steel, and lately lil' Yak seemed to inherit some of Angus' vigilant and ill-mannered ways. Unbeknownst to Yak, Germ was starting to notice the change also, but it was bound to happen eventually. As long as he and Pintz stuck around, Yak would be hood; or so he thought. Yak was his lil' cousin, and he would protect him, even if it meant losing his own life. There was no way that he and Pintz would be able to face uncle Marv if Yak became a victim of the streets under their care. So, as the days would continue to churn, they promised to keep a watchful eye on the youngster, especially when it came down to him spending countless hours with the likes of Angus. Satisfied with the numbers, the four of them sat around getting high contemplating on how their new grind would take place. *Would they make boat loads of money like all of the other blocks in the south end, will they attract the police to the point that their block will be shut down and end up stuck with a bunch of work in their possession or would they get robbed by some anxious bump needy fiends or*

56

even some jealous envy dealers from the neighborhood? They wondered if elevating to another degree of selling drugs would get them killed in the process. But then, like all other drug dealers, they summed it up to the lifestyle, and one they would live until they met their maker. For the M.H.B's, it was until death they do part.

Chapter 11
Hand to Hand

T he work was carefully separated into five zip-lock baggies. Four of them contained a hundred dimes, equaling a stack. The fifth zip lock held the remaining one-hundred and sixty-dimes, which would be flipped repetitiously by Germ himself. He chose to take on the responsibility of rinsing this particular pack, seeing it was for the security of their lives and operation. After cleaning up the basement, discussing the layout and what should be brought back off each gee-pack, they hit the pavement.

The work Big-Meat sold them was pretty decent, which gave them the strength to run with all the other blocks. Fiends were starting to hear about the block and began to make it a regular Stop 'n Shop. Not to mention a smokehouse was nested in between Capitol Ave and Russ Street. Being that the smokehouse was in close proximity made it very convenient for the neighborhood fiends to cop, get high in private, and then cop again, if need be. It was no doubt that the 'Money Hungry Boyz' had something brewing fast, and I ain't talking about no coffee.

The *'block'*, Babcock Street, stretched out about a quarter-mile in length, with three-family houses littering both sides of the one-way street. It wasn't a poor neighborhood by far. You had more than your normal social class tenants residing there, then you had the smart tenants, who kept to themselves, all except for Ms. Mary. She'd be the only thorn in their sides, seeing she was constantly on some *rally-block-watch-bullshit*. But not even some elderly woman and a few *'Drug-Free-Zone'* signs would stop their long road to riches.

$$$$$

Asia, Melodie and Courtnee were all on three-way talking about their plans for the day. Avonne could clearly hear the loud chatter, blaring from the speakerphone from where she was inside the bathroom. Prancing out the bathroom, a large bath towel tightly wrapped around her curvaceous body, and a smaller one bee-hived around her doo.

"What's up, bitches?" she smiled, demanding their undivided attention.

"Aye...hoe," Asia spat.

"You's the bitch, 'Vonne!" Melodie said playfully.

"And where you going? You up all early?" Courtnee questioned her baby sister; she was known to sleep in late.

"I wanted to hit the mall. A bitch could use a new outfit," Avonne answered honestly.

"I know Wendy's ain't paying like that to be copping new fits on the reg' hoe! Where you get mall money from?"

Melodie knew better. She had to be tricking with some baller from around the way. She was right. Her check was only $78.34 after taxes, and the type of gear Avonne loved to rock was out of that range. Unbeknownst to her girls and sister, she'd been dating this older cat named Jerry. He was getting money over on Grand and Broad Street. They'd been on the low, fucking for four months now, and Jerry had no regrets pushing that scrilla her way, and in return she'd put that snapper on him. She considered him to be her 'sponsor'.

"Mind your business...BITCH!" Avonne said playfully, then dropped her towel and began lotioning her yellow skin.

She had no insecurities about herself, after all, she was a twin, so her and Courtnee held similar assets. Only Avonne's ass was two inches phatter.

"That's alright hoe, because what happens in the dark, always comes to light!" Melodie assured. "Listen y'all; I'll get up with y'all later tonight, after my shift is over."

"Bye, bitch," Asia yelled through the speaker.

"Yea hoe, see you after work and don't forget to bring us some Butterfinger's too," Avonne spat. They all laughed.

Melodie didn't care, they always threw the 7-Eleven jokes at her whenever they were in play mode. The convo continued between Asia and Courtnee. McDonald's had a full line-up of girls to full-up their shifts. They decided on hanging out in the hood today, since they both had the day off.

Avonne caught the bus to West Farms Mall after swapping some head, for a few extra dollars from Jerry. He would have taken the ten-minute drive out to West Hartford to drop her off, but his block was banging like the first of the month, so he chose to stick to the script.

Courtnee and Asia met up an hour later.

"What's up bitch? I'm feeling that jean-skirt and top girl," Asia commented on Courtnee's outfit.

Courtnee sported a blue-jean, thigh-length, skirt by Apple Bottom, and her top was all white with the words 'Dyme Bitch' embroidered in red and blue rhinestones lined across her 32DDs.

"Thanks hoe," she replied. "Sheeit...Angus gonna rape dat ass when he see you in those tight ass leggings girl, and look at dat little ass halter you're rockin'. Ya lil' nipples are screaming, suck me!"

Courtnee knew Asia dressed this way to keep her   thug-love

J. Alexander

tempted and only interested on one thing – her.

"You think so?" Asia smiled, noticing her perky tits standing at attention.

"Bitch, you probably just finished gettin' off, with yo' nasty self," Courtnee teased.

"And you didn't?" Asia questioned, knowing it was something they both were accustomed to doing on a daily basis. It was the freak in them. "That's what I thought," she smiled.

They were having their usual girl talk as they trooped it to Babcock Street. Bending the corner, they noticed Pintz had a crowd of fiends around him, and some more were coming out of the small alleyway where Yak normally posted up to safely catch his sales. It was the crew's way of keeping him off the frontline and away from the dangers of being busted by the cops.

"Damn, this shit is really jumping out here today. It's fiends everywhere!" Asia said, looking at the abundance of fiends swarming Pintz ready to get their high on.

"Yeah, you know my boo gets dat pa...per." Courtnee gave Asia a high-five, and then walked up on the crowd. "Hey you," Courtnee said to him with a huge smile.

"Aye, what's hood, lil' mama?"

He was happy to see her on deck. She was not only his fuck buddy, but also his good luck charm.

"Yo block! I see y'all got it poppin' off out here."

Courtnee's mind was doing some calculations, as she watched him exchange drugs for money, and couldn't wait to help spend his earnings.

"No doubt, we 'bout to turn it up around here. We on some

61

Jeezy shit, soul surviving."

"I heard dat!" Asia cut in. "Y'all out here like y'all starving, hungry as hell. Anyways, where's my boo?" Asia asked, referring to Angus.

"There he goes right there," Pintz answered, seeing Angus hopping out of a Toyota Tundra that belonged to a fiend they'd stolen weeks ago from the Grand St. Hustler's.

Angus noticed the girls standing with Pintz and joined the small crowd.

"What's good shorty?" Angus walked up on Asia and wrapped his arms around her waist, letting his arms drift down to her thickness. "Damn ma', you looking tight today. Gimme kiss."

"You, and thank you, babe! You know you don't have to ask for no tongue, you can have it whenever you want, boo," Asia replied, then gave him a succulent tongue kiss.

"Y'all ned to get a room with all dat. And you ain't scared to be hopping in and out those cars like dat, Angus?" Courtnee asked, not really concerned, just making some small talk.

Feeling as if that was a dumb question, Angus raised his white-tee up brandishing his steel, "Hell nah shorty, you know a nigga don't mind peeling a niggas shit back." and meant every word too.

It was the gangster in him; he was a young thug foreal.

"If dudes get it fucked up wit the M.H.B's, I'll have 'em coughing up dey lungs, you know where I'm from? Hartford son, ain't nothin' nice…niggas can definitely get melted over they ice; believe dat!"

All they could do was shake their heads, because they knew

it was true. Germ might have been their leader, but Angus was extremely dangerous and feared in the hood for a sixteen year old. His thirst for guns and catching bodies was similar to blood and vampires since being first-bitten. A first kill does that to a newbie.

"So what, y'all came to cop or kick it with us?" Pintz asked.

They both looked at him strangely. They weren't offended, because he always joked around like that.

"Nigga, don't get it twisted!" Courtnee barked, while her hands rested on her hips.

To smooth things over, Pintz let them know he was just kidding. Joking with the girls was just his way of having fun. No pun intended.

Germ was in a yard three houses down observing the flow of traffic and his boys. His pack was moving just the same as theirs, mainly because it was a spot he had been trapping out of for weeks now. He was on some low-key shit and could see up and down the block with no problem, which was perfect. Slowly, but surely, his pack was disappearing as the early hours soon faded to black.

Tied to the hood, Asia and Courtnee chilled on the block until nightfall, watching out for the M.H.B's safety. Like always, the blue van blitz through causing the traffic to slow heavily, and the hustlers to call it a night, where they retreated back to Germ's crib. With a feeling of comfort and safety consuming their entire being, they relaxed, smoked and played XBOX into the wee hours of the morning.

Chapter 12

Real Shit

About 1:30 a.m., Germ got a call saying the jump-outs had bounced and mad money had been coming through the block for the last hour or so. He woke everybody up. It was back to the script. His goal was to go 'from nothin' to something as fast as possible. Germ was different from the others, in his dreams his envisioned Lambo's and yachts, not public transit and ten speeds.

"Damn Germ, is money all you think about?" Asia asked through a set of sleepy eyes.

She was in another world as she lay across Angus' lap. To her it was an honest question, mainly because this side of him she hadn't seen before. Yes, they had always been hustlers, but now they were really on their grind 24-7, leaving her less time to spend with her dude. Just as Asia lifted her head off his lap, Angus smacked her in the back of the head.

"Watch your tongue ma, or next time it'll be your mouth!" he threatened. "Now get your shit and get the fuck home! And don't make me say it twice."

Germ desperately wanted to check Asia, but Angus had done so already, which he was happy he did because he might have been a little more brutal with a verbal assault. He wasn't with laying hands on a woman. Asia looked at both of them through evil eyes, but knew better than to challenge either's authority. She and Courtnee gathered their things and hit the pavement as ordered. During their walk, Asia complained about Angus tapping her nugget, but knew not to get it twisted, he was something short of crazy, and she wanted no parts of his thuggish ways. Courtnee and Avonne came from a good home with a mom and step-dad who implemented a curfew that she constantly ignored, so Asia decided to walk Courtnee to her house in hopes to keep her out of the doghouse with her parents. When they reached Courtnee's doorstep, the two shared a sisterly embrace and said their goodbyes.

"Foreal, go home, Asia. Don't be out here all night on your bullshit," Courtnee urged.

She was well aware of Asia's all night affairs and cared very much for her wellbeing.

"It's way too early, girl, I'm about to holla at this baller I met a few weeks ago. Don't worry 'bout me, a bitch is straight!"

Asia hugged her girl again, and then, headed towards the payphone at the corner of Broad and Russ Street. She was looking for some late night dick. It was just Asia's luck, because her desires became a reality. She stood at the Russ and Broad Street payphone only five short minutes, before the platinum Buick swerved in front of her. The window rolled halfway down revealing its driver, and Asia smiled happily.

"Aye, Big Money, you got room for a cutie like me?" she said seductively.

Without saying a word, he popped the door locks and rolled the windows back up. There was no need to answer, she already knew the deal. Ten minutes later, Asia's thick brown legs were locked behind her head, while she endured pleasure and pain from the older man's pounding thrust. He was struggling to tame his young thing in the backseat of his Buick, so they ended up at a Motel 6 out in Wethersfield, off Exit 20. Now it was the headboards turn to endure some pain, since Asia's head violently banged against it every time he pulled out, then rammed his dick back inside her womb with brute force. She loved every minute of it too!

"Damn...you a freak, foreal," he managed to say in his

exhausted state.

"That's why you love me! Now let me taste dat big black dick, daddy."

$$$$$

Melodie's shift was just about over and she dropped her register's total in the stores till, as her pops strolled into the store.

"Aye, Daddy, you're here kind of early tonight," she said happily, though surprised to see him.

The night was young, her feet were killing her from standing on them all day, and she was definitely ready to be out. She missed Germ immensely and could use some sexual healing.

"Hey, sweetheart, I've got some inventory and ordering to do, so if you can give me twenty minutes to handle that, I'll have you out of here in no time 'kay?"

"Sure, dad, go ahead."

Melodie was cool with that, because she knew Germ was on the block getting money anyway, and the only thing that separated them was time and distance; two things she planned to close soon. As promised, Melodie's dad finished his work quickly and told her she was free to leave.

"Thank you, Dad, and I'll see you at home okay," she bided after hugging him tightly.

Exiting the store, Melodie unlocked the driver's door from her keyless remote and then climbed into her dad's MKT. She made sure the coast was clear; Melodie began pulling on a half smoked blunt from earlier. She knew it would not be until next week when he would expect his truck back, so it was cool to get her nightly ritual on.

J. Alexander

She did have a car of her own, but it was in the shop getting some bodywork done. While stopped at a red light, a mini-van rear-ended her Acura TSX, so instead of renting a car, she'd been using her dad's truck until hers was finished. All alone, traveling in the early morning hours, Melodie enjoyed her high and the sounds of the 'Quiet Storm' on 89.9 Cute FM. She effortlessly sang along with 'Tina Marie.' "Let me be your angel; let me be the one, for...you-ooo ooo ooo! Damn this is my, jam." Though she hadn't been born back in the day when Tina's song was a smash hit, she inherited the old soul from her parents. Turning off Maple Avenue onto Park Street, Melodie cruised at 25 mph until she reached Babcock Street. She took the right onto Babcock Street and cruised down the one-way strip. Very observant of her surroundings, she noticed a few people strolling by foot, most likely in search of a hit. Melodie knew the clubs had just let out, which meant the drug traffic was going to pick up tremendously. As she passed Grand Street, she noticed a dice game going down and decided she would pull curbside to the action. After blowing the horn, she said her hellos to everyone and continued to observe the illegal gambling.

"What did you do Mellz?" Yak asked. "You're out kinda late I see. Where's my boo thang at?"

"Boy, you know Avonne ain't messing with you. You's a flirt, and...you ain't tricking like you weigh! Maybe when you step your ones up, she'll let you smell the poohnani," she teased.

Everyone, including Pintz erupted into heavy laughter.

"Damn, Yak, you ain't doing no tricking? You getting money now and best believe 'Vonne's into those baller types. Plus, I heard shorty got some major head." A dude from the neighborhood said, stamping Melodies' prior address right before he went to roll the dice.

"I ain't paying for none of that fish, I'll take dat shit if I have to," he said seriously. "She'll come around, you'll see. A nigga's 'bout dat scrilla, so fuck dat gold diggin' ass trick!"

Yeah, he might be seeing some chips right now, but that didn't mean he was obligated to trick it off on the likes of Avonne, who had been nothing but a tease since the day they'd met.

"You better watch that tongue boy, fo' I cut that little shit off!" Melodie warned, holding up a fresh box-cutter she had taken from work. "Aye Angus, where's my peoples?"

"Hol' up Mellz, I'm tryna scrap these fools."

It was Angus' turn on to roll. He shook the dice around in his hand, and then let 'em rip the runway. After hitting six-one, he scraped up his winnings, said thanks for the free paper, and then hopped in the truck with Melodie.

"Let's bounce, ma', he's down the block."

"Well hello…to you, too! So rude." Melodie shifted the SUV into drive and proceeded down the block as he instructed her to do.

"Oh, my bad, ma, morning," he replied gripping his winnings. "Suckas," he boasted, as his eyes feasted on the dead presidents.

Now, all he had to do was get them a suitable coffin and bury them accordingly. There was nothing like free money in his eyes.

"Where's Asia? I'm surprised she ain't out here going hand-to-hand with you, or at least watching your back," Melodie inquired, knowing it was the norm for her girl to be posted up on the block whenever Angus was, it was damn near to the point where she thought Asis was selling crack herself.

"She got out of pocket, so I had to check her stupid ass. Her and Courtnee walked home not too long ago. She's probably sucking some niggas dick right now, wit' her stankin' ass."

Melodie thought about what Angus just said and knew Asia well enough to know that what he said was probably right. Sex, thugs, and ballers came first to anything else in her life, and out of spite, she was probably fucking someone close to him.

"No she ain't, boy. She's probably under her sheets dreaming about you."

In her best defense, she tried defending her honor.

"Yeah right," his sarcasm heavy. "Humph, whatever. Come on, Germ's down the block."

Chapter 13
Nightz Like These

Melodie caught a glimpse of Germ as he was hopping a fence. He had just finished selling his pack and was heading in the house for the night. It had been a long day of hustling, and he was extremely tired. All he wanted to do was get a few hours of sleep before he took it back to the block As Germ did a slow bop down the right side of Babcock Street, he noticed the halogen angel-eye lights flicker. Someone was obviously trying to get his attention, but to no avail. He wasn't into stopping for cars when he was out of work.

"Too late," he mumbled, feeling it was a lick lookin' to cop some he didn't have.

The lights flickered again, but this time it was followed by a soft voice.

"Slowdown baby boy, you scared of me or something?" The voice had a sultry intonation.

Suddenly she noticed his blue fitted turning in her direction causing her to smile heavily. He noticed Melodie's voice and moved with caution towards the SUV. Germ slowly approached the truck surveying the area for jack-boys. There was no mistaking he didn't want Melodie being caught up in some bullshit she had nothing to do with. Finally at the truck, he peeped his right-hand-man relaxed in the passenger's seat with his hat dirty low on his head. Once the window rolled down, the two greeted one another with daps.

"Sup Germ?" Angus spoke first.

"Shit. I was 'bout to take it in, I'm tired ass fuck, plus a nigga done rinsed crazy."

"Dat's what's up. Here, you might as well hold on to this change, my nigga."

Angus had also rinsed his work. He handed Germ a whole stack and hopped out of the SUV.

"You gonna need to call ol' boy ASAP."

"Damn homey, you checked a whole gee out dat work?" Germ said after skimming through the huge knot.

"Nah, I hit the crap game when your shorty rolled up and helped me bail out on them fools. I definitely wasn't tryna let them win it back, ya heard. You know me...I might've laid everybody down and took mines back had dat happened."

They laughed, giving each other dap. Angus decided he would just fork over the winnings from the crap game to help their quest in getting rich. He was definitely one who lived by the phrase, 'Get Rich or Die Trying.'

"Angus, you know you need to stop. Someone gonna push your shit back one of these days," Melodie warned. "You need to be more careful out here with these dudes. Nobody's playing fair you know!"

"I got this, Mellz, but yo' Germ, I'll holla in the A.M. I'm out, one-up!"

"Fo' sure, one-up, Kik." Germ watched his man look around before becoming one with the dark night.

As soon as Germ hopped in the SUV, he cuffed the wad of bills in the pocket of his fatigue shorts, and then pulled out a blunt.

"Where you coming from, anyway, girl?"

"Work, and hello to you, too!" her sassiness bellowing in the

71

car.

"My bad, wassup, pretty? Yo boy just got a lot on his mind right now. I'm trying to get this paper right, feel me?"

He reclined his chair and lit up the blunt he rolled as soon as he finished his pack.

"Of course I do, but I hope you're not planning on hustling forever, Germee!"

She had other plans etched out for them, and selling drugs was far from them.

"What do you mean by dat, ma'?"

His complexity was evident. He wasn't sure where this had come from. However, after many blissful nights of sexing, Melodie would share her desires to spend the rest of their lives together. Even with the tears, Germ never took her fantasizing serious. That fairytale life had never knocked at his door, so what real reason did he have now to start thinking of that white picket fence life? The streets would be his lover and stacks of dead pressie's would be that fence.

"What I mean is that you're gonna have to get yours and get out. Don't be like the rest of these clowns out here selling drugs like it's a full-time job, Germee. There is more in life besides the block, Angus' crazy ass and your two cousins, boy. I love you, Germee, and I want a life, a real life without all the headaches and heartaches associated with you possibly dying out here in these damn streets, or ending up in prison for the rest of your natural life, Germee. I swear y'all just don't get it sometimes."

Normally Melodie would break down when discussing their future, but she was so exhausted her tears never showed their presence.

J. Alexander

"Like what, ma?"

For the first time, Germ seemed skeptical to what Melodie was spitting, although he knew exactly where she was going with it. He loved to press her at times. He wanted to see how far she would take things, and how much she really loved him. Germ was looking for those crocodiles to swim ashore, but she surprised him by keeping her cool, and this shocked him. Melodie used her right hand to caress Germ's leg. She then turned her whole body towards him and said, "Uh...like fucking marriage...asshole, careers and children for starters," with that, tears began to cascade down her pretty face as she divulged her aspirations about building a life together with him. Germ was her first boyfriend, her first love and her first sexual partner, all she knew was him, and she could not get enough of him. She would die for him and did not mind displaying her affection for him. Her emotions were definitely worn on her sleeves. Germ listened attentively as Melodie spoke, which touched that soft spot in his heart. Surprisingly, she could tell that she had broken down that iron shield he kept erected ninety-nine percent of the time when faced with things of this nature. His reasoning for being so tough, was solely because he had never known what it was like being loved by a woman. He had been raised without a mother figure, so affection never plagued him. He knew how to be hard and defensive. However, there was something about tonight. Melodie had touched his soul deeply. He inhaled on the blunt, blew the smoke into the air and then took pride in running the crocodiles away from her face.

"I feel where you're coming from, Mellz, but right now...all that fairytale shit gone have to wait. Me and boss status got a rendezvous...and real soon, too!"

There really wasn't much Melodie could say or do to persuade Germ at this point, so she reluctantly gave in to his wishes. However, that did not mean she would give up on him for any reason. She was his 'til death. She was happy knowing that she had turned on a light in his dark room.

"Well…why don't we head on over to my crib, let me ease some of that tension you've been carrying around with you all day."

The real shocker tonight was when he told her that he loved her.

"I love you more, babe, now come on…I'm horny and tired."

First, she instructed him to pull his shorts down. Once that was taken care of, she reached for his manhood and began to massage it slowly until he grew to its full potential. By the time the SUV pulled into the driveway, he was ready to explode, and she knew it. Putting the truck into park, Melodie adjusted herself into a position that allowed her full access to his rod and took him into her mouth, swallowing him whole. She performed her felletio act as if this would be her last time on stage ready for retirement. Feeling the large boa start to constrict, Melodie steadily continued her strokes allowing his semen to sail down her throat.

"Ummmm…now come on, let's go get it in for real, babe."

Chapter 14

Fresh Start

Melodie was up early, as usual, when Germ filled up the empty void in her bed. Her father would be walking through the doors at exactly 8:30 a.m., and she had to get any trace of her night and Germ out of there. Even though her mom saw nothing wrong with her little affair, her father was very stern and would castrate any man found in his house, let alone her bed. It was 8:14 a.m. Eastern time, as Germ slowly crossed the threshold between trouble and freedom. After buttoning up his shorts, he then put his fitted hat snug over his head. Melodie stood in the doorway, admiring her thug walk away bare-chested, wife-beater draped over his shoulder.

"C'ya later, Germee," she shouted, as he bent her staircase.

Though he never replied, she knew he said his goodbye's with that last kiss. He had things to do, which involved money. Shortly after, Germ entered his crib through the rear-door that led to the kitchen. Upon closing the door, he noticed that his dad was in the kitchen, filling his glass up with some orange juice.

"Sup pops?"

"Germee, you've been down at that pretty little Indian's crib all-night huh? Well whatever you're doing, you'd better be strapping up, because I'm too young to be a grand-dad," he said seriously and then began drinking from his glass.

"Nah, Pops, ain't nothing like that. I know how to strap that magnum on tight, plus Mellz is checking for school and a real life outside of Hartford." Germ spoke from his kitchen chair, thinking back to his and Melodie's conversation hours ago.

"Oh yeah…sounds good. So, what are your plans?"

He was shocked to hear at least one of them had brighter ambitions and goals. Uncle Marv was all the father and mentor Germ could ask for. He worked hard knocking down two shifts at the Colt Firearm's Plant, where he rarely found time to be home and spend time with his son. He spent his free time at a girlfriend's house, so they barely saw each other, but when they did, it was all love.

"I hate to say it, but you know me, pops, I'm addicted to the life. You've done your job, but right now, school don't interest me, marriage and kids neither."

His answer cut through Marv's heart like a Ginsu knife. Marv felt as if he had failed his only child, more so deprived him, of a good nurturing life, which could have possibly led to the American Dream.

"You know, it wasn't supposed to end up like this, Germ. You know, after your moms passed...I—"

"It's all hood, Pops. I know what you mean, and this is the life I chose, no matter if moms were here or not. You've done more than your best, and I'll always love you for that!" Germ cut him off to let him know what's done is done, and one day there would be a good chance he would revert to being a law-abiding citizen.

But for now, it was the streets. With that said; Germ parted ways and went about his business. Down in the basement, Germ sat on the couch. He hated to feel as if he let his pops down, but he was a man now and could fend for himself. After a brief sigh, he emptied his pockets, placing everything on the glass table. Yak walked out of a backroom in some plaid boxers and no shirt.

"Sup cuzzo, you just getting in?"

"Yeah, I stayed at Mellz crib. I was just counting this here work money. Sup wit' you?"

"Man, I'm tired as shit, but hold up, let me grab this paper for you!" Yak headed back into the room.

When he returned, he tossed a knot onto the table.

"That's $820.00! Shit was popping out there last night after you disappeared."

"No doubt, where big bruh at?"

"Right here," Pintz answered.

He had just come in with a bag of food from McDonald's for him and Yak.

"What's good, peeps? I see you brought food," Germ smiled.

His stomach was growling like a muthafucka. After digging Melodie's guts out half the morning, he was spent.

"Nah cuz, you can't be hungry. I'm sure you ate some snapper all night and probably all morning," Pintz and Yak shared a laugh.

"Fuck you two niggas. You probably spent yours with that fiend Amanda!" he shot back humorously.

"Sheeit...she's got some good-good, but not good enough to snack on. Here my dude."

He threw the hot bag at him.

"Aye, how you looking on dat gwop?" Germ asked.

"I been done, catch." Before getting a chance to count it, Pintz confessed." That's seven-ninety, I owe ten."

"Don't worry 'bout it, I know we eating it now," Germ responded.

Germ tallied everything up, and then separated it into stacks. On the glass table sat three gee-stacks. Off to the side, was five-hundred-ninety dollars, also the odd gee pack. Germ had taken a sixty dollar loss, but it was expected.

"Aye, toss me dat cordless." Germ said. It was time to hit Big-Meat.

Chapter 15

Da Re-Up

The phone rang and rang and rang, unfortunately, there was no answer.

"Fuck!" Germ shouted impatiently.

He knew the last gee-pack wouldn't last two hours, seeing it was the first of the month.

"Wassup, cuz, everything alright?" Pintz questioned.

"Dis fuck-nigga ain't answering. I'm 'bout to try him again, though."

This time someone picked-up, "Hello?"

"Who's this?" Germ asked annoyed.

For some reason he could not decipher the voice.

"Lil' nigga, this Fluff! Fuck you want this early, fool?"

He wanted to disconnect the call, but he feared they might have wanted some more work. Just off the strength of money and not wanting to hear it from Big-Meat, he complied.

"You know what it is. You ain't got no pussy do you? Therefore, it's got to be about some paper! Where Big-Meat at?"

He had no love for Meat's right hand at all and displayed every chance he got.

"Watch your tongue, youngin', you're gonna need that for your shorty. Now wassup?" Fluff replied agitated.

Germ gave him the low-down, and then agreed on a time,

they already knew the place. About forty-five minutes later, Germ rode on a tricked-out Mongoose bike to Baby Park. He was tempted to let Yak ride out with him, but felt he was already moving a little too fast for his age, so he had Pintz ride shotgun on the back pegs. There were certain things pertaining to the streets that he did not want Yak to deal with, and copping large weight was one of them. Germ had the re-up money stuffed inside a brown paper bag, cuffed in the lining of his waist. The adrenaline rush he experienced just counting up the dead pressie's was life altering, there was definitely no turning back now. He swore nothing, or no one, would come between him and the hustle.

"Aye, here they come," Pintz said, noticing the Platinum Lacrosse easing up the block.

"Yeah I see 'em." Germ laid the bike on one peg, and then walked to the door of the Buick.

The window rolled down and right away he noticed Big-Meat was absent. He'd sent his yes-man, but what was more apparent was the lavender knock-off Coach purse resting on the rear-seat. Something wasn't sitting well with this picture. Just when his mind flashed back, Fluff called out to him, disrupting the sudden revelation.

"Yo homey, you gonna get in or what? A nigga ain't got all day!"

He hit the automatic button and the tinted glass shielded any further visual into the car. Germ totally forgot, or let's say, put his thoughts on the back burner for the sake of business.

"Here's thirty-five-hunid, I need five O's this trip. Can you fade dat fat-boy?"

Fluff laughed at Germ's stupidity. Didn't he know Big-Meat had whatever, whenever.

J. Alexander

"Damn…you lil' niggas rinsed that work mighty fast. Y'all got the block jumping, huh?"

He never got a reply, Germ hadn't come for small talk. It was a cop and go affair.

"Here lil' nigga, keep up the good work, Big-Meat loves fast earners. He might even put y'all on his payroll." Fluff said through a smirk.

"M.H.B's don't push no man's pack. If anything, niggas gonna' work for us, ya heard?" Germ barked, and then hopped out, slamming the door behind him. "Fuck outta here, errand-boy."

As they rode-off, Fluff yelled, "Watch yo' self youngin'!"

Paying Fluff no attention, he kept pedaling on the bike. He was adding up some numbers in his head, also trying to figure out where he'd known that Coach purse from. Either way, it was worth storing away in his mental.

$$$$$

By now, the moon's crescent had overwhelmed what little light the day's sun strained to cast upon the city, which happened to be just perfect for the M.H.B's. All five of the ounces were broken down into huge dimes. At eight dollars a rock, they would bring back eleven-two, plus they still had another gee-pack from their first flip, which Angus had been moving since early this morning. When the rest of them hit the block, fiends were circling around Angus, trying to compensate their daily fix. Although the odds were stacked against him, he had it under total control, but that didn't stop Yak from running up on the crowd. He wanted in.

"Yo, I got dem stones!" he yelled to the fiends.

Angus smiled at his young protégé's drive. You see, what

Yak failed to realize is, that at the end of the day it all went into the same kitty, so it really did not matter how much either one of them made as a solo hustler.

"Yeah holla at my lil' mans, I'm out." Angus instructed.

He had sold his last three rocks just as Yak bombarded the crowd.

Down the block, Angus found Germ and Pintz doing them. He made his way through the mini-crowd, and then acknowledged his homeys with some dap.

"Wassup my dudes? Yo, Germ, I'ma need some more work, it's bangin' out here."

"Damn, you rinsed all dat? You ain't even been out here long."

To show and prove, Angus pulled out several knots. He hadn't had the time to separate the money properly.

"I can show you better than I can I can tell you."

"No doubt, I'ma go snatch it out the spot for you right now."

Hearing that the block was in an uproar, Germ made off with the quickness. He walked to their secret spot in the alleyway and grabbed two gee-packs, cuffing them in the lining of his waist, then stored the rest back into the opening of a brick wall that was close to six inches deep and eight inches wide. Other than Twan, who was now an afterthought, there were only four people who knew about their stash spot, so they were safe.

It took him all but two minutes to get back. After giving Angus his packs, they all stuck to the strip like magnets. They had gained the necessary rest to stay outside far into the wee hours of the morning. And with an abundance of crack to rinse, it was going to be an all-nighter for the M.H.B's.

Chapter 16

Uh Day 'n Da Hood

Today was another smoldering heat wave summer day in Cunnuck. Babcock St. was flooded with its normal pedestrians, while those who did not have air-conditioning sat on their front porches. Their two and three speed fans were no help at all. Up and down the block, the neighborhood kids played in the open fire hydrants and sprinklers, while others played two-hand touch football in the middle of the street. Across the street from Ms. Mary's house, a group of young boys and girls were enjoying what appeared to be a water balloon fight, and hitting every passing vehicle. Of course, you also had your hot-in-the-ass girls prancing around in skimpy attire in hopes of enticing a d-boy. Mellz and her crew were definitely on deck. They were outside leant up against her dad's MKT, looking fly as hell.

"Ooh...turn that up, girl. That's my shit," Courtnee said.

It was that hot track 'Everyday I'm Hustling' by Rick Ross. Old...but still hood! As Courtnee and her girls danced to the drug selling music, that's exactly what the M.H.B.'s did. It was like a block party today that had not discriminated against the neighborhood fiends. In droves, they shadowed the block, mainly because Germ had beefed up the dimes to attract more clientele, and seeing that the quality was better than normal, Babcock was the street to cop from. Definitely a lucrative move on his part.

"Aye bruh, this shit is live out here," Yak spat, admiring the abundance of traffic flowing through the strip.

In his money hungry mind, they were going to be where they wanted to be in no time should this continue.

"You ain't lying, bruh. If we could only get some type of

J. Alexander

breeze out here, I'd be hood. It's hotter than nine-eleven out here."

Pintz then peeled out of his white tee. He'd been diligently working out in the basement when not smoking or playing XBOX with the others, and what better way to show off his new six-pack. Of course he knew Courtnee was looking, which made it all the better.

"Stop faking, Pintz, you see them hoes over there checking for niggas. Now, all of a sudden, you wanna peel off!" Angus checked Pintz in a homey kinda way.

Everyone laughed, knowing Angus was right. This was a first for Pintz, so they saw right through his boastful antics.

"Aye, where's cuzzo?" Yak asked.

He hadn't seen Germ since he came out of the alleyway.

"He went to grab some more work from the spot, plus he had too much fetti on him. You know Germ don't play dat shit."

It was one of their golden rules to never carry big wads of cash around while pitching on the block. Just as Angus stopped talking, they heard a set of screeching tires. When they looked up, they saw a pack of mobbing kids assaulting a blue SUV with a flurry of water balloons. It had been weeks since they'd last encountered this particular SUV, so they were surprised to see T-Kill's two goons hop out in an angry fit.

"Yoou, yyou, yoo, you stu-stu-pid, little kids!" Zoe barked.

Luda was to his left, wearing a mean-mug. The young mob ran off, in fear of being beat down from the older cats, also their parents. On many occasions they were warned against throwing the water balloons at passing motorists, of course, they disobeyed and were now subject to the backlash of T-Kill and his crew.

85

"Aye Gus, you see these fools?" Yak pointed. "That's T-Kill's shit. The youngins done thrashed they shit."

Luda caught it the worst, he was soaked from the head down. Standing on the curb, you could see small pieces of balloons stuck on his face. Yeah, someone had tagged his ass real good.

"Fuck 'em! That'll teach 'em to ride through our block with the windows down like shit is sweet. They lucky I don't shoot dat shit up for dat bullshit he tried at the park!" Angus spat nonchalantly.

Until today, they hadn't seen T-Kill or his flunkies nowhere. For them, it was out of sight out of mind.

"Fuck outta here, lames!" Pintz yelled, gripping his nuts.

He wasn't the least bit scared of T-Kill and his crew, especially seeing that they were on his turf this time.

"You lil' cats gonna learn to stay in your lane," Luda returned.

"What? This is our lane, homey! You're on the one-way, or hadn't you noticed?" Pintz countered.

"So, what you sayin', Pintz?" Luda spat.

"Ain't nuffin' over here but an ass-whuppin', fuck boy!" Pintz said disrespectfully.

He sized Luda up a long time ago and figured his thump game wasn't up to par, so in his mind he didn't deserve no respect.

"Wassup?"

T-Kill sat inside the truck observing the verbal exchange between his goon and the M.H.B.'s. His soldiers were loyal by all means, but he wanted to see how this would play-out. He had other plans that didn't involve his mug being remembered by any witnesses, so for now he planned to stay put. With a simple head nod from T-Kill, Luda ran up on Pintz, leaving him no time to react, catching 'em flush with a two-piece to the face, dropping him hard to the ground.

Luda stood over him taunting, "I told you to stay in your lane, youngin', now get up, lil' nigga!"

From Pintz' point of view; he thought Luda looked crazy still wet from the water balloon. Seeing his brother laid out on the ground, Yak started to jump in, but Angus stopped him.

"Let 'em rock, young. He's got to man-up and get dat OG-respect, plus, it's too many shorties looking. Pintz ain't going out like dat, trust."

Angus knew Pintz had a mean hand game, so he was going to let them do their thing head up for now. If he saw that Luda was getting the best of his people, that was when he would intervene.

"Get up!" Luda towered over him yelling, spit spewing from his mouth.

Zoe was laughing and pointing from the side, while sizing Yak up as well.

"Yyoou, you–ne-ne-nextt!" Zoe stuttered.

He was punching his left palm with his right fist, showing that he too wanted some wreck. Yak paid him no mind. He was ready to go at Luda. What no one knew was that Pintz was stalling because Luda's punch blurred his vision, and he was trying to get his senses back. Pintz had fully recovered, and was ready to get it popping. Just when Luda turned to the SUV's window to see T-Kill's expression, he was caught with a flurry of haymakers.

"Now what, fuck-boy? Hold dis!"

Again he started whaling on Luda. Hook after hook, Pintz administered an ass whooping Luda never saw coming, thanks to the boxing camp his moms kept them in as youths. She was not into having wimps living under her roof for one minute.

By this time, Yak had stole Zoe, dropping him with the quickness. Soon after, he found himself being stomped out something crazy.

"Talk dat shit now, stuttering mufucka!"

T-Kill had seen enough and hopped out of the SUV. He couldn't believe his eyes as he walked up on the fight. He was in some knock off Roc a Wear sweats and a matching sleeveless tee. The sight of his biceps were threatening, they were so huge. Witnessing T-Kill's true framework put Angus in a state of pause. He had no intentions on going toe-to-toe with the OG, nor was he going to let him intervene with the head-up that was in progress. Instead, Angus pulled out his deuce-deuce and slowed the OG's roll.

"Hol' up big-fella, dis head-up ain't it?" Angus questioned, and then chambered a round in his ratchet.

In fear of their lives, the crowd of onlookers quickly dispersed. Mistakenly, T-Kill began to bask in his glory for seeing the crowd disappear like magic, however, his smile soon faded, realizing that he hadn't caused this. He noticed the pistol in Angus' hands and quickly went for his own and kicked himself for leaving his in the car. The one thing he was sure of was Angus had no problems letting his bark.

"What it's gonna be, OG?" Angus calmly asked.

J. Alexander

In compliance, T-Kill raised his hands high in the warm air, symbolizing he wanted no trouble. He was going to take this one for the team.

"Come on pussies, y'all makin' a nigga look bad!"

Like loyal soldiers, they stumbled back to the Escalade, both dripping blood from various cuts and bruises they inherited from their scuffle. Inside the SUV, T-Kill shook his head in disgust. He quickly started the engine, revving it until the RPM's nearly redlined and then skirted off in haste.

"Fuck outta here, faggots!" Yak yelled; his middle finger high in the air.

An array of vengeful thoughts plagued T-Kill's mental as he rode by smiling. In his mind, someone had a reservation with death, and he planned to speed it up for them.

Courtnee and the others walked up on the boys, "Y'all straight, right?" Asia asked.

"Fuck yeah!" Yak responded, brushing his shoulders off.

"Dat's my boo!" Courtnee said, clutching onto Pintz arm, proud that he put in some work.

She always knew he was rough, rugged, and raw, but to actually see him throw down was sexy in her eyes.

"Ummm!"

"Damn, Yak, I ain't know you could throw hands like dat," Avonne licked her lips.

She was definitely turned on by Yak's display of toughness.

"Dat's because you won't give a nigga no slack, but yeah, these things work!"

89

He threw a few punches into the air, appreciative of her compliment.

"No, dat's because you always up in these ratchet bitches faces," she rebutted. "Nah, foreal though, you cool?"

For the first time since he'd been trying to holler at her, she licked her lips seductively, thinking that maybe giving some could become a reality.

"Like a room full of A.C's."

"Here, take my number. Call me sometime, handsome."

Yak happily accepted Avonne's digits. He couldn't wait till they sold out, so he could call her.

"So, you gonna let a nigga hit?"

"You want know unless you call, now, will you?"

"In that case, lemme make sure I get nice and tipsy, I'm trying to make you love me after the first stroke."

He gripped his crotch to let her know what he was working with. Tonight would be his first time ever digging her guts out, and he wanted to make a good impression on the pussy.

"Well, at least you got more than what I thought you had, boo. Call me, 'kay."

"Fo' sure,' he promised.

Asia looked around at all the nosy people still in attendance and thought it would be best if dude got out of dodge before the cops rolled up.

"Angus, you need to bounce. Too many people…including nosy-ass Ms. Mary done saw you with dat heater," Asia warned.

J. Alexander

"She's right," Pintz said, backing up her warning.

"Come on, let's go for a ride, y'all. Where Germ at?" Melodie questioned.

"He shot to the crib to grab some work. He should've been back by now though."

"Alright, I guess we'll catch him on the way," Melodie said, and they all loaded into her truck.

As Melodie pulled off, they heard a concession of shots that appeared to come from around the corner. Nearing the corner of Russ and Babcock, the worst began to set in.

$$$$$

Zoe and Luda were feeling some type of way. It wasn't the fact of getting beat down, it was by whom they'd had taken it from. Something they weren't taking too well.

"Yo, T-Kill, let me see yo strap, I'm about to body something," Luda said way passed pissed.

"Ye-Yeea...yeah, T-Kill!" Zoe was also displaying his feelings being that Yak had really put a whooping on him.

"I guess next time you'll watch who you hop out on Zoe, but don't worry. I've got this." He already had his .9mm rested on his lap.

T-Kill was ruthless to the core. Even though it wasn't him who'd taken an L', he felt humiliated by today's actions. Had he not left his gun in the car, it would have been hell on earth for a lot of people. As T-Kill slid out his mother's womb, he had large traces of larceny in his heart. It actually surfaced when he and his baby-sister were playing in their auntie's swimming pool. For kicks, he wanted to see how long she could hold her breath, so he held her under water by her shoulders until she stopped moving, then got out the pool, sat on the ledge and watched her lifeless body float aimlessly. When his parents found her body, he said he'd fallen asleep on the lawn chair and hadn't noticed; crazy fool! He wasn't even of age yet, and his first death, by way of drowning, was his little sister.

As one hand gripped his nine, the other banged against the wheel. T-Kill took several sips from his warm St. Ides malt liquor; letting *"What's Beef"* by the late Biggie Smalls consume his every thought. Just as the SUV was about to bend the corner of Broad St., Luda pointed.

"Yo, there goes that nigga, Germ, let me see dat heat."

He desperately wanted to put in some work. T-Kill was stuck in a daze, his eyes fixated on Germ's every move.

"I got this! Watch and learn, lil' nuts!"

T-Kill hopped out of the truck so fast, he forgot to put the shit in park. With no mask on, he ran up on Germ and put the muzzle into his chest. Unfortunately for Germ, he had no chance to react. Staring death in the eyes, Germ prepared himself to join his mother in heaven. For the first time, he'd been caught slipping while in the streets, and he could kick himself for walking with his head down as he made his way back towards the block.

"Wassup now... nigga? Go fuck wit' some nigga's yo age."

Germ knew they had beef with the OG, but he was thrown by T-Kill's sudden appearance.

"If you plan on using it, use it, bitch nigga!"

First, Germ was blinded by the muzzle's flash, and then, he felt the impact of the .9mm's kick, which dropped him right where he stood. Sadly *"bitch nigga"* were the last words Germ spoke before he blanked out. After the fourth shell found shelter in Germ's chest, T-Kill ran between some houses that led to the next street over, where his SUV picked him up around the corner. For now, he'd gotten away with a possible murder.

After hopping back into his Escalade, T-Kill suggested Zoe whip back around the block. Zoe protested in fear that the area would be swarming with blue and whites. He also wasn't expecting T-Kill to smack him upside his shit before demanding he do as told.

"You better just hope we get in and get out before they do, you stuttering muthafucka! Now swing the fuck around the block, pussy!" T-Kill shouted.

With no other choice but to comply with T-Kill's orders, Zoe bent the corner of Grand Street nearly running over two of Jerry Mafia's workers in the process. However, by the time his workers pulled out their heaters to fire on the reckless driver, Zoe was whipping the Cadillac around Babcock on two wheels, evading any retaliation from Jerry's crew.

The loud sound of T-Kill's juiced up motor roared as Zoe floored the gas pedal. The adrenaline rush had taken over any rational sense of thought in his mental as he swerved at any pedestrian in his path. Zoe zig zagged the Escalade down the street, and even jumped the sidewalks, in attempt to run down any witnesses. In doing so, he flipped Harold ten feet into the air, leaving a rusted Ford Pick-Up to break his fall. His body lay, mangled, in the rear bed, in a pool of blood. At this point, T-Kill had his arm out the window, letting his gun talk to the crowd. As each shell spat out the muzzle of his gun, he felt pleased, seeing the many bodies diving for cover.

"Now, dat's how you bow down to a Gee!" he barked out of the passenger window.

From Boyz To Men

What really set him off was seeing the tricycle wheels spinning rapidly as it sat upside down. He took pleasure planting the hollow tip in little Jameka's stomach. Out of shells, T-Kill demanded that Zoe get out of dodge.

Chapter 17

Life or Death

Following the loud gunshots, Melodie whipped the MKT wildly around the corner. Her worst fears became a painful reality seeing Germ's limp body sprawled out on the sidewalk in a pool of blood. Sparing no further seconds, they all hopped out and ran to his aid, hoping they weren't too late. In the midst of today's mêlée, crowds of people began rushing out of their houses wearing the faces of concern. Billowing in the distance, a variation of women's voices could be heard echoing with pain, sorrow, and grief. Staring at Germ on the ground, Melodie felt like she had also taken a bullet. She wanted to lie down and die with her man it hurt so badly. Germ was in very bad shape. Nevertheless, Melodie kneeled down beside him and attempted to revive him with CPR. Melodie's quick thinking might have saved Germ's life. Seeing him regurgitate his own blood let her know he had some internal bleeding and desperately needed medical attention. Surprisingly, she was doing a good job resuscitating him.

"Pintz, Angus come 'ere. Help me get him in the truck. If we wait for the ambo, he'll bleed out!"

"Hold up, he's probably dirty," Pintz said and quickly searched Germ.

Luckily for Germ, his clique rolled up when they did, seeing he had a couple of gee-packs in his waist. Had he been caught with all of that work on him, it would have easily sent him to the East Block (Youth Tier), in H.C.C.F (Hartford County Correctional Facility), for a nice stay. Thinking fast, Pintz retrieved the packs and cuffed them in his nuts once he was safely inside Mel's truck.

Together, they lifted Germ's bloody body into the back seat.

From Boyz To Men

In dire need of reaching the Hospital, Melodie sped through every city light, nearly wrapping out twice, before pulling into the u-shaped driveway at Hartford Hospital. Outside the emergency doors, several doctors and nurses were congregating while smoking cigarettes when the MKT's tires screeched to a final halt.

"Help! My friend has been shot!" Melodie shouted. "He's got three, maybe four, shots to the upper-abdomen area," she repeated, sounding like she'd been registered with years of experience as a medial physician.

Everyone, including the doctors and nurses eyed her suspiciously. Her medical French was overwhelming, but hopefully life saving for Germ. As the paramedics rushed Germ into the emergency room, a female nurse probed Melodie for any pertinent information she might have had concerning Germ's name, allergies, etc. In compliance, Melodie relayed his age, government name, and where his father could be reached to the nurse, who in turn passed it onto the admittance desk. Soon after, she and the others found seating in the emergency room's waiting area.

It took some time; however, Uncle Marv was contacted through the hospital's emergency records. He was on lunch break at the Gun Plant when his name echoed over the loud intercom system. He figured it was his supervisor needing something he was too lazy to retrieve himself. He and some co-workers were enjoying cold-cut sandwiches and Pepsi Ones. Reluctantly, he excused himself from the crowded table to go answer to his supervisor's call.

"Don't go getting yourself fired, Marvin. Randle seemed to be in a bitchy mood when I came in," Eddie, the Assembly Foreman said.

"I'm too focused for Randle to get under my skin, be right back though," he responded, walking out the break room.

Marvin approached his supervisor's office carrying the eerie feeling that he'd have some strange request, nonetheless he still went inside.

"Hey, Randle, you paged me over the intercom?" Marvin asked, standing in front of his supervisor's cluttered desk.

"Umm, have a seat Marvin."

Hearing those words brought on a weary feeling in Marvin's stomach. Something did not feel right. He just couldn't put his finger on it. He just hoped he wasn't on the lay-off list that had been circulating throughout the Plant all month. He witnessed some old-timers, who had nearly reached their pension status, catch the first wave of lay-offs, and he did not want to be a part of the trickling affect that had been plaguing the job site recently.

"Sure, but what's going on Randle, on my lunch break and my food's getting cold."

Randle took a deep breath before he shared his news with Marvin, "Well, the Emergency Room over at Hartford Hospital has been trying to reach you for some time now." Randle paused to grab a piece of paper from off his desk. "Here, they left a direct number to the admittance desk."

Randle knew of Marv's temper and did not want to risk it flaring, so he carefully pushed the yellow post-it paper across his desk towards Marvin.

"The Emergency Room, for what?" he repeated confused, immediately Germ and the boys popped into his head. "Did they say who was in there?" His voice began to harden.

"Sorry, but they informed me that because I was not a parent or legal guardian they weren't at liberty to pass on any information concerning the well-being of the patient."

Right there told him this was very serious, and it was indeed one of the boys.

"Well, how long ago had they called, and why the hell am I just being notified?"

This was exactly what Randle was afraid of.

"I…I just got the…"

"Never mind, I swear you people…"

Marv used Randle's phone to call the Hospital.

When he learned that his only son was laid up in surgery, he shot Randle a stern look and warned him, "You better hope my son is okay!" then stormed off without saying another word, letting the cheap door slam into the wall.

Marvin knew it wasn't Randle's fault. He just happened to be the closest thing to an excuse for him to wild out because he wasn't there to protect his son.

$$$$$

The glass doors of Hartford Hospital swung open wildly; and there stood Marvin full of rage and fury. For a brief second, Marvin stood still in the archway of the entrance, trying to gather his awareness of the busy and death scented area. To the right and left of Marvin were people coughing, in blood-covered linens, some on crutches, and even those who had streams of tears littering their faces. He let his desperate eyes wander the crowded room. With timely success, he found a red and white sign labeled, 'Patient Admittance'. In giant, hurdling steps, he made it his only priority to reach the sectioned off area that sat two Hispanic women and one black male, doing intake of patients for their proper identification and insurance.

J. Alexander

Through the glass partition, he looked an elderly Hispanic woman, who wore a blue, white and pink nurse's jacket filled with happy teddy bears dead in the face who said, "Hello, may I help you, sir?"

Marvin began to feel light-headed, however he still answered.

"I'm here for my son, Germee Rivers. They say he was brought in with multiple gun shots."

Reviewing the hospital's records, she located Germee's name.

"Yes, he's in surgery, and the doctor could use any relevant knowledge, such as: allergies to certain medicines; blood-type and donor information; family illnesses and so forth. Here you go, sir." She explained and politely handed him a clipboard to start the long process for admittance.

Marvin was trapped in a state of despair. He had been down this road before, only the last time he'd lost someone very dear to him, Germ's mom. It took Marvin ten vigorous minutes to fill out the lengthy forms, thereafter, she directed him to the third floor where he could await any further news concerning his son's well-being. Wasting not a second more, Marvin rushed off to find his son. Right off of the elevator, Marvin located the nurse's station. Thereafter obtaining all available information concerning Germee, Marvin was told that it was just a waiting game, and he could take a seat in the waiting area, and the doctor would be out shortly to speak with him. This didn't sit well with Marvin one bit. His stomach began knotting, knowing there was little he could do at this point. Before taking a seat, he looked around at two families that were obviously enduring similar atrocities. Marvin mourned for the family and then took a seat on the burnt-orange couch. Feeling helpless at this point, he rested his head deep into his lap and drifted off to sleep.

Chapter 18

Too Young to Die

The tempers of the remaining Money Hungry Boys were at their peaks. No one was more upset than Angus. His feelings were weighing on an unbalanced scale. He regretted not handling T-Kill and his flunkies when he had the chance, *'there were just too many people out there,'* Pintz kept telling him, but he wasn't trying to hear it. Soon, death would be knocking at several doors in Cunnuck.

"Yo, what we gonna do 'bout these fuck niggas?" Yak asked.

He wanted some get back for his big cousin's shooting.

"Oh, don't you worry 'bout dat young, I got dis! Them clowns don't know who they fuckin' wit!" Angus had a devilish sneer on his face as he spoke.

He was definitely going to get his man, and if all went bad, then murder would be the case they gave him.

"Well, whatever you got planned 'Gus, we definitely want in!" Pintz added.

He was tired of playing games with the washed up OG's who continuously staked their claim on young niggas' time.

"Yo, we need to rinse these last few packs, too. You know ole boy from VA coming up in two days with dat heat, so I wanna be on point."

"Yeah, dat's right," Angus agreed. "Come on, let's bounce. We can come back to the Hospital later, about 6 o'clock; two hours before visiting hours are over. It's Monday, and by then, second shift will be on, so we won't have to worry about   the jump-outs, feel me!"

Agreeing with Angus' plan, Pintz called Amanda for a ride. They had some major shit to tend to and didn't need nosy ass Melodie and her girls medaling in their affairs. It took her all but seven minutes to make it across town to the hospital, and like always, they could count on Amanda and the use of her Honda. Before dropping Amanda off to the crack house, Pintz gave her a fifty piece for her services, which she had no problems with. She was just interested in getting on one. Minutes later, they passed around a blunt as Angus directed Pintz through the city in search of their prey. The hunt was now on and in a bad way.

$$$$$

Uncle Marv was in a deep snore when he felt a light tapping on his left shoulder. In his mind, it was all a part of a dream until his vision finally focused in. Then, after wiping his eyes, he realized the horrid reality was as genuine as the President's signature.

"Oh excuse me, I must have drifted off," Marvin admitted.

Sitting straight up in his seat, he used his left hand to wipe away the drool that amassed around his mouth. In observance to his surroundings, he took notice that there was only one couple remaining in the waiting room. To the right of him, stood a doctor, clad in grey dress pants and lab coat; a stethoscope dangling from his neck. He could clearly see that Marvin's thoughts had faded off from his prior dreary state, so he politely introduced himself.

"Hello, my name is Dr. Malloy." He reached a hand out for a proper greeting. "I actually operated on your son...I presume?" He paused to get a reaction out of Marvin. Not receiving anything but a blank stare, he continued. "You can relax a bit, sir, we've done our best. Your son had the best doctors working to save his life."

From Boyz To Men

"Please Lord...let my son be okay," he silently prayed. "Yes, I'm Germee's father, how is he?" visibly concerned, he asked.

"Well, as you know, when he was brought in, he was in bad shape. The bullets caused severe damage to two of his main arteries. He's endured a lengthy surgery. However, I am pleased to say that the surgery was successful. I must say though, seeing as he sustained four, point blank range shots to the upper torso, he did extremely well. Now, had the caliber been anything larger or an inch closer to his heart, I'm afraid we would've lost him."

He paused and shook his head at how the youth of today were being cut down by way of the gun. Just two nights ago, he lost young men that were also brought in with multiple gunshot wounds, which he was unable to save. It was always hard for any doctor to make a parent or loved one relive the possibility of their child dying behind the bullet, or any tragedy for that matter.

Nevertheless, he could tell his words cut Marvin deeply. He noticed how Germee's father cringed as he spoke. He also knew words, of course, were the most powerful drug used by mankind, which is why he practiced everyday on how to relay pertinent and vital information to the grieving family.

"So, my boy will be okay?"

A single tear of relief and happiness welled in the corner of his eye hopeful to hear, again, that Germ would be okay.

"I'd like to think so," he smiled. "We'll be moving him to ICU status shortly. Then you will be able to sit with him. May I ask you a question, sir?" Dr. Molloy was curious about something.

"Sure," he replied.

Marvin thought it would pertain to the whereabouts of Germee's mom, seeing she was not in attendance.

J. Alexander

"I've noticed that there were two shootings in your neighborhood today, by any chance, would you happen to know a Jameka, she's the little girl who was brought in minutes after your son. The report lists them being a short distance away from one another, and if I'm correct, the same gun was used to carry out both shootings."

Marv's face contorted, symbolizing he was in his mental rolodex, searching for a name and face. Finally, his eyebrows rose with a tale only he could tell.

"That's Ms. Mary's grandbaby. Her mom was into the streets and sadly died from a heroin overdose a few months back. How is she, I mean, is she going to make it? She's so small and young!" Marvin could see her racing down the sidewalk on her tricycle clear as day enjoying life as a toddler.

"I'm afraid…things aren't looking too good for her. You spoke of a grandmother. She's with the Hospital Chaplin right now. If you have any questions concerning Germee, please feel free to have me paged. My shift doesn't end for another two hours."

In his years of visiting hospitals, Marvin had never encountered such a charismatic doctor besides the one who consulted him sixteen years ago when his wife gave birth to their son.

"Thank you, doctor." he said sincerely, and then left in search of the chapel.

Chapter 19

Comeout...Comeout...Wherever You Are

Behind the dark-tinted windows of Amanda's Honda, Yak, Pintz and Angus rode around the south end of Hartford trying to get the one-up on T-Kill and his two flunkies. Yak had a mini bat dangling from the left corner of his mouth, while Pintz and Angus sipped on a half-pint of Remy V.S. It was nothing to call up bootleg-J any time after 8 o'clock p.m. and get whatever you desired. Bootleg-J was the neighborhood liquor store on wheels. With every toke and every sip the trio took, their minds became flooded with nothing but vengeance. Someone was going to pay, even if the drama had to retrace its steps back to granny, T-Kill's only living relative.

"Man, this nigga ain't nowhere in sight. I say we drive by his crib once more," Yak said.

He was a little sluggish from the weed smoke, also tired of turning corners looking for T-Kill's Escalade.

"He's right 'Gus; we should run through his grannies spot and see if dude is camping out yet. We gotta get the rest of this work off, too," Pintz added, other than emptying a clip into T-Kill's dome, hid mind was on making enough money for the VA gun connect when he came up.

"Do it, drive through there," Angus responded.

He knew even if T-Kill wasn't at home, his karma would soon catch up to him regardless. However, to take it to every, and anyone who opposed them from this point on, they would have to meet ole boy from Virginia; and to do that, they still needed to hit the trap.

Pintz guided the Honda towards Capitol Ave., headed for T-Kill's spot. Angus guzzled the last of the Remy V.S., and then tossed the empty bottle out the window.

"Turn right here," Angus said.

As told, Pintz cut a right onto Hungerford St., then drove slowly down the one-way street hoping T-Kill's SUV would be parked somewhere along the road. Unfortunately, T-Kill's truck wasn't in sight.

"Yo, dude's truck ain't out here. Maybe he put dat hot-ass shit up." Yak said, still searching both sides of the road, being there were no backyards in which cars could be parked.

"Yeah it looks that way," Angus replied, only they couldn't see the sickening smirk on his face.

He had some plans that didn't involve Germ's cousins.

"Come on, let's hit da block."

Before pulling off, Angus noticed a light turn off on the first floor, meaning it was bedtime for someone.

"See you in a few, ma, believe dat!"

$$$$$

It was now 2:00 a.m., the M.H.B's were down to their last few rocks, well at least Yak was. Angus and Pintz had rinsed theirs and stood off to the side, conversing about future things and ways to clip T-Kill's wings, also LateNiteSnackz's, should he continue to be a threat to their movement.

"Aye, Yak, what's hood, you done yet?" Angus asked.

"Nah 'Gus. I got bout thirty-pieces left, why what it do?"

From Boyz To Men

"We trying to go hit Money Ross' Spot, throw some bones, probably get some head or somethin'. You got dis?"

"Hell yeah, I'm playing the yards til' I'm clean, then I'll be through, ya heard."

"You sure, lil' bruh, cause a nigga will stay and hol' you down til' you rinse dat work," Pintz offered.

He knew the clubs were letting out, and Yak could handle his own, but as his big brother, it was his duty to inquire when it came to Yak's safety.

"I got dis, y'all bounce." Yak said, hailing down a sale.

"A'ight young. You know where we at, so holla when you done." Angus said, and gave him some dap before he and Pintz walked off.

They cut through some backyards, which was a faster way to reach Money Ross' Spot. They were eager to get a little down time in with all that had transpired today.

As Angus hopped the first fence, he felt that he was leaving his protégé for dead. He started to dump his deuce-deuce on him, but knew down at Ross' he and Pintz could easily get into some shit, so he held on to it. *"He'll be okay,"* he told himself, then hopped the last fence into the Bodega's backyard.

Chapter 20

Two Heads, Always Better Than One

Yak eased his head out of the darkness, peering down both sides of the block, only to pop it back in, seeing nothing profitable in sight. He was aware of the fiends that would be lurking at this hour and was eager to get through the end of his pack. He wanted to go get it in with his comrades.

"Psst...Psst!" was a call most of the regulars would use when they could not see a face, but knew they were in the vicinity.

Upon further observation, Yak noticed it was only Amanda. He felt safe and knew some money was involved, so he surfaced out the darkness and stood on the sidewalk.

"Sup girl?"

"You, are you holding?"

Amanda's pale face twitched as she spoke. She was wearing a thin, white top with no bra, which exposed the hardness of her erect nipples and a pair of cut-off shorts that raised tightly into her crotch area. Her thickness was very evident.

"Always, now hurry up...a nigga gotta stay on point. The under-cover's been riding through all damn night. I swear, if a nigga gets busted on some dumb shit, I'ma fuck you up, girl."

Yak was just being careful and cautious. Just as he'd said, the police had been patrolling the area all night due to the new block watch program that had been implemented by Mayor Perez in hopes to salvage this part of the South Side. Little did the Mayor know, but not even some block watch could halt the movements and progression of the M.H.B.'s. They were about to go from *'boyz to men'.*

"Well…I was wondering if you wanted to, you know," she ended, broadcasting a sexual smile.

She only had six-dollars and hoped the youngster was feeling horny as usual.

"Damn, you smoked those rocks we hit you off with already? I know you toting some type of change, Amanda." Still, his tool began to harden with the opportunity to get some head.

"Yeah, I got $6 on me, and if you want, you can rent my car for the whole night. Your peoples left the keys in it. I'll even run some sales for you until you're done," she promised, completely exhausting all her remedies.

Yak was in deep thought. He searched the block for any custee's, when he saw none he made Amanda follow him into the dark alley.

"Let me get dat change you said you had on you," he said, staring at her nipples. "You didn't think you were getting off scott free, did you?"

Amanda passed Yak the crumbled up bills, at the same time his shorts hugged his ankles, ready for some of her bomb head. Amanda never replied. Instead, she dropped to her knees and took Yak's tool into her mouth, deep throating him. Yak was leant up against a wall, which gave him some good leverage, or else he would've collapsed by now. Amanda could see he was already gone from her vicious headlock as she studied the whirling of his eyes. It was similar to a ballet dancer, practicing pirouettes. Amanda sped up her motions on Yak's dick. Her mouth was wet and warm, which made Yak's balls stiffen up. She then tickled each one of them with her free hand until she noticed his eyes doing cartwheels. Unbeknownst to them both, they had a peeping tom, one who was seriously admiring not only Amanda's head

J. Alexander

game, but also Yak's dick size.

"Damn boy, you're holding for a little nigga! I should've been put this snapper on you." The peeping tom said, feeling her kitten drool at the mouth. She didn't down play the youngster because she knew all d-boys got head and sex from fiends at this hour. *"The game could get stressful, and what better way to relieve yourself,"* she reasoned.

"Uhhh...oooh, faster faster!" he pulled on her bronze hair causing her to gag momentarily, but she was used to a ten or eleven at best, so Yak's seven, eight didn't pose too much of a threat to her throat.

After pulling him out of her mouth, she jerked him vigorously until she felt the muscles in his rod pulsate, only to cram each inch back into her warm mouth. Twenty seconds later, Yak began convulsing, and then shot a hot load of cum deep into the back of her throat.

"Urgghh!" he grunted out of breath, while Amanda watched satisfied with her work.

"That should get me three rocks!" she said to herself. "You good?" she mumbled, letting his sperm marinate in her mouth.

"Yeah...I'm hood. Fuck you learn to suck dick like dat?" He shook his head at how easily he could get addicted to her fellatio game.

She hadn't answered him just yet. She wanted him to see how she swallowed every last drop.

"Pornos, of course," they both laughed.

Just as he was wiping himself off with some napkins he had in his short pocket, Avonne appeared out of the shadows.

109

"Damn, Yak, dat's how you get down?" Avonne looked in Amanda's direction. "Yuck!"

Yak wasn't too sure what she meant, so he said, "Gotta get it somewhere," his dick still out with traces of semen glistening off the tip.

"Don't get me wrong, I know all of y'all boys get it in, I was referring to that thing in your pants!"

"Oh, this thing?" he looked down, surprised he was still rock hard. "Here 'Manda, that's four, I'll see you tomorrow, I got work to do."

Amanda brushed by the younger girl, looking her dead in the eye. She was offended by Avonne's presence and open remarks.

"See you, big boy!" Amanda said through a smile, and then disappeared into the night; she had a date with the pipe.

For a moment, the air was very awkward until Avonne broke the silence, "You want me to post-up out here with you?"

"Yeah, do dat, and if you're lucky, I'll let you taste dis big ole thang." He gripped his rod.

"I'm a big girl, if you hadn't noticed," Avonne did a quick two-step, and then turned around. "I got no problem siphoning some of your gas, so act like you know, boyee!"

Avonne was a freak by nature. Her three idols were the sexy vixens: Trina, Lil' Kim and now the black Barbie-doll herself, Ms. Nicki Minaj. They played a big part in her salacious ways. In the blink of an eye, Yak found himself on that dark path once again, only this time his big head violently crashed into the brick wall.

"Urggghh!" He wasn't sure what plane his flight crashed on,

J. Alexander

but it was invigorating, yet well-worth it. "Ahhh!"

"Put it back in...Put it...back...in!" he demanded, as Avonne
squeezed him tightly, riding his pole with her hand.

Her head might have been better than Amanda's, and he
desperately wanted back inside her warmth. After another quick-
nut, Yak was exhausted, but very determined to rinse the
remainder of his pack. The two stood in the alley's darkness as
fiend after fiend either rode or walked up to satisfy their habitual
cravings. There were also a few cars he hopped in and out of to
make his work disappear. Tonight was all about da Benjee's, and
he planned to get it how he lived on the hustling. Yak was in
between serving Marlin and Rhonda when Avonne noticed the
same late model Dodge Intrepid pull up and turn its lights off. She
wondered why the couple never got out when they came to cop.
At this hour, Avonne figured they might be on some bullshit, so
she pulled out her razor and cuffed it in her back pocket. Fiends
were often known to pull off with a hustler's pack when not
getting out of the car. Other than the young features of the black
male driver, Avonne knew the overweight woman wouldn't be
much of a problem should things get out of hand.

"Hurry boy, you got these two fiends out here geeking,"
Avonne urged.

Yak looked and noticed it was his peoples; Bruce and Dawn,
and sped up his current transactions.

"Hoe, shut up, I'm coming now."

After getting rid of Marlin and Rhonda, he jogged out to the
passenger's side door of the car.

"Wassup Bruce, Dawn, y'all back already, what's good?"

He hoped it was a hundred again, because he would be able
to take Avonne back to the crib and bang her back out.

111

"Let me get six this time," Bruce said, counting out his money.

"Sheeit, as much money as we spend, Pac, I know this one hundred and twenty dollars will get us an eight-ball, right?" Dawn intervened, she knew those dimes wouldn't last them but twenty short minutes, and she wanted to get high.

Yak laughed, hearing Dawn spit out the name *'Pac'*. It was the name he gave to all of the fiends, so there'd be no trace to him should anyone decide to flip and turn rat for the police.

"Ain't no weight right now, but here y'all can have my last ten for eighty, dat's cool?"

"I guess so," Bruce answered, giving Dawn a peculiar look.

The two shared a sinister look then smiled, knowing they had gotten the best deal of the night. While Yak was leant over into the passenger window pulling his pack out, Avonne knelt down by the rear tire, blade out ready to slice a hole in it if they tried to pull off.

"Damn...what's that smell?" Dawn covered her nose, looking at the brown plastic baggie Yak held in the open.

"Dis dat good shit, girl. All my regulars get the good shit!" Yak joked, he wasn't used to cuffing his packs just yet, or else he would have had the baggie wrapped in a napkin.

"Boy, don't tell me that came out of your ass!" Dawn was disgusted and frowned at Yak and his display of poor hygiene.

Before Yak got a chance to respond to Dawn's question, a slew of masked-men, dressed in all black tactical gear, rushed the Intrepid with their guns drawn. Avonne was in awe as the masked marauders appeared out of the bushes like lightening bugs from across the street and just about every yard five houses down. She quickly went into ratchet mode and started kicking and screaming obscenities at the officers.

"Fucking...P.I.G.S.!"

To shut her up, Detective Dawanna Jones of the Vice Squad popped her in the head with her flashlight, and the two began to tussle.

"Get off me, you fat bitch! Dat hurts!" Avonne yelled.

Being larger, and trained in these sorts of things, Dawn had gotten the better of Avonne by using her weight to hold her on the ground, then straped some plastic T-strap cuffs around her wrists.

"Shut up you little trick. If your young, fast ass was in bed, instead of playing big girl at two a.m., with a dick in your mouth, you wouldn't be in this predicament," Dawn bashed her.

While she and Bruce handled the manual labor, which consisted of purchasing the drugs straight from the dealers, her team had been doing surveillance for over an hour now and had obtained some very circumstantial evidence.

"Fuck you, bitch!" Avonne didn't care who saw what, the cuffs were killing her far worse than any words could at this point.

"And you nasty, too! You went and put that lil' thing in your mouth right behind some crack head? Pitiful and nasty! Get her out of here."

She was too through with the young girl to continue to even go back forth. Yak had been rushed face first to the ground, when he looked up, he noticed Bruce standing over him with a blue nylon jacket on with *'Narcotic Vice Squad'* in bright yellow letters. In his mind, he couldn't understand how this had happened to him. He had been extremely careful up until the point where Amanda and Avonne came through on some sexual shit, and now he had become part of the statistics of men who thought with their little heads instead of their big ones. By now, more officers had arrived on the scene and combed the area for more drugs and possible weapons, but came up empty.

"Hey, is this her purse?" a blue and white asked, holding up a lavender bag.

"If it ain't, it is now." Dawn said, hoping it had some type of drug paraphernalia inside it.

Shortly after being subdued at the scene, they were brought to the sub-station on Affleck Street and booked. Inside Avonne's bag were three nicks of green and two more box cutters. After being stripped out and fingerprinted, Avonne was allowed to make her one phone call where she phoned her stepmom. It was hard, but she informed her of her charge and bond, which was five hundred cash or surety. She was bailed out at five fifty-five and being blasted by six a.m.

"What a night," she thought.

As for Yak, his parental guardian, Uncle Marvin, could not be reached. He was asleep on a plaid chair next to his son, therefore he would be placed in the custody of J.D.C. until Monday morning or someone came for him. One thing's for sure, Yak definitely had several years of problems ahead of him.

Chapter 21

High Stakes

Through the rear entrance of his Bodega was a large doorway, closed in by a thick, steel door. After the steel door became ajar, there lied a steel gate that was locked by a state-of-the-art deadbolt and a three inch wooden slab, interlocked with a metal hook. His juke joint usually opened around seven p.m. on weekends, and ten p.m. during the week. Inside the small establishment, were two large pool tables cushioned with eggshells for the dice games. In the back, were two rooms with full size beds, 32" TV's and DVD players; of course, which would cater to the four girl escort service he provided to his patrons.

"Nigga, hurry the fuck up!" Someone in the crowd impatiently shouted.

"Chill nigga, heaven ain't called on you just yet, but after I roll this 7/11 and rape you for all your scrilla, ole Angie gonna put a bullet in dat ass." Pintz antagonized.

Pintz was on the dice, taking forever to roll as usual. It was part of his nightly ritual. He loved to talk cash-shit before shooting. It was his way of taking cats out of their game. He had forty dollars on his point and thirty around the board to several players. He was about to roll the dice but took a quick glance around the table to check on his bets due to the scandalous niggas that ran through Money Ross' late night playhouse. I'm talking grimy to the point their green backs couldn't be trusted. Counterfeit money was on the rise once again, and Money Ross himself, was a connoisseur in the field. In any event, Money Ross was not to be trusted. Pintz finally rolled the red, transparent bones along the table. The first die stopped on a six, and Pintz began talking hella shit.

"Six-one gonna get chu done!"

Then the second die bounced off the steel-grey eggshell and rolled onto one. Pintz yelled out while glaring tauntingly at the niggas who bit the dust behind him, hitting his fifth straight number. So far, he had raked in almost four hundred dollars. Angus wasn't into dice. He loved to play 21 Blackjack. Money Ross' chic, Mya, had just brought him a nip of Remy and a fried whiting dinner.

"Good lookin', ma'."

He slapped the older woman on the ass then slid her the fifteen dollar charge for his order.

"Boyee...you a little too young for all this ass, but I got a new P.Y.T. for you in back whenever you're ready to pay like you weigh."

Mya ran Ross' stove and stable of young whores. She was an ex-prostitute who turned wifey. So what, she was a little run down, she was still voluptuous and thick in all the right places. Mya never lost her sensuality or her looks, and because so many of Ross' customers often propositioned her, he had no quarrels with her making him some extra cash, but in her mind, she had changed and was not having it.

"So, what's it gonna be, handsome?"

"You know how I like 'em, Mya. She better be tough, or I'll bend that ass without a tip," he warned.

"Well, it wouldn't be the first time. I got this, just let me know when you're ready, okay baby?" she said and went off to meet the other player's necessities.

J. Alexander

Angus was in deep thought while dousing his last piece of fish with some Durkee Red Hot Sauce. After stuffing a piece of wheat bread into his mouth, he studied the two bricks (face cards) in front of him.

"Hmm…" he mumbled, contemplating whether he should split them or pass.

Satisfied with his decision, he knocked on the wooden tabletop passing, the play to the next player.

"Yeah, lil' nigga, you should've split those tens," Snackz told him.

He had been watching from the side to see where his game was at. He also favored 21 Black Jack. LateNiteSnackz was not alone tonight. He not only had his goons with him, but two badass chicks that went both ways. He kept 'em by his side when out enjoying some leisure time. Mona and Rachel were his personal playmates and would do absolutely anything for him. When Angus looked up from the table, he noticed Mona had a purple bikini top and some coochie cutters on. They made brief eye contact until he noticed Dex and Dro sizing him up with gangster grills. They were obviously still salty from their last encounter on the 'Law'.

"You think so, ol' head?" Angus replied.

"No doubt, youngin'." Snackz answered with a head nod.

"Well, if you think you know so much…here, bet this deuce, I would've busted splitting my tens smarty."

"Nah, how 'bout we bet five-hundred, you should've split those bricks, young," Snackz said, testing his gangster.

Angus was leery at Snackz's proposal. Unbeknownst to the table, splitting the two tens was, in fact, what he was

117

contemplating a few minutes ago. *'Ah what da hell!'* he thought. "Hol' up, dealer." Angus dug into his knot and peeled off five bills. "Let's do it, OG!"

He was feeling cocky and confident as he tossed his paper on top of the table.

"Shit, ain't 'bout nothin'," Angus concluded, displaying a grimace.

He was a thug first, and a go-getter second, so being afraid of a simple bet from the likes of Snackz was out of the question. Pulling out a large knot full of twenties from out of her bra, Snackz held a tight face as Rachel did the honors for him. It was obvious she was the more loyal of the two and his favorite, seeing she held onto his bankroll. Rachel counted out the five hundred and threw the wad next to Angus while giving him a stern look.

"Play cards, Phil!" Snackz urged.

From the dice table, Pintz could see things with Snackz and his goons could get out of hand. Taking his turn, he quickly rolled the dice, crapped-out, and then went and stood by Gus' side.

"Wassup, peeps?" Pintz questioned, looking around the crowd of people, waiting to see how this would play out.

"Ain't shit, 'bout to take this fool's paper," he boasted, looking from Rachel, then to Snackz.

Money Ross was viewing the sideline action from a standing position. He knew how grimy Snackz and his crew could be, but knowing how Angus got down told him it wasn't going to be a good night, at least for the ambulances. As Phil looked to Money Ross for any specific signs as to why he should or should not continue, his heart rate sped up immensely. Money Ross nodded his head in approval, giving Phil the green light to continue dealing the cards. Phil reached the first player after Angus, who busted with twenty-two. The player next to him also flat lined, only he busted with twenty-five. The next one stayed with a three showing, leaving the next card on Phil. Phil had a king of hearts showing.

"Dealer takes one," Phil said, and then, flipped a four of clubs over.

The room fell silent anticipating what Phil's next card would be, seeing he had to take another hit: in black jack it's a rule that the dealer must hit up to seventeen, and then, stay afterwards.

"Dealer shows fourteen," Phil announced.

When he flipped the seven of diamonds over, Snackz smiled, knowing that had Angus split his tens, he would have gee'd up because the two bricks that busted the two players after him, would have been his.

"Dealer has twenty-one," he announced and took in all of the house's winnings.

"Get dat paper, Ray. Youngin', lemme know when, and we can get it poppin' head-up," Snackz said and walked off.

He was in need of some down time, so he headed to one of the back rooms.

"You got dat old school. See you on the rebound," Angus said nonchalantly.

He wasn't in the least bit upset, because had he went with his first instinct, he would've cashed in. To him it was a lesson learned, but one he also had to teach Snackz very soon. Angus felt played being there was a crowd that witnessed his loss, however, he vowed that it would never happen again. When Angus looked up from the table, he noticed someone was giving him the eye.

From Boyz To Men

"Wassup, ma'," he asked curiously.

"You're cute but a fool. Have a goodnight."

Before walking off, Rachael blew him a seductive kiss; a tale that told a defining ending. A light quickly went off in his head, he figured she could be the key to getting close to Snackz. Angus was turned on by the display of exoticness from Rachael and stood up to let her view the wood he had grown in such a short time.

"Yeah you and your man can get."

With another hundred dollars to burn, Angus played two more games, unfortunately losing both. Fifteen minutes later, Pintz and Angus were side-by-side, tag-teaming Mya's newest P.Y.T. in one of the backrooms.

Chapter 22

Oh...You Ain't Know!?

E arly the next morning, Angus and Pintz woke up with major hangovers and Lolita, Mya's newest dick peddler, in between them. Lolita was just too fly and tender to leave without having another taste. After thirty minutes of tossing her every which way but loose, they gathered their things and shot out of Money Ross' on the double. Exiting the juke joint, Pintz' recollections of the night had no signs of his younger brother. He had not come through last night as he said he would. It was now imperative that he get back to the block to see what was up with his little brother. As he approached each wire barrier, he conquered them like a true track star, hurdling them with ease. It wasn't the first time Yak pulled a no show when he was supposed to meet them at Money Ross', but for some reason his big brother intuitions was telling him something was out of place. Hopping the last fence, they saw a few of the regulars lurking aimlessly about the block, so Pintz knew Yak was nowhere in sight. If so, he would have had a major crowd around him, but that was not the case.

"Yo, where the fuck is Yak?" Pintz said loudly, his mind racing in different directions.

"Calm down Pintz. He's probably at the hospital with Germ," Angus said, which made good sense.

"Yeah right, where we should've been all night," he said, feeling some type of way about getting his swerve on while his cousin was laid up with tubes running in and out of him. "I swear...if that old-head T-Kill has anything to do with my lil' bruh's absence, I'll snap his old ladies neck, then his!" He uttered through clenched teeth.

From Boyz To Men

"Oh, we gonna handle T-Kill and those two flunkies of his. And old Grammy just might see Heaven a day earlier than planned," Angus assured, already having things capered up.

With no sign of Yak, the two made to Uncle Marv's. As soon as they stepped up onto the porch and was about to enter the crib, Avonne ran up the small flight of steps behind them.

Out of breath, she said, "Where have y'all been? I've been looking all around for y'all all morning!"

"Girl, fuck you been around here for? So, you really checking for youngin' all of a sudden, huh?" Angus said, knowing the mind games she played with Yak before, witnessing him thrash Haitian Puffy yesterday.

"Psst...! You ain't gotta act all grand, Angus, I just thought y'all'd like to know that we got knocked by the deeze this morning!" She said snapping her neck back and forth in a ghetto like fashion.

"Fuck you jus' say?" Pintz asked not sure he'd heard correctly.

"I said; we got knocked by the deeze. All night he'd been serving these two under covers. You know; those two in the Intrepid who usually spend heavy?"

"Who you talking 'bout, fat ass Dawn?" Pintz asked still confused.

"Yeah, dat's her," Avonne answered. "And dat cracker Bruce! They the deeze though," she added rubbing her sore wrist.

Detective Dawnna Jones was fatigued with her fat girl jokes every time they faked coming to cop drugs, so she made sure to get a little vengence by tightening the plastic t-strap cuffs on her wrist.

122

Pintz was no dummy. His sixth sense told him that something was not right with Yak. He also thought about the countless times he sold to Bruce and fat-ass Dawn and knew he would probably have a bench warrant coming out soon also.

"Yo, 'Gus, I done served them too many times to fucking count myself, so what now?"

"First things first, we meet Germ's connect from VA, then we put that work in on T-Kill and his two flunkies. Little bruh's a minor, and knowing them dirty ass cops, they've got crazy undercover sales on him, but that's something Uncle Marv's going to have to handle we too hot evidence to even go to court for him," Angus said, making mounds of sense.

He might have been a school dropout, but he was street smart to the tee.

"I guess you're right," Pintz agreed. "Hold up...how the hell you get out, 'Vonne?" He was curious.

"Oh hell...to da nah! You ain't asking a bitch that, like I'm some fucking rat snitch?" she threw her hips to one side and mean-mugged Pintz. "And for your information stupid...I'm sixteen with a mama, unlike you!" she snapped her fingers in his face, unappreciative of his comment.

Without a thought or care in the world, Pintz backhanded her for the disrespect of his dead mother.

"Bitch...if you ever...come out of your mouth like dat again, I'll beat fire out your stu...pid ass," he barked then spit in her face.

It was a side of him no one had ever seen before. Angus was in tears as he watched the scene unfold.

"Nigga, you's one crazy fool. Come on, let's go count this

money up."

They walked away in their own thoughts. Angus' mind on Germ and T-Kill, while Pintz' mental was consumed with Yak and the bench warrant he knew he would have to face one day. For now, meeting up with Punchy from VA was their main priority.

Chapter 23
Now What

Avonne finally got up off the ground, holding the left side of her face. Although she could not see it, Pintz left his hand print embedded across her yellow, butterscotch skin. Obviously, one of the downsides to being a red bone. Brushing herself off, and then snatching the lavender Coach bag off the ground that she'd borrowed from Asia, Avonne walked down Russ Street desperate and full of rage. For one, the nickel bags of weed the deeze's found were not even hers. Asia forgot to transfer them when they swapped purses a couple of days ago, now she was subject to doing some major C.S. (Community Service) or probation for their blunder. However, that didn't bother her as much as the vicious backhand Pintz leveled her with.

"Ole bitch ass nigga wanna put hands on a sista! He must don't know," Avonne blanked-out, as a wicked thought sedated her mental.

Once Avonne's inflamed, vengeful, thoughts brought her to Lawrence Street, she noticed the crowd of niggas she remembered bringing a move to Yak not long ago, and a venomous sneer plastered her face. Step after step, Avonne's voluptuous goodies bounced, catching every eye in the crowd; their thoughts vividly explicit.

"Hey y'all," she said, finally standing in front of them now wearing a fake smile.

"Fuck yo young ass want?" Slim asked.

He was the oldest out of the crowd and saw right through her innocent façade the moment she bent the corner. She was known as a flirt in the hood, which would usually end with her getting some free leisure money from dudes without giving up the goods, leaving them with massive erections.

Avonne turned her nose up at Slim's remark, she could care less how he felt about her right now, she had some major get back to tend to, and he was not going to throw a monkey wrench in her plans today.

"Not your tall old ass, now fuck off, lame!"

"What's up then," Blaze, a short, dark skinned cat, with growing braids, asked. He'd love to trick some of Snackz's drug money on the young tenderoni.

"Well, I came to holla at Dro," she licked her lips from corner to corner. "What you got goin' on, cutie?" she asked, staring Dro dead in the face.

Not easily falling victim to her bullshit, he replied, "Wassup wit' you?"

"I got something for you. That is, if you can handle it?" She replied seductively.

Who was young Dro fooling? He'd die to hit that young stuff. His rod was rock hard long before she spoke directly to him, which she happened to notice when she looked down at his crotch. With that, Avonne directed all of her attention towards him. She was young, sexy and street smart and planned to use those attributes to her advantage today.

"What you got dat we all can't have?" Dex asked, he wanted in as well.

"Well...now that you asked, I guess you can play, too, sexy."

She licked her lips. In her twisted little mind, Avonne figured Dro might not be enough for what she had brewing, so he was

126

J. Alexander

definitely about to be added to her evil plot. This wasn't just your average act of vengeance. It was against the M.H.B.'s, but mainly Pintz.

"Are you driving, Dro?"

"Fuck you think…I look like a young wannabe?" he barked, then pressed a button on a keyless remote to a 2010 Ford Escape, a rental car from Enterprise he'd been in for two weeks now. Yeah, all of the hustler's on the 'LAW' were seeing chips like Pringles and had no problems splurging on the things they desired.

Avonne smiled, knowing she had struck oil with Dro. He was young, ruthless and did not give a fuck.

"Let's go get a telly then," she suggested, her eyes flirtatious as could be.

"Say no mo'. Yo Slim, I'll be back in a few, hold the fort down, kiko."

With that, he, Dex and Avonne hopped in the small SUV and headed to the Super 8 in the Meadow district of the city.

Thinking about the good time they were about to have with Avonne, it only took Dro ten minutes to make it across town. After stopping at the Package Store and grabbing some dutches, the trio entered the lobby of the stuffy hotel.

"Hello, may I assist you with a room today?" the middle-aged desk clerk inquired, eyeing Avonne with a disgusting look.

From the petite frame and kiddish features, she knew she was young and probably about to get into a freaky threesome with the older boys.

"Yeah, I need a short stay rate," Dro said in a   snappy

baritone.

He caught the resentment in the clerk's eyes, also her tone of voice when asking about renting them a room.

"I'll need to see a driver's license or some form of identification. Our short stay rate starts at forty dollars for three hours."

Dro tossed his driver's license onto the counter and shot the woman a nasty stare. He could care less how she felt, he was about to twist Avonne's back out and hers too, if she dared to join them. The clerk quickly found a room at the far end of the 1st floor, and then, processed two room keys for them. After handing Dro the key cards, she offered them a sarcastic farewell.

"Have a good time."

"Oh…we will!" Avonne sneered wickedly.

$$$$$

Inside the small room was a queen size bed with the usual floral print quilt, an ancient 25" color TV, a large desk that had obviously taken a beating over the years and a nightstand, which held an eggshell colored push button telephone and lamp on it. Dex quickly found his place at the round dinette table and began rolling some trees up. He loved to smoke dust, so of course, he rolled up two separate blunts of wet. Although Avonne previously showered from her little stay in lockup, she excused herself to the bathroom to freshen up. While Avonne was doing her, they both stripped down to their boxers ready anticipating the ménage trios. Dro then cracked the top on some Hennessey, and then lit up a blunt.

"Don't be touching or looking at my shit neither, nigga!" Dro said playfully, but he was very serious.

He knew the wet would have Dex doing all types of crazy, freaky shit, and he wasn't playing that gump-shit now or never.

"Fuck outta here, nigga, I ain't wit' dat gay shit!" Dex said in his own defense.

Avonne exited the bathroom in her bra and panties, her thick bush protruding from the sides of her pink hi-cut bikini underwear.

"Let me hit dat weed," she said, smelling the exotic weed throughout the room.

Smoking was one of her daily pleasures. The sight of Avonne's curvaceous body mesmerized Dro and Dex. Although she was only sixteen, she was fully developed. Her nipples were fully erect pushing her bra out about a half-inch, as her wide hips let them know her ass was just as fat.

Dex passed her a blunt with the quickness, and even though it was one of the blunts mixed with wet, she hit it twice before passing it back for a regular one.

"Yeah, I dabble a little bit, but I ain't trying to be off my square, Dex. Let me hit dat Henny, Dro, damn!" she giggled.

He was stuck on stupid still casing her thickness. Dro was also surprised that she indulged in smoking wet.

"Oh, here you go, ma', drink up. Take all dat down," Dro encouraged, wanting to get her lifted to the point where she would do any and everything they wanted sexually.

And just as planned, they fucked and sucked her for over an hour.

"Okay, now that we've gotten our sexual frustrations out, y'all need to pay attention, 'kay?"

They two of them listened attentively to how she planned, rather gave up the valuable info, on Germ and his clique.

"So, dat nigga, Germ, is layin' up in the hospital right now?' Dro questioned, his attention was stuck on a come up, although he hadn't felt the M.H.B's were seeing no paper like that. "I swear you better not be lying, girl."

"Are y'all even listening to me?" Avonne shouted as she stood in her underwear in front of the TV giving them the rundown on their operation.

She was growing tired of talking and wished they would start taking what she said seriously instead of some type of hoax. She wanted them to run in there on some gun-ho shit, but Dro was a little smarter than that.

"Yak, the youngest one is in juvi as we speak, so y'all only got Pintz and crazy ass Angus to worry about."

"So, what about Germ's pops, he ain't around these days?" Dro asked.

He knew and heard of Marvin's reputation from his hay days in the city and really didn't want to go up against dude, if so, he wanted no parts of what Avonne had brewing.

"He'll probably be up at the hospital 24/7 or at court for Yak. You know that's his nephew, right?" She let be known, just in case they didn't know they were tied by blood.

"A'ight, we got dis, don't even worry 'bout it," Dro reassured her. "Here light dis and come give me some head...we got about a half an hour left on this room."

With that said, Avonne took a few totes on the blunt and pleasured Dro as requested. While she was riding the length of his dick with her mouth, she grew hopeful that her plan to bring the

M.H.B.'s down to a leveled playing field was just moments away. Avonne swore Pintz would pay for not only smacking the dear life out of her, but also spitting in her face like she was some stranger of the streets. The true meaning of a person's pride getting in the way of friendship. Her vengeance against Pintz was in the looms of darkness.

Chapter 24

In God We Trust

A ngus and Pintz were in the basement, counting the money they had accumulated thus far, also the money they scraped up the night before. Yak had been arrested with over $2,000 worth of work, but that was a loss they could handle. That money was actually was going towards their gun connect.As Pintz counted bill after bill, he wondered how his little brother was doing in lock up. What he was going through? Was he okay? Was he eating right? Were cats getting out of pocket with him? They had never been separated before, and it seemed strange, even though it had only been a day since last seeing him.

Angus could see the lost look on Pintz' face, so he questioned him, "Yo, my dude, what's on your mind?"

"Man, I'm just thinking about my baby bruh. I ain't never been without him before. I mean, I know he can take care of himself, but I've always been by his side, feel me."

"You already know, kik. Shit's fucked up right now, and it's up to me and you to keep it together. We gotta get these straps and wet those fools for Germ. Therefore, you gotta pull it together. M.H.B.'s to the death!" Angus swore.

He never knew what it was like to have real brothers, his comrades were the closest things to brothers he ever had, and he considered them to be of the same blood. Angus' little pep talk seemed to pull Pintz back into reality. He finished counting his pile of money and started on another. In the end, they actually had a nice piece of change stacked up, which surprised them both, and it was time to make shit happen.

J. Alexander

"That's it homey, $9,875. With that loss we would've had over ten racks easy. I hope we'll be able to bond Yak out," Angus said.

Yak was his little dude, and it pained him to know that he was caged up like some wild animal with an unknown date for freedom.

"Yeah, I feel ya. I gotta holla at my Uncle Marv. He probably don't even know Yak's in Juvi since he's been up at the hospital with Germ all night. Shit ain't looking too good right now 'Gus, but we going to handle T-Kill one way or the other." Pintz made that clear.

While Pintz packaged up the money, Angus decided to reach out and touch Punchy, their gun-connect from Richmond, VA. He informed them that he was on the highway and promised to be at Melodie's crib within the hour. It just so happened he had other business in the sheisty capital, so he hit the road a day early.

Out of the nine G's, Angus took out thirty-five hundred for some artillery. The plan was to be well equipped from now on, and that meant carrying heavy all day, every day. The remainder of their money would go to some work from Big-Meat. Although the block was hot from the recent shootings, it would eventually die down, and they would be ready to pick up right where they left off.

$$$$$

Marvin found Ms. Mary right where the doctor said she would be. He silently crept up on her and bid his sorrowful feelings for his family tragedy.

"Sorry to hear about little Jameka, Ms. Mary. She is so innocent and didn't deserve this. How are you?" Marvin asked consolingly, his heart went out to them as a whole.

133

Still caught in her prayer, Ms. Mary stood quiet. She so desperately wanted to relocate to a better section of Hartford, but there really was none. Today's youth controlled every inch of the city with their drugs and gangs these days. In addition, her low income would not allow her to reside in the more secure, gated communities Hartford offered. In addition, her SSI check wasn't enough to provide them the lifestyle she longed for. It was just barely helping her situation as it was, and now her grandbaby's life resided in God's hands.

"Thank you Marvin, but I'm sure the Lord will choose whether or not it is Jameka's time go home. It was pre-ordained for today to happen, so all I can do is pray," she said finally breaking her prayer. "Help an old lady up, will you, Marvin?"

"Sure Ms. Mary." He extended both hands out to help her up from her crouched position.

"How's Germee?" she asked gracefully.

Through the grapevine, she had heard about him being a part of today's unthinkable tragedy.

"He's in ICU as we speak. From what the doctors are telling me, I'll be able to see him in a few. I just wanted to check up on you."

"You're so sweet, Marvin. Beverly would be so proud of you," she referred to Germee's mom.

They were good friends and both worked at Hartford Hospital back when Jameka's mom was alive.

"Yeah I'm sure she would be." Marvin pictured life with his soul mate back when times were good and raising Germee in the city was not as bad as things are today. "Thanks. Are you going to be okay down here, Ms. Mary?"

J. Alexander

"Yeah...I think I'll stay and chat with the Lord awhile. Thanks for the company, too! Bless Germee's young soul. Please give him a kiss for me okay."

"No need for thanks, Ms. Mary, I consider you guys as family. You take care okay," he said, and then went to be with Germ.

Marvin made it back up-stairs in no time. After a short wait, the desk clerk showed him to a private room guarded by a police offier. It was policy to keep close watch on all shooting victims in case the shooter wanted to finish the job after rumor spread that they had survived.

The clerk let the officer know he was cleared to go in as his parental guardian. The cop glared at Marv as he passed, which stunned him. He chalked it up to him being pissed he was placed on guard dog duty. *"Too bad,"* Marv thought.

Finally inside the room, he viewed his only child, asleep on the full size bed with tubing running in his nose, mouth and arms. This would mark the third time he had shed painful tears in sixteen years and twice in two days. It hurt him severely to see Germ in this fashion.

Marvin tried his best to shield his son from society's crime-stricken ways, but a boy has to transform into a man eventually, and Germ had done just that when he chose the street life. Marvin, himself, led a similar life, so he had never condemned Germ's choices, all he could do was stick by him the best he could. In light of the fact that Germ was practically on his deathbed, he felt that he had failed him as a father. Maintaining his faith in the Lord as well as the doctor posing there was a good chance of survival, he was clinging off the possibility of Germ coming out of this ordeal in one piece. And should this be the case, Marvin planned to get Germ as far away from Connecticut as possible. He would no longer leave Germ's life in the hands of Corrupt

135

Cunnuck. As soon as he left the hospital, he had a phone call he needed to make.

As a concerned and loving father, Marvin sat with his son for hours. He watched as doctor after doctor, and nurse after nurse came in and out of the room either changing an IV or taking Germ's vital statistics. Had Marvin never viewed the wall clock, he might have never known how late it was. Although he was eligible to stay over with Germ, he knew a hot shower and some food were essential, not for just his sake, but Germ's as well. He would sleep once he knew for sure that Germ was okay.

Marvin slowly stood up, gripped Germ's hand, and in a prayerful manner said, "Poppa's here, and I always will be. I love you, son, and please get better. I need you, son."

Marv attempted to let go of Germ's hand, but he felt a firm lock onto his hand. When he looked up, he saw a stream of tears trickling down his face. Marv smiled widely, as a sigh of relief washed over him. To at least know his son was coherent, gave him the blessing from God he had been praying for.

"Thank you, Lord, I will lift up my eyes to the hills from whence comes my help. My help comes from 'He' who have made this possible! God bless you!" he graciously praised for saving his son's life, and then walked out of the room.

Chapter 25
Strapped Up

The phone rang loudly in the basement where Pintz and Angus sat smoking weed and playing Madden 2005. They put the game on pause in hopes that it was Melodie, saying her peoples were in town. It was 9:45p.m., and he should have been on deck two hours ago.

"Hello?" Angus spoke into the receiver.

"Hey 'Gus, my peeps is here. Y'all were coming through right?"

"No doubt; we'll be through in a hot one," he said, and then, ended the call.

"Who was dat?" Pintz asked, pulling on the weed.

"You already know. Come on, bag dat gwop up. I'm trying to holla at dude, then take it to them fools, feel me!" Angus said with hatred.

He was anxious to get back at them lame ass niggas for putting his man's in the hospital. Pintz took heed to what Angus said and gathered up the buy money. Shortly after, they left out the back door that led to the Babcock Street side, where they had a stolen Cadillac STS not a day old out of West Hartford waiting. Angus knew of some car thieves from around the neighborhood. He put in an order for something fast and nimble that would assist them in a high-speed chase should one arise and for only three grams of hard, he 'd come up. Amanda's Honda would do, but that was an everyday rental they used, so it would be too obvious for a drive by and a getaway. After turning a few corners in the neighborhood, the STS pulled into Melodie's driveway. They immediately noticed the VA tags on a black Dodge Magnum with darks lenses and chrome feet.

"I like dat bitch right there, 'Gus," Pintz said, looking at the out of town whip with admiration.

Down south, where he came from, they rode old schools whips, but for some reason the American made car held his undivided attention.

"Yeah," he nodded in approval. "She is looking tight, huh?"

"Like virgin pussy," Pintz smiled, picturing himself behind the wheel show boating around the hood.

"Come on, let's get dis shit over wit'," he urged, cocking a round in his deuce-deuce in case shit got out of hand.

Pintz smiled, knowing Angus wasn't playing any games tonight. "You got dat shit off safety, bruh?"

The look Angus shot him said enough, but for good measures he answered. "No doubt."

"Dat's wassup, kik. Let's do this!"

Angus knocked on the side door to Melodie's crib. They heard a light shuffle inside of her apartment, and then noticed a head peep through the mini blinds. In precautionary mode, Angus drew his ratchet and cuffed it to his side. He wasn't taking any shorts, not at this point in their come up. Catching a glimpse of Angus gearing up for war brought a frown to Melodie's face. She knew she had to smooth things over with her boys quickly, because she did not want a wild shoot out ensuing over trust issues. Rushing to the door, Melodie latched onto the door knob and pulled on it until it swung ajar.

"Hey, y'all, everything's cool. So, Angus, you can put dat heat away…this is my family y'all dealing wit."

"It ain't nothin' like dat, ma', you know how I get down. I stay strapped and ready for whatever." He replied. "I'm just protecting M.HB interest. You can understand dat, right?"

"Whatever, boy, like I said, these are my peeps, and y'all have nothing to worry about. Oh yeah, I know y'all haven't been up to the hospital to see Germ, but he's doing okay, and they think he's goin' to be fine."

Melodie thought that it would be a good idea to switch up the subject. From personal experience, Angus was known to be a hot head and could pop off at a drop of a dime, and she was not about to lose a piece of her bloodline due to ignorance.

"Good looking Mellz, you know we can't go up there right now, we probably got warrants out for our arrest on some drug shit," Pintz said. "You know Yak and Avonne got knocked by the deeze last night, right?"

"Nah, I ain't know that. I haven't spoken to anyone since dropping Germ off earlier. I've been up at the hospital sitting with Germ. I thought I saw Uncle Marv's pick-up out there, but I never saw him."

"You know Unc, he was probably pacing the floors or in the chapel praying for Germ's speedy recovery," Pintz replied, knowing his uncle like a book. "So, what's hood, where your peeps at?" They were very eager to get things in motion.

"Come on, follow me," she responded.

Melodie ushered them into the garage where Punchy and one of his boys stood, sipping on some Remy Martin. Upon entrance the aura was awkward, that is until Punchy broke the eeriness.

"What's good, y'all trying to do some business or watch us sip all night?"

He, too, was eager to get things poppin' and hit the road.

"No doubt, let's see what you're working wit'," Angus stated.

"Now dat's what I was hoping to hear, and before we set shit in motion, I'm sorry to hear about your man's, too. But don't even sweat it, I brought some real act right for y'all. These'll help y'all get some revenge on them fools, ya heard," Punchy declared, knowing the fire power he was about to sell them was enough to win a waging war of any sort.

Punchy nodded to his mans, he in turn opened a large suitcase full of handguns and rifles.

"I got 44's, .9 milli's, .45's, .40's, .357's, Calico's, AK's, Uzi's, it's whatever," Punchy said and watched as their faces lite up with amazement. "Not to mention, they're brand new, squeaky clean, and I've got a ton of ammo free of charge, too!"

"Dat's what's up. Listen, I got thirty-five hundred, take care of us," Angus said and nodded at Pintz.

Thereafter, Pintz tossed Punchy a brown bag full of dead presidents. Punchy caught the bag and then tossed it to his mans who then took a peek inside to make sure the count was on point. Punchy was about his business, however, trust was an issue he felt he didn't have to worry about dealing with her cousin's people. So, wasting time counting it up was out. If it were off, he'd definitely be back for his and some blood.

"Looks right P'," his mans admonished and tucked the bag in his waistline.

"Your paper's good, so y'all good. I'm extending my arms in ways I don't do for many, but your man is my people's people, so like I promised, I'ma make sure y'all straight, feel me?"

Punchy was a big deal down in the south and prided himself on being an arms dealer with great service, money and protection was his thing, not to mention he loved to see youngin's on their come up. Punchy grabbed a large duffle bag he brought with him and began stuffing it with an assortment of guns. In the collection were, four of the Glock 40's, two .50 caliber Eagles, two AK 47's, two Mac 90's, and two riot pump shotguns. The ammo was of the most elite, deadliest bullets known to man. He even threw them back five hundred dollars just because he knew what type of customers and bond he just formed.

"Hold up, take these new .44's I got, real pit-bulls, too! And trust me, their bite is definitely worse than their bark," he nodded with a scowl. "Shit if you gotta target, I can show you better than I can tell you."

"I like your style, P', but we gon' handle this ourselves. Thanks for the offer though. They gon' know M.H.B.'s don't take no shorts after we six-feet something," Angus stated.

In completion of a good transaction and a chain well linked, the four of them shook hands and enjoyed a toast. Pintz suggested they smoke on some of Ct's Purple Haze before they hit the road. About thirty minutes later, Angus and Pintz headed out the same door they came in, only now they were armed to the tee and ready for war.

$$$$$

The hour struck twelve. The city was extremely quiet for the moment, it was as if everyone knew something tragic was about to take place in the nearing hours. Could they really smell death in the air? Had the inner city civilians predicted heavy blood showers in the forecast? Anything's possible in Homicide Hartford. Angus and Pintz covertly loaded up the heat they intended on rolling out with for their mission into the STS. They were clad in all black fatigues and black Timberland Field boots.

Pintz laced his fingers with a pair of thin nylon gloves and his face with a ski mask, letting it rest on top of his head until it was time to get busy, and then, tossed Angus a set also. There would be no trace whatsoever of tonight's massacre.

Angus made sure he gassed up the stolen car in case they got into an all-out chase with T-Kill or the police, should something go array. All the clips to their weaponry were extended and loaded to the max. Inside a medium size gym bag were the two riot pumps, two .50's, two Mac 90's and two .44's. Their plight hadn't called for so much heat, but Angus was a warrior and thought like Germ; 'what if'. So he over-packed with the possibility that things could get out of hand.

As they crept up the creaky steps leading from the basement, Pintz could hear Uncle Marv on the phone. His conversation caused him to halt and be nosey.

"Yo, 'Gus, I'll be out in two seconds, ya heard?" He told Angus through a whisper.

As Angus kept it moving, Pintz eavesdropped on Uncle Marv's conversation. In revelation to his nosiness, he overheard Uncle Marvin talking to who he thought was their Uncle Big-Rod, out in Magic City, Birmingham, Alabama. *"Hmm...what's this about?"* Pintz mulled.

"Yeah bruh, my boy is shot the fuck up in ICU right now," Marv informed him.

"What?" Hearing his nephew, a Rivers, had been violated and was laid up in ICU disturbed him immensely. "You need me and my boys to roll-up north? Just say the word, bruh, and we'll be in Ct in no time!" He said angrily.

For years, Rod had been trying to get Marvin to pack up and move the boys down south, but he continuously declined, saying his life was in Connecticut. Subconsciously, Big-Rod felt guilty

142

J. Alexander

for not making them come down after Germ's mom died years ago, because being who he was in Magic City, he could have protected them from all harm.

"Relax bruh, Germ's going to be okay. However, I'ma need you to keep him right while he recovers. I wanna send the boys down your way for a little while, feel me?"

While on his knees in the hospital chapel, Marvin had made his mind up, Germ and his two cousins were getting out of Homicide Hartford.

"Shit...dat ain't no biggie, bruh, I got 'em. When are they coming?" Big-Rod was antsy to see his family.

"As soon as possible," Marv replied.

"Fo' sure. Oh yeah, what's good with Yak and Pintz, they straight?" He asked, seeing that Marv never mentioned his other nephews by their sister Bianca.

"Wow, with all this shit going on I haven't seen them two, but I'm definitely sending them as well. If I know Pintz, he's out there right now looking to murk something," Marv knew Pintz had Bianca's street savvy running through his veins and would not lie down while Germ was laid up in the hospital.

"A'ight, dat's what's up, bruh. I'll be waiting on your call. I got dis!" Big-Rod assured.

"I'll holla back soon bruh, one!"

"Hmm..." Pintz mumbled as they ended their phone call.

He then crept out of the house with the Uncle Marv's secret, which would right on time. Now they had the perfect getaway to go with a perfect plan. *"We put T-Kill and his two flunkies to bed, and then get out of dodge for a while. It couldn't get any better,"*

143

From Boyz To Men

he thought. Moments later, he climbed into the passenger seat of the stolen car.

"So, what's up, Pintz, everything straight?" Angus asked, seeing a little extra energy in Pintz's demeanor.

"Yeah, no doubt, kiko. I just heard Uncle Marv talking to my Uncle Big-Rod out in Magic City. Dude is caked the fuck up, too."

"Fuck is Magic city?" Angus questioned.

He thought Magic City was a strip club down in Atlanta, so he was a little thrown.

"Magic City, Alabama, crazy…" he laughed; Angus could be so off point at times.

Ok, so, what dat got to do with us?" Angus was still confused.

"Oh, my bad, Unc' plans to send us all down south, so Germ can heal up, which is good, seeing we about to peel these dudes shit back, feel me." Angus saw the light in what Pintz said.

"But where would that leave me?" He thought. *"How they gonna just pack up and leave me here all alone? Fuck am I gonna do wit' out my dudes?"* In Angus' eyes, things were just getting worse instead of better. First Germ caught some hot ones, and now, Uncle Marv was planning to separate them by thousands of miles, and he disapproved of it all.

"Chill peeps, you coming, too!" Pintz said, giving him a brotherly punch in the chest. "We M.H.B.'s for life."

"Let's catch some bodies then!" Angus said and chambered a round in his life taker.

"Let's do it!" Pintz agreed.

144

Chapter 26

Revenge At Its Worst

A little after 1 o'clock in the morning, Marvin found himself in a very agitated state. Even though Dr. Malloy reassured him that things would be okay concerning Germee, the thought of losing Germ weighed heavily on his mind. With all that has happened today, the anticipation of misfortune caused him to breakout into a cold sweat. Marvin sat quietly in the dark night of his bedroom, ingesting warm shots of Bourbon, hoping to ease the estranged quiver throughout his body. Every so often, he would share stares between an innocent photo of him and Germee when he was much, much younger and the Greek Orthodox Church, through an open window in his bedroom. In the midst of remembrance, he allowed his mind to stroll down memory lane. He recalled a specific moment with Beverly, his girlfriend at the time, and Germee's mom where they were young, happy and content with life and the hand they were dealt. It was a time where they clung to one another for everything. They shared a small one bedroom apartment after Beverly was thrown out of her parents' home upon the learning of her pregnancy that she so cleverly attempted to hide. Nevertheless, as the months elapsed, her swollen belly continued to swell, alerting her parents to her deceit.

Feeling misunderstood and unwanted by her parents, Beverly drank and smoked during the early stages of her pregnancy, ultimately falling into a slight depression, which caused complications during delivery. With no way to stop the unwavering loss of blood, she died soon after delivering their son, which kick started the first stage of depression for Marvin, and now it seemed he was traveling down that same road again. Continuing his pity-party for one, Marvin slowly fell into a drunken stupor, oblivious to his surroundings.

$$$$$

The later the morning became, the warmer the temperature seemed to get in Connecticut. Dro had the air on low inside the rented Ford Escape, while he, Dex and Avonne rode down Park Street's bumpy asphalt, smoking blunts of wet. The SUV was cool, foggy and reeked of mint. Overly excited about the task at hand, Dro knifed the Ford Escape up Park Street, making a fast left onto Babcock Street causing everyone in the backseat to wallop over one another.

"Whoa!" Avonne yelled over the music, too through with his driving.

"Shut yo ass up, fo' I kick you the fuck out!" he barked over his shoulder.

The wet had Dex high ass shit, his uncontrollable laughter said it all.

"I'm just saying, Dro, we don't want to raise no unwanted eyes," she concluded.

She was desperate to get in and get out without incident. She'd seen enough of the police sub-station for a lifetime.

After a heavy sigh, Dro said, "Whatever hoe, I got dis!" then oozed down the one-way strip like molten lava.

Dro finally brought the SUV to a halt four houses down from the three-family house at the corner of Russ and Babcock Street. He shifted the truck into park. The V-6 engine became silent, almost non-existent. Just before exiting the truck, Dro made sure that both Dex and Avonne knew the risks going in and going out, and that he would not hesitate to put a bullet in either of their heads if they fucked this caper up.

In a ninja-like fashion, the trio crept towards the rear of the yellow house. Dro maneuvered as team leader raiding Hussein. He eased leg after leg over the railing of the porch until his entire body was over the banister; next came Avonne, then Dex.

"Shhh," Dro said, as Dex made an unnecessary thud when his Timbs became one with the wooden platform.

"My bad," he whispered apologetically for is blunder.

"Stupid nigga, I swear…"

Instead of bashing Dex, Dro played with the gold doorknob until it made a slight clicking sound. He knew then that someone had left the rear door unlocked. And like seasoned cat burglars, the trio crept inside. The first room they came across was empty, except for a full size bed, and a cheap looking dresser with a cracked mirror fastened to the back in a tilted fashion. Although Avonne revealed earlier that the M.H.B.'s stash would be downstairs in the basement where the trio slept, Dro told Dex to begin a search there. He considered this to be check-day, so he wanted all that he could find.

Tiptoeing very lightly, Avonne followed Dro into the kitchen at a snail's pace. It was there that they, rather Avonne, pointed out the door leading to the lower level of the house. Just when they opened the door, they heard a noise behind them. Dro drew his steel and turned around with haste. Seeing that it was his crimey didn't stop his heart from speeding up.

"What the fuck, Dex? You need to get it together!" Dro spat heatedly.

"My bad, Dro," he answered in a cowardly tone.

He knew not to fuck with Dro and his explosive temper.

"You ain't find nothing in there?" he asked.

There was no doubt that they got down together, but when it came to easy come ups, he had to check and see where his mind was at.

"Nah, it was clean like a fucking maid been through here." Dex replied truthfully.

With the anticipation of coming up, Dro accepted his reply, but that didn't mean he wasn't pressed to put one in his dome for the moment of fright.

"Come on, and keep the noise to a minimum."

Dro shook his head as they continued their search into the basement. There was another room they hadn't hit yet, but Dro needed to get in and get out as soon as possible.

After indulging in several shots of the warm Bourbon, Marvin felt the urge to piss. He hadn't had a need to drink in some time, so his tolerance level wasn't peaked at all, though just standing up made him experience a woozy feeling. After rubbing at his throbbing temples, he attempted to walk but found himself flat across his bed. He laughed it off, and then raised himself to a standing point once again. This time he was more successful in his attempt to walk to the bathroom.

Marvin stumbled from out of the room Dro and his bandits hadn't rummaged through. Surprisingly, Marvin made it into the bathroom by the kitchen.

"Uhhh!" he moaned, as the dark urine sprayed out of his urethra.

He wasn't sure how, but he managed to tuck himself back inside his pants. Leaving the bathroom, his stomach began to growl, thus his new agenda was to visit the fridge for a bite to eat. Grabbing a cold slice of pizza out of the refrigerator, he started his journey back to his sinkhole where he could drink comfortably.

J. Alexander

As Marvin began his journey back to his bedroom, he not only noticed the door to the basement open, but a little noise also. Not seeing the boys since Germee's brush with death, he ventured towards the steps.

"Hey...Yak, you there?" he slurred, "Pintz?" No answer.

"Oh...shit!" Avonne whispered. "That's Uncle Marv. I thought you checked all the rooms out, Dex?" she stated nervously. "We're fucked!"

"Shhh..." Dro ordered, he was not about to let them fuck things up.

"What are you boys...doing down...there? And where...have you's been?" he furthered slurred, and began his descend down the steep steps.

"Hurry up, y'all finish looking for the shit, I got dis!" Dro whispered, and then stood along the creaky steps.

Avonne had seen where the boys had often removed a metal door on an old furnace, so she immediately ran to the large white cylinder.

"Bingo," she said, pulling out several brown bags.

In a split second, she reached inside one of the bags and cuffed a knot of money. Thinking fast, she tucked the knot into her panties before creeping into the darkness to Dro's side.

"You got it?" he asked.

"Yeah," she whispered in response.

Marvin was now at the third step from the bottom of the landing when he saw Dex crouched low by the ragged couch the boys used for some of their fuck sessions.

149

"Hey, who's…"

Just as Marv went to finish his question, Dro grabbed his legs causing him to take a hard tumble down the remaining steps.

"Urgghh…" Marv moaned as he lay at the bottom of the stairs in pain.

Out of fear, Dex blurted, "Fuck, what are we gonna do now, he saw my face?"

"This!" Dro said and did what most robbers would have done in the moment of fret and assurance that escaping unscathed was the only thing at hand.

Bloc…Bloc…Bloc…Bloc!

Dro put four slugs in Marv's heaving chest, as he lay helpless in his inebriated state. The four deadly shots echoed loudly throughout the basement, scaring Avonne to the point she soaked her panties. Witnessing Marv's death, left her physically immobilized as she watched the surprise of her involvement cast through Marvin's cold eyes; his life slipping away by the second. Avonne's temperature began to rise. She had no clue of what would come of this, and panic soon set in. In a state of shock, Avonne charged at Dro with speed. When she finally met him face to face, her flailing arms drummed against his muscular chest.

"What have you done, Dro?" She screamed loudly. "Are you fuckin' crazy? Fuck did you shoot him for?"

Dro gritted his teeth while giving her a stiff warning, "Bitch…if you, ever…lay a hand on me again," he nudged her in the head with the tip of his gun to let Avonne know he was serious, "I'll leave you in an alleyway slumped! Now get your stupid ass the fuck outta my face!"

Although Avonne was shook by Dro's sudden actions, she stared him down like a lioness protecting her young. In the back of her mind, she contemplated where her karma would hit the hardest; from Dro or the M.H.B.'s. *"What have I gotten myself into?"* She mulled.

"Come on…let's get the fuck outta here," Dex shouted, thinking about the authorities catching them at the scene of the unfortunate murder of Uncle Marvin.

Scared and indecisive of what to do next, Dro and Avonne took heed to Dex's orders. Finally inside the Ford Escape, they escaped into the early morning hours a few thousand richer, with the blood of Marvin on their hands.

Chapter 27
Armed and Dangerous

H

ere, you wanna hit dis weed?" Angus asked Pintz.

"Nah, I'm good my dude," Angus replied, his mind was strictly on finding and murking T-Kill and his flunkies once and for all.

The two rode in silence as they searched for any sign of T-Kill or his old ass Escalade. Angus knew Pintz had a lot to deal with at the moment. His little brother was in juvi, while his cousin was shot-up in Hartford Hospital.

Angus decided to swing back by T-Kill's grandmother's spot in hopes of catching him and his click.

"Damn, we've been riding around this bitch all night. It's 2:30 a.m., where the fuck are these niggas?" Pintz spat, breaking the silence.

"Shh, shh. Hol' up…" he smiled, noticing T-Kill's Escalade double-parked right in front of his grammys crib. "Look, that's his two flunkies inside playing Play Station. I can see their heads clear as day."

"Yeah, dat's them, come on, let's get this blood, bruh!" Pintz said as he went to open the door, but Angus stopped him.

"Chill, chill, I'ma swing around the block and park. I wanna catch 'em off guard, feel me. Even if we miss T-Kill coming out the house, we'll be right behind 'em."

Angus wasted no time making it around the block. He found an open parking space that took up two spots for an easy getaway.

J. Alexander

As a covert tactic, he popped out the fuse to the dome light in the stolen S.T.S., so once the doors became ajar no light whatsoever would give them away. Pintz had a .50 cal tucked in his waist and a .44 in the small of his back, and a black riot-pump shottie in his hands. He really wanted to push some shit back. Angus had a fully loaded .50 cal and a Mac-90 ready to get it cookin'. Together, they slowly crept up to the Escalade in a crouched position. Every so often, Angus checked all of the neighboring houses and windows for lights and peeping toms. Just before setting his attention back towards the SUV, he noticed the porch light on T-Kill's house come on, and out of the doorway, T-Kill appeared, devouring a sandwich. The frowns on Pintz and Angus' face were venomous. They paused as if they were professional hunters hunting in the wild.

T-Kill made his descent down the stone steps without a care in the world, which is why he would never have to worry about another thing in his life ever again. Pintz never replied to Angus' earlier statement, mainly because his stare was stuck on T-Kill. When T-Kill finally reached the bottom step, a Ford F-350 bent the corner of Hungerford Street, its bright lights shone directly on Angus, blowing his cover completely.

Angus and Pintz shard one last look at one another before Angus whispered, "It's now or never bruh."

Realizing his life was now in danger, T-Kill immediately tried to bail. However, his legs froze up, allowing him no possible chance of escaping his blind date with death. In pursuit of his prey, Pintz ran with the speed of a cheetah dumping shell after shell at T-Kill's dome. He was definitely on his duck hunt shit tonight. While Pintz was in kill mode, Angus sprayed the T-Kill's Escalade with the powerful Mac-90, giving it a complete face-lift. Caught off guard, Zoe and Luda paid a grave price for their poor lack of awareness of their surroundings. Angus was now on the side of the SUV, knocking all the dark tinted glass out with every shell that spat from his Mac-90, and in the process, Luda was   the

153

first to catch a dome-shot, leaving him slumped over in the front seat. Through all of the gunfire being let off, Zoe somehow managed to get his .9mm out and return some fire of his own. But from the opposite side of the SUV, Pintz nailed him with a direct shot from his .50 cal, killing him instantly, making it a two-on-one death party. In a desperate attempt to elude death, T-Kill was tripped up by his own feet. Thus, in the process of regaining his footing, T-Kill scraped his knees against the cold concrete. Even though Pintz' anger was seething through his pores as he watched from the rear, he had to laugh, knowing that T-Kill's days were numbered, and he would be the one to send him to hell.

Boom...! Was the sound of the first shot Pintz administered in the enemy's path.

Pintz let the riot-pump shottie bark, and once the hot lead made contact with T-Kill's leg, it blew it off completely and landed a few feet away from where he now lay squirming in a world of dire pain.

"What's up now, OG? You ain't looking so tough now."

T-Kill looked up at Pintz with eyes of forgiveness; he was hoping God would spare his life. *"Y'all lil' niggas gotta either cop work from me, or it's tax season'."* Pintz quoted some of the rules T-Kill threatened them with in the past. "Imagine that. Nah, bitch nigga, it's casket season!"

Pintz walked directly up on T-Kill as he lay on the ground crying and begging for his life like the fuck-boy he really was. He had no fight left in him; absolutely nowhere to go and bowed down to Pintz.

"Please no, please don't kill me...please," he begged, sobbing.

Boom...Boom, the shots echoed into the still night.

Pintz had no sympathy for T-Kill and his bids for mercy. Without a care for T-Kill's life, Pintz hit him with a direct bull's eye to the face. From the impact of the shotgun blast, his melon exploded like a pumpkin dropping off a four-story building. For a brief second, Pintz stood, stuck on stupid, observing T-Kill's lifeless body; incoherent to Angus' call.

"Come on, let's go! We got to get out of dodge, kik!" he continued to shout until Pintz snapped back into reality and ran for the stolen STS.

Had Angus had more time, he would have chased down the F-350 that rode through as the deadly mission ensued, just for good measure. However, as soon as the thunderous barks from Pintz' .50 cal broke wind, the pick-up sped off with haste. It was obvious he didn't want to risk being placed at the scene of the gruesome murder.

"You a'ight, kik?" Angus asked.

"Yeah, I'm hood, my dude. Let's hit da crib though!" he returned and hopped into the car.

While Angus whipped the STS at a precautious pace through the capital city, Pintz placed all of the guns back in the duffle bag along with their masks. They kept their gloves on while inside the stolen car; careful not to leave any prints behind for forensics to determine whom they belonged to. Shortly after, Angus dropped Pintz off on Putnam Street. He was in charge of disposal. Angus was very smart when it came down to things of this nature and had another car they had rented from a friend waiting in Putnam Heights. He quickly made the switch but not before setting the STS ablaze. Strange, but before knifing away from the blaze, he turned and admired the orange and red ball of flames wafting in the skies. Satisfied with his work, he eased the switch car away from Putnam Heights and found a parking spot two houses down from Uncle Marv's house on Babcock Street, getting away   scot-free. Just to be on the safe side, Angus hopped a few fences, and then, crossed the street into the rear yard of Uncle Marvin's house, where he met up with Pintz. Prior to entering the building, they surveyed their surroundings before coming out of the shadows. Once they assumed that the coast was clear, they made their way inside the house, stopping in the doorway. Entering the three-family house, a wave of paranoia consumed Pintz. He felt as if people were watching from afar; as if they knew and was well aware of the triple homicide he was just involved in. Shaking the paranoia off, he continued inside the house safely. He hadn't taken notice that their back door was ajar because of the adrenaline rush he experienced. Again he looked around, only this time he called out.

"Yo Unc, you here?" Nothing. "Uncle Marv, you home?" This time he yelled loudly, then went to his Uncle's room, figuring he was in there fast asleep, tired from being up at the hospital.

Entering the room, he noticed an open bottle of Bourbon tipped over on the dresser.

"Damn, Unc' I know exactly what you're going through, but it's going to be okay. We got 'em…we got 'em all!"

Pintz knew his Uncle was grieving over his son's sudden tragedy and sympathized with him. Not finding Uncle Marv in his bedroom, Pintz continued his search throughout the house. Making his way through the kitchen, Pintz saw that the door to the basement was open wide as well, which was very peculiar. They never left it open, and Uncle Marvin rarely frequented the basement, unless he really had something to discuss with them, so something was off.

"You must be downstairs looking through Germ's things to bring up to the hospital," he reasoned. "Unc, you down there?" he called out; still nothing.

J. Alexander

He continued the journey down into the basement and upon reaching the bottom step, Pintz found the dead corpse of his beloved uncle in the deep end of his own blood. Unable to bear the sight of his lifeless family, Pintz fell to his knees, cradled Marvin's head into his chest, and began sobbing uncontrollably. Through the sobs, Pintz heard footsteps, but never looked up.

"Hey, what the fuck happened down here?" Angus asked, startled.

His eyes bulged seeing the puddle of blood where the two sat, also that the basement was in shambles. Then it hit him like a ton of bricks; someone had violated them by breaking in their sanctuary and killed Uncle Marvin in the process. He wondered if it was T-Kill and his flunkies before they got to them. If so, they had paid a dear price for the six thousand dollars they had hidden in the basement, which was their entire stash. Now they were back to where they started as 'boys' on a long journey of becoming 'men'.

Chapter 28

No Pain, No Gain

The predicted forecast for a warm, sunny day somehow slipped away rapidly, as the phantom shadows in the sky hovered massively in several obscured cloudbanks, causing a heavy down pour of thick rain over the city. It was clearly visible that every thick puff had a distinctive silver lining; a picture perfect depiction of life's skyscraper. And just as Pintz always believed as a youngster growing up in Florida, *'that when it rained heavily such as today, God was crying for whatever reason he was'*, Pintz knew different, it was for his Uncle Marvin's tragic death. With the weight of Germ being shot-up, his younger brother being in juvi and the loss of the only guardian left up north, he sat stone-faced in another world, staring into the pounding rain through a window.

"Hello...hello...?" the deep baritone shouted repeatedly into the receiver. "Hello?" still no reply, and then the line went dead.

It was obvious the person in the 205 area code was deeply concerned with the call. Not two seconds later, the cordless phone stuck in the tight grasp of Pintz hands, chimed in a loud repetitious tone. Surprisingly, Pintz snapped out of his daze and answered the phone.

"Hello...," his voice faded in a sense of distress.

He was so thrown by the recent events that he had totally forgotten that not even forty seconds ago he dialed the cell phone number starting with the 205 area code.

"Aye, what's good? Who dis?" the voice spat.

"Oh my bad, it's Paul, I mean Pintz," he corrected, "I was looking for Big-Rod, my uncle?" he managed to get right under the circumstances.

"It's me, fool…What's up with the weirdness, boy? Everything cool out there with Germee? Marv told me what happened," his southern drawl lingered.

"Yeah, I guess so, its Uncle Marv though," Pintz' voice again trailed off in distortion; it was hard for him to fathom the loss of his uncle.

"Nigga, you better talk fast, fo' I come through dis phone!" He was starting to get livid at the mention of his big brother's name.

Since young boys, Big-Rod had always fought and defended his younger brother when faced with altercations up until state lines separated them.

"Someone broke in our spot and deaded him last night. Ya' Velle is in juvi for an undercover sale. So, it's just me now, Unc." Pintz sounded defeated more than anything, which was evident in his tone.

He might have been street savvy, but tragedy had not graced his doorstep since losing his mom many years ago, and he didn't know how to cope with it.

There was a brief moment of silence before Pintz said, "Uncle Rod, you there?"

Still, nothing but silence on Big-Rod's end of the line; he was at a loss for words with the revelation of his brother's death.

Seconds later Big-Rod replied, "Yeah, I'm hood, young, I'll be there sooner than you can bury the niggas responsible for killing my peeps. Go get yo' self a room somewhere. Make sure when you get there you call my cell and give me your room number, ya heard?" Big-Rod paused. He was flushed with grief.

"You getting all this, Pintz?" He was extremely concerned about his nephew's well-being, being he was so young and had no one there to help him get through the adversity of losing yet another loved one.

"Yeah, I'm reading you a hunid percent, Unc, but whoever murked Uncle Marv, also hit our stash up. I'm hit on bread, Unc."

After sobbing for what seemed like forever over his uncle's death, he decided he would check the furnace for their stash, seeing that the basement was in disarray, which was when he discovered that their entire stash was gone. They were dead broke; no drugs, just a small arsenal to their name.

"Don't worry, young, everything's gonna be hood. Listen; go to the closest Western Union in about one hour. I'm about to send you a stack, so get yo' self right, ya heard. It's going to be a'ight nephew," he added for a sense of assurance.

He knew Pintz was all alone now. However, that crazy Rivers blood ran through all of their veins, and Big-Rod knew Pintz was libel to do some heroic shit, which would solve nothing. Sending Pintz the money to get a hotel was his way of keeping him safe until he and his goons arrived in the city, but after that, the green light for murder would be given. The chance at vengeance was a few hunid miles away and in the hands of a true BOSS; Big-Rod Rivers the don of Magic City, Alabama. Little did he know, but murder had already darkened a section of the city, just not the one's responsible for his brother's death.

"A'ight, one. I'll hit chu soon, unc."

$$$$$

It was late into the afternoon when Pintz finally got back in touch with his peeps out in Magic City. The city coroner did their part by briefly examining the body of Uncle Marv and then hauled him away in a body bag. In addition, the annoying homicide investigators questioned Pintz on the scene about his knowledge of tonight's mishaps instead of bringing him downtown. But like a cd stuck on repeat, he explained to them that he had nothing for them; that he came home and found his uncle slumped. Tired of his repeated lies and bullshit, they wrapped up their brutal inquiry, which would be labeled as a robbery homicide for the time being, and vacated the scene.

Once they were gone, Pintz took a quick shower, and then dressed for the rainy weather. He knew of a Quick Collect spot down in the Sav-Mor Plaza on Park Street, which happened to be a hike in itself. Nevertheless, he zipped up his water repellent North Face pullover, then buttoned up the matching pants and hit the pavement; his Gortex boots splashing in the many puddles during his travels.

Pintz made it to the Quick Collect in less than eight minutes flat and was successful in retrieving the stack Big-Rod promised. Now it was another race in the torrent downpour seeing no gypsy cabs were in sight. He would have waited it out, but he forgot the number to Big-Rod's cell, so it was imperative that he go back to the crib to let him know that, that part of the plan had been accomplished. The faster Pintz ran, he could feel the .50 cal slipping out of his waist to the point he had to stop to readjust it's housing properly. Finally, in front of the V.F.W., he felt relieved. Their house was six, maybe ten feet away. Out of the corner of his eye, he caught a quick glimpse of a dark figure hopping the small fence that separated their building from the Oliver's house.

With extreme caution, Pintz decided he would take the long way around the building to investigate. At the beginning of the concrete walkway, he pulled out the chrome cannon from his waist and crept slowly in the storms irrigation.

The path was muddy and obscure. His Gortex boots sank into the earthy soil with every step. However, he so desperately hoped whoever was lurking on the premises was Uncle Marv's killer, so he could dump the entire clip into their heads.

"Yeah, muthafucka…show yo' self!" he demanded under his breath, only no one emerged, so he cautiously continued his stride.

There was a small bend in the structure of the building where a person could mask himself or herself from sight and the rain. Just above the area was a small roof that capped the diminutive area safely. Pintz was two steps away, his new toy level with his waist. Moments later, he jumped out of the rainfall, pistol now pointed at the midday-marauders temple.

Noticing who it was creeping around his crib, he breathed a sigh of relief, and then he spat, "Fucking, Angus…you know I almost popped your cherry, lurking around my spot like you was one of them fools coming back to hit us up again?"

"Chill out P. Come on let's go inside, I need to change out of these wet clothes," he retorted in a vast shiver.

He was soaking wet and extremely cold with nowhere to run, nowhere to hide, except here.

"Come on, let's go inside then, nigga," Pintz said, leading the way.

Once inside the basement, Angus wasted no time removing his soggy clothing. Pintz found him some of Germ's Akademic jeans and a hoodie. He wasn't quite soaked to the boxers, so he was good there. Pintz then tossed him a fresh pair of socks and some wheat Timbs.

"So what's the deal, 'Gus, fuck you out here in the rain like dat for?"

"Hol' up, let me dry my hair off. Here dry dis off for me," he said, and then passed Pintz a .44 Magnum. "Be careful too,   dat's my baby, and her stomach full to capacity," he smiled devilishly.

Pintz was very careful with Angus' heat as he sat on the couch doing what was asked of him, also studying Angus' strange behavior. He couldn't make anything of it, so he chilled out, being Angus was always in and out of time; literally bugged-the-fuck-out!

"A'ight my dude, dis the 411. Real shit though…dis goes no further than us, you got it?"

He knew Pintz was thorough when it came to things like this and would never snitch him out, but it wouldn't have been him if he didn't put it out there. Caution was a virtue in his book.

"Miss me with dat bullshit, 'Gus, what's hood?" he was a little thrown off and offended by Angus' previous remarks.

Though he let it go, he wasn't in the mood to go back and forth about the topic of whether he could be trusted with this so called secret.

"You know when I saw you all fucked up over Uncle Marvin's, dat shit had a nigga vexed, so I went and camped out in the backyard over by T-Kill's Grandma's spot…"

"And? That shit still hot as hell, bruh, fuck's wrong with' you?" Pintz interrupted.

"Damn, chill out you antsy mufucka, and hell is hot, P' nigga, Angus ain't never scared. And I ain't built for nobody's steel cage neither, so you already know I'm going shell for shell if shit gets thick wit' them boys in blue!" He smiled, but was serious. "Now…as I was saying, I was on deck while those stupid CSI and news people tore the area up for clues and shit. You know, dat fake ass 48 hours shit. I think I even seen the C. Lyons out there on some investigative shit."

"Who, retired homes who be doing all that cold case shit?"

"Yeah, that's dude. Anyways, T-Kill's old lady is out there putting on a good show for the news, acting all fucking hysterical and shit. You know…crying and screaming and shit, feel me?"

"Yeah no doubt 'Gus, I hear all dat, but what the fuck happened, kik? Spill da beans," Pintz said, growing agitated not knowing what Angus had to say.

"You know me, I laid on 'em until they jetted and then crept in the old bitches spot and domed her old rotten ass for Uncle Marvin, feel me?" he confessed with no remorse whatsoever; a cold-hearted hood nigga foreal.

Pintz was in awe at the sudden news. "Damn kik, you on some broad-daylight type shit huh? I pray to God you was careful, bruh, ain't nobody peep you doing your thang right?"

"No doubt P', you know I move like a ghost wit' mines." He made a small whistling sound as he flailed his arms in the air as if he were flying.

"Why you always gotta be on joke time, fool? Dat shit is real, kik," Pintz said.

Too much had happened in the past few days for Angus to be acting all crazy and nonchalant at the same damn time.

"On some real shit, I think I'm good though. But you know that old folks' home looks right out onto Hungerford Street, so there's always that possibility that some nosy old fart could've seen something."

"Oh well, fuck 'er! Let 'er old ass sleep wit' them fishes," Pintz spat.

His emotions had superseded any rational thought of

164

compassion for the elderly woman. He felt as though she deserved the same fate as Uncle Marv. A member of his family was gone, and one was laid up in the hospital. Somebody had to pay, so why not it be her.

"Peep it, Mo' body's on her way over to grab a nigga, so we're gon' chill out at the telly till my Uncle Big-Rod touches down."

"A'ight, but you cool with dis fiend bitch being around us like dat right now?" Angus asked

He wasn't sure if it was a good idea for her to be in their presence at this time. In his mind, she was expendable too and would not hesitate to let one of his hot shells lay dormant in her mental should the cause arise. Except from sales, sex and renting her whip, they really didn't know her like that, so Angus was passive about her mouthpiece and the world of trouble they could possibly face if she leaked to the cops.

"I got dis fam, she's cool. But if she asks too many stupid, while girl questions, we'll trunk dat bitch."

"A'ight, but I swear…if dat crack-head even blinks wrong, I'll let 'er meet Eastwood on a personal level. Let 'im finger fuck her ass to death. Dat's word to me!" he swore and then kissed his chrome .44 Mag on the nose.

Chapter 29

Too Close for Comfort

T he dim lighting, in Dro's small bedroom, cast a grim but normal to average feel. At twenty-one years old, he still harbored the mind of a teenager. Inside his cramped bedroom were 30x40 size posters of his favorite rappers and B-ball players masking the limited wall space. Scattered about the floor were your normal stacks of sneaker boxes, piled high against the far wall. Though most of them weren't filled with shoes, the insides were over capacitated with weed, different calibers of handguns he collected and of course his crack. He never kept his profits with any of the other incriminating evidence. Instead, he used his hoodies, jeans and coat pockets to store his paper in, feeling that they were the safest places.

After splitting up the bag of money they took the M.H.B.'s for, the trio smoked several blunts, drank and engaged in a risqué orgy. Avonne had gotten over her fear of being pegged as an accomplice to Marvin's murder, not to mention counting out her cut from the heist made it all worth the beef with whomever. Dro was the first to get his rocks off and then used the little sense he had to clean his .9 milli of finger prints, because later that night it was going deep into the Connecticut River; *no gun – no conviction*, he concluded.

From where Dro sat, he watched the two as they lay sound asleep and wondered if he made a bad choice in letting Avonne live. She would be the only tie to the murder besides Dex. He assumed Dex would never rat him out, but shit, Sammy the Bull turned on Gotti up, T-Lee took the stand on Pekeno (the head of the Solido's), so why would he be any different? For the time being, he would let them both ride, just to see how things would pan out. Nevertheless, he swore he would bury him and Avonne if he felt leery or deception of any kind.

After taking care of his business, he woke them up, it was time to bounce. He wanted to hit the block. The mere fact that Dro hadn't known if their rented Ford Escape was seen leaving the scene of Uncle Marvin's murder, he decided it would be best to ditch the SUV. It was going back to Enterprise A-SAP.

Together, they strolled down Broad Street headed for the 'Law', which was just around the corner; the rainfall sparing them no pity. Today's winds were at full gust, blowing the loose branches and leaves around like a two-dollar whore on Huntington Street.

Avonne was thoroughly pissed. Her seventy dollar hair-do was ruined. "*A total waste,*" she cringed shaking her head upsettingly. Dro and Dex was hood, they were dressed from head-to-toe in North Face rain suits.

"You know, you could've driven us to the block, Dro. Fuck you got us walking in this wet ass shit fo'?" Avonne complained.

Unbeknownst to Dro and Dex, she could care less, being she cuffed over eighteen-hundred dollars from the robbery. As soon as she got the chance to break away from them, she was going to her mother's hair stylist, Joy, the renowned owner of 'Head-To-Toe', located on Main Street, to get her doo back intact.

"Shut da fuck up...yo silly ass ain't happy unless you got a dick in you or tricking niggas paper off at the mall. You lucky I ain't slump yo stupid, ungrateful ass and left your body for the coroner to find!" he spat, thoroughly tired of her shit already.

He now regretted not putting her young ass out of her misery. As usual, Dex laughed at the exchange between the two. He was the quiet type. He just hung out, made his bucks, and enjoyed the hood as it be.

"Fuck you, Dex, wit your little-dick-ass! All you're good for is laughing at dis fool and playing the flunky roll...hoe ass nigga!" Avonne spat heatedly, her head bobbing side to side in the rain.

Just as Avonne finished cutting into Dex, they noticed a white Honda stopped at the red light at the intersection of Russ and Broad Street. When suddenly the front passenger window lowered just enough to reveal the brim of an UConn fitted hat. Avonne's frown displayed surprise and severe guilt. Dro paid the car no mind. It was Dex who had seen the Honda too many times to forget and knew it was a half-a-crack, so the fitted cap told him who was inside. A sense of panic washed over him. He was flushed with fear as he noticed the barrel of a gun poke out the window before the car proceeded through the light.

"Whew..." he mumbled.

He figured that Pintz and the M.H.B.'s knew he played a part in the heist, also Marvin's death and was about to return the favor. However, God was on his side today, which he was very thankful for. It was Avonne who felt threatened because she had now been seen in the company of Dro and Dex. A light went off in her head where she thought that she could somehow use this to her advantage in the plot to subtract her involvement in the caper.

"Hey, y'all, I'm out. I've got some things to take care of. I'll see y'all later, 'kay" she said and then disappeared into the downpour.

"Fucks up wit' her?" Dex asked warily.

"Beats me, come on, I see some sales down the block," Dro advised and continued to the fiends on deck.

Chapter 30

M.H.B.'s, We All We Got!

Taking a left off the I-91 North Highway into the Metro Meadows area, a three-car caravan was being led by a '77 Chevy. The triple black candy paint was well worth the stacks Rivers' spent on his pride and joy. The limo tint gave the old school a dark mysterious look as it passed two police cruisers headed towards the HPD headquarters just off the highway. Behind the Chevy were two big boy Denali trucks, dipped in an oil-black coating, sitting on chrome Jordan's, its windows faded to black. Although the cars fit right in with the Connecticut traffic, their Alabama license plates gave them away. Inside the Denali's were eight country ass niggas who'd murder something at the drop of a dime if given the order.

Sitting at the last stop light before the hotel, Big-Rod instructed his driver in which direction he should take next.

"Make this here left and hit the Red Roof Inn, playa."

As directed, his lil man did as told, and the caravan followed close behind, making the turn onto the hotel property.

"Look for room 214."

It was the hotel room Pintz was supposed to be laid up in. It wasn't long before the grim looking procession from out of town parked directly in front of the city's most frequented fuck-nest.

$$$$$

Angus was on his way back from the McDonald's that was directly across the parking lot from the telly with a handful of hot food and a tray full of sodas. Caught up in his own world, Angus

From Boyz To Men

was oblivious to the all-black caravan in the parking lot. It wasn't until the Chevy's passenger's door opened, and a 6'1", 250 pound male stepped out draped in all black with a fitted hat low on his head. Next, he saw a littler version of the big fella, only he was about 5'8" in height, also in all black. The only differences between the two were the corn rolls hanging from under a black doo-rag worn by Big-Rod's right-hand man.

Off instinct, Angus dropped the tray of sodas and went for his best man when he saw the other six goons hop out the SUV's, looking like they were ready to reenact the hotel scene out of *'Street Is Watching'*. He tried to remain inconspicuous as possible while following the group of men headed in the same direction as the hotel room that he and Pintz were occupying. His co-d Eastwood was down by his waste as his head hung low, trying not to appear as if he was trailing them in any way.

$$$$$

Inside the hotel room, Pintz laid across the mattress in a wife-beater and some jeans, while his boots overlapped the edge of the bed. He kicked his heels together as he and Mo' Body were heavily engaged into the movie, "American Gangster". Growing weary of Angus' whereabouts, he insisted that she check into it.

"Aye Mo', look out the window and see what's good with Angus fo' me," he said, his eyes remained glued on the TV screen.

He was at his favorite part where Frank peeled Tango's shit back for refusing to pay up on his percentage.

"Sure, but…" she replied in a jittery tone.

She was sober and desperately craving a bump; the signs were written all over her face. Amanda was hoping they had some work on them, because she planned to use her last twenty dollars to cop a hit.

"Pintz baby…?"

"What's hood, Mo'?"

"You got a lil something on you?"

He wasn't into discussing the intricacies of the M.H.B.'s dealings and movements with her or any crack head for that matter, so unless she had some knowledge about who it was that took them off for their drugs and paper, she was out of luck.

"Nah Mo', we're dry right now, ya heard?"

Reluctantly, she got up and walked to the blinds as Pintz asked her to. Peering through the small slits of the blinds, she observed a group of men in all black, and Angus not far behind toting his heat.

In a panic, Amanda shouted, "Oh shit Pintz, hurry…hurry! I think Angus is about to shoot some dudes out here!"

Hearing the urgency in Amanda's voice, Pintz wasted no time grabbing his .50 cal and then raced to the blinds. He needed a look for himself. Looking into the crowd of men, he smiled seeing that his uncle Big-Rod was leading the pack. Then it dawned on him that if he didn't hurry up outside, there was a good chance that there was going to be a massacre on the hotel's grounds.

Wasting not a minute further, he rushed to the door, opened it, and yelled, "Chill out 'Gus…dat's my peoples from Magic City."

Caught off guard by Pintz' sudden cries to chill out, Big-rod's trusted goons quickly turned around with their guns drawn ready to air some shit out. And the looks on their faces said they weren't taking shorts.

"Wassup neph, what's dis here?" Big-Rod asked, hoping for the sake of God the youngster carrying a bag of McDonald's and toting the large cannon was from the home team, because if he wasn't, he was about to become their target practice.

"Yeah, dat's Angus, he's peoples, Unc'," Pintz answered quickly, which apparently saved him a one-way trip to hell.

"Good thing too, neph." Big-Rod knew they were almost caught slipping, and he didn't like it. Nevertheless, they would have dropped Angus with the quickness. "Old boy ain't playing though. I see y'all holdin' some heavy shit too, nephew," he referred to Angus' .44 and the .50 cal Pintz was clutching very tightly.

"Yeah, Angus ain't around for all the small talk when it comes to drama. Come on, let's take dis party inside y'all, I'm sure someone seen our little standoff, feel me," Pintz suggested, being they were drawing too much attention when they were supposed to low.

"Nah neph, we're sitting ducks now. And you had to get a room right down the street from 5-0! Pack dis shit up we're going somewhere else. Let's get it," Big-Rod concluded, which was very smart thinking on his part.

Big-Rod's goons turned around and hopped back into their vee's awaiting their next orders; most of them with murder on their minds, the others consumed with money.

Pintz told Mo' Body she could leave and thanks for her help, but they had some B.I. to handle. She left happily. That rock was calling her. There was no doubt she was going to spend that last twenty dollars she'd been holding onto since arriving at the room.

J. Alexander

Amanda peeled off, while Pintz and Angus hopped in the Chevy
and rode off, feeling at ease for the moment.

$$$$$

During the ride, Pintz filled Big-Rod in on the accounts prior
to today. He also showed Big-Rod where his little brother Yak,
was being held. The Juvenile Detention Center on Broad Street
was enormous and known for housing mostly car thieves and drug
dealers and on occasion an under aged killer. The next morning,
Big-Rod made a trip down to the JDC building and inquired about
his nephew, Ya'velle, and sadly, it was a day too late. Being no
one had come for him, thus receiving word from the HPD that his
parental guardian had been murdered, Yak was awarded to the
custody of the State and tried for his crimes.

They convicted him on numerous counts of selling narcotics
to an undercover officer and possession with the intent to sell.
They placed a no-bond hold on him and revealed that Yak would
more than likely be transferred to Young Cheshire out in
Wallingford, CT., where he would remain until his eighteenth
birthday. The Judge had thrown the book at him, to say the least.
Once Pintz heard the news about his little brother, he felt as if all
life had been sucked out of him in one breath. He wasn't sure how
he was going to survive everyday life without Yak, but knowing
he had Germ and Big-Rod to help him through, he was hood.

Despite Yak's current predicament, Big-Rod was able to get
in a 15-minute visit in the far section of the visiting room. The
only catch to his visit was that a guidance counselor would
supervise attentively for legal purposes. As a plus, Big-Rod was
added to his list of relatives. That gave him visiting privileges for
the duration of his incarceration, which was good on Yak's
behalf.

"Vellee, Vellee, Vellee...wassup, youngsta?" Big-Rod said
full of energy and stood to embrace him.

From Boyz To Men

The two shared a brief hug and took their seats at the small table. His baritone was just as Yak remembered it being as a kid. It had been such a long since the two had been in each other's presence, and Big-Rod was surprised at how big he'd gotten. They were both appreciative of the contact visits they offered. Because once he went up the way, it would be all glass time.

"Uncle Rod, gotdamn…it's been years." Yak wore a huge smile that made his uncle's heart tremble.

Big-Rod hadn't felt this type of love in some time now.

"Ain't nothin', Unc, I'm glad to see you, but what's got you up north?" Yak questioned, being he'd never made the trip up before. "What's good with my big bruh, Germ and Uncle Marv?" he asked out of concern.

Yak's inquiry made Big-Rod think, "Hmm, so you haven't heard, huh?"

"Heard what? Wassup…?"

Just that quick, Yak began to perspire, fearing something happened to Pintz. Since being nabbed by the deeze, he had no knowledge of the murders.

"For starters, Germ's in I.C.U., but he's doing good. They're going to release him to me, so I'm taking him down south with me to recover. You know your big bruh is fucked up about you, right?"

"I already know, Unc. I know he's going through it," Yak confessed. "Okay, now what's hood wit' Uncle Marv? I know he's wrecked behind Germ getting' wetted up"

Big-Rod hated to be the bearer of bad news but he had to know, "Your uncle was killed in a robbery."

"Killed...? A robbery...? Fuck is you talking 'bout, Unc?" he banged his hands on the table, causing everyone including the C.O.'s to jump.

"Keep it down, Rivers, or I be forced to terminate your visit early!" C.O. Jones blared across the room.

"Man fuck all dat, you hoe ass cop!"

C.O. Jones immediately stood from his desk and made a beeline towards Yak's table. "What was that, Rivers?"

"Chill brother, I got 'im," Big-Rod iterated to C.O. Jones, at the same time displaying a grimace. He could tell that it worked because C.O. Jones took the same beeline back to his station. "Ya' Velle," was all Big-Rod had to say for him to calm down.

"I know, Unc, but damn...Uncle Marv's dead?"

This was too much for Yak's young mind and heart to accept. Feeling like the walls were starting to close in on him, Yak put his head down onto the table to mask the evident.

"It's gonna be okay, young; I promise!"

In Yak's mind, they hadn't even packed their belongings nor hit the highway yet, and Yak was feeling desolate. They were all tight, but he and Pintz' relationship was like identical twins, joined at the hips. With Uncle Marv being dead, them about to be separated by hundreds of miles, Yak knew he had to man up.

"So, what happens now, Uncle Rod?" he asked with his head still down.

"Hol' up a minute young." Big-Rod quickly stopped Yak from talking, fearing what was next to come out of his mouth.

He caught the nosy counselor bitch attempting to be indiscreet in her eavesdropping. Her ears were like two drones

175

gathering information for the highest bidder. Catching onto his uncle's sudden change in demeanor, Yak changed the subject.

"Listen, tell big bruh I know why he ain't come through, and it's all hood. I'ma be here for a while, feel meh. Make sure he sends those kites and photos on time. Watch him for me, Unc."

Ending his wishes, Yak forced a painful smile to ensure the levee's had no chance of breaking its hold. It was one thing to be emotional at a time like this, but to let the other youthful offenders in the room catch him at a low, would be detrimental to his survival for the next three years.

"I got 'im, young. Don't you worry 'bout nothin'. It's family first wit' me. I gotta tell you though, Dat Angus is straight hood wit' his. Yeah, youngin' ain't playing no...games, bullshit ain't nothing!" Big-Rod concluded.

Hearing enough vulgarity for one day, Mrs. Stevenson interrupted their visit. "Alright then, I think that's it for you two."

Feeling like she was on some bullshit, they shot her menacing stares, which made her turn away. They laughed hysterically and then said their goodbyes. Big-Rod walking away feeling at ease, Yak reminiscing about the life and times he shared with Uncle Marv.

"Damn big Unc...I'ma miss you, dat's word to meh!"

Big-Rod promised to keep his commissary stacked up and told him to call at will; the line was open.

As soon as Big-Rod pulled out the JDC parking lot, he went and put twenty-five hundred on his books. He figured that should hold him down for a few months. He then made all of the funeral arrangements for Marvin and then visited the hospital. He and Germ kicked it for two hours and discussed everyone's situation on the outside. Germ broke down into a crying fit learning that his pops passed away before he got the chance to kick it with him. The fact that he was in disposal, really tore out a piece of his heart.

"You can't be serious, Unc! Niggas done murked my dad? I'ma comb the city 'til I find his killer, and God bless the soul of whoever fucked wit' a River!" Although Germ was in physical pain, the emotional pain was much greater.

It took all the strength he had not to break down alongside his nephew. Nevertheless, it was Big-Rod's duty to hold his composure for Germ's sake. Showing a sign of weakness at this point would lessen any hopes of Germ becoming a man, and he was not about to let that happen. As it was, Germ might be down two parents, but he still had a boss for a guardian and uncle, and that would take him to heights he never thought were obtainable. It was time to go from being a *'boy, to a man,'* literally.

Germ knew leaving Yak behind was wrong, but Uncle Marv really wanted him to go down south and recover, so he agreed. The meds had soon kicked back in causing Germ to drift off, never seeing Big-Rod as he broke out.

"Take care young Germ. We've got work to do. Magic City, prepare yourself for another generation of Rivers."

Chapter 31

It's So Hard To Say Goodbye

U ncle Marv's funeral was just as any other parting service. From all corners of the world, the Rivers family flew in and drove out to Connecticut to pay homage and their respects for his time on earth. The services were being held at the Hopewell Baptist Church. Marvin and Beverly had been devout members of the clergy, though he had not attended service in the days before his passing. Nevertheless, he was saved, and the Lord turns no saved soul away at crossing.

Recently enduring major reconstruction, Hopewell Baptist had new Palladian high arched doors, two expensive stained glass windows with all of Heaven's Angels and Disciples etched on them. Its new high cathedral ceilings were painted with more Heavenly beings. It was very imposing, a place you would feel comfortable and solemnly sound. In the front pew, Big-Rod sat next to Germ in his new ride, a wheelchair. He was tailor-fitted in a black suit and alligator shoes by Ferragamo. Germ was grateful to have his Uncle Rod by his side. Without him, he would be lost. From where he sat, he observed a huge photo of his dad, then another one with them together almost life-size, as hundreds of floral arrangements decorated the internment with a touch of class.

When it was time for Germ to say his goodbyes, Big-Rod wheeled him up to the mahogany casket that was lined in off-white sheathing and gold accents. When the four-wheel sedan halted in front of the casket, Germ let out a deafening cry. His insides felt as if they were rotting with every breath. Losing his dad was a grieving process he thought could never end.

When the interment concluded, the procession rode off to Cedar Hill Cemetery with a stretch limo leading the way. Germ,

J. Alexander

Angus, Pintz, Big-Rod and Melodie rode inside, while two other limousines ushered all of Marvin's close relatives. Just like in the church, Germ wept uncontrollably and spoke in tongues, which only Pintz and Big-Rod could make out. He spoke of how he had never met his mom, and now he has lost his father. He felt damned and began talking under his breath!

"Have I been cursed for not taking the right path," his queried God *"I'm sorry Dad, this is all my fault. Had I not been stashing work in the crib, this would have never happened, and we would still be living our lives as a family. I will always love you, Pop."* He made a cross over his chest and then bided his farewell. *"Hold the fort down...and please tell momma I love her.! Gone but not forgotten!"* He ended with and watched the handymen of Cedar hill seal his grave with soil.

After Marv's body was laid to rest, the family and friends of Marvin gathered at the V.F.W. directly across the street from their home, where they enjoyed an array of food, beverages and mourned a great man. For Germ, it was a leap into manhood. He vowed to be the best man he could with what he had, knew and learned from his pops. However, revenge weighed heavily on his mental, as an abundance of uncertainty hovered around him, leaving him full of hate.

Knowing it would more than likely be some time before he saw the likes of his first love again, he decided to spend the night with Melodie. The two made love as if it were going out of style. Melodie begged Germ not to use protection, but he declined in fear of destroying what life she had in the makings. There was no way he was going to get her pregnant and leave her in CT., to raise his child all by her lonesome. His father had instilled better qualities and morals in him to do such a thing. Through torrents of tears, Melodie finally accepted his reasons and gave herself to him every which way he desired. In the morning, Germ pleasured her with a final orgasm with his tongue and then dressed.

"I love you, Mellz." He promised to keep in touch, but he was off to the Magic City to start over.

"I love you more, Germee," Melodie professed before breaking down into a crying fit.

They had come so far as friends, which soon transitioned into young lovers, and now he was walking out of her life just like that.

"I'm going to miss you, babe, take good care of yourself," she mumbled, gripping her bed sheet close into her cleavage as she continued to mourn the separation of something she thought would never cease.

Germ felt as if he was abandoning her, but he had to go. Pausing in the doorway of her bedroom, he took one last look at his heart, blew her a kiss, and then disappeared in his wheel chair.

Chapter 32
Ease on Down the Road!

Today the luminous sun, radiant as ever, was obscured by Premium 3mm-Scotch Limo-tint, as Lil' Tone, Big-Rod's right-hand, cruised the smoothly stretched highway. For some strange reason, I-95 was being very social to its motorists. The normal cluttering traffic was slim and uncongested. The only thing other than rap music heard in the car was a light snore from Big-Rod.

In the back seat, Pintz and Germ were lost in their own thoughts. Their faces steady with every passing vehicle; life for them seemed unfair in all ways. For Pintz, he had no parents, and his only sibling would be lost in the criminal system for the next three years. In Germ's case, he lost the only parent he'd ever had. He never had the privilege of growing up with an mom. He never had the chance to rest his balding-head in the softness of a mother's bosom. He never experienced the warming smile of a mother displaying her proudness of her child's accomplishment, or a mother's over-protectiveness when he was tackled too hard in a little league football game, and because so, he was tainted deeply.

Through the rearview mirror, Lil' Tone could see the subtleness from in the back seat and broke the silence.

"Aye, you two straight back there?" he asked, his voice lingered heavily in a southern drawl.

"Yeah Tone, we trill, just thinking dat's all." Pintz responded, letting him know that the two were just laid back taking in the view.

"Laid back? Who can think with all this Webbie and Boosie shit you playing! If it ain't them, you blasting some Pastor Troy shit," Germ complained. "You ain't got no Gucci Mane or my dude Jeezy up there?"

He was in deep thought, and all that dirty south music was aggravating him to the point he couldn't think straight. Lil' Tone laughed it off. Knowing Pintz was from down south, Lil Tone knew the transition for him would be nothing, but for Germ it would be crazy because most dudes from up north didn't entertain their choice of music.

"Here, light this up!" Tone said and tossed Germ a huge blunt for him and Pintz. "Maybe this'll help ease all dat tension."

Germ lit the blunt took a few deep pulls and then passed it to Pintz. While they was getting their burn on, Lil Tone popped in a new DJ Drama cd into the player.

'All I do is win, win, win..,' blared loudly throughout the car.

It was the remix to Khalid's newest street banger.

"Damn, Khalid got a remix for dis?" Germ became amped hearing Busta Rhymes, Jada Kiss, Fabolous, Fat Joe, and the Black Barbie doing their thang – yeah he was wide-awake now.

"Oh, you like this shit, huh?" Tone nodded his head, taking a quick peek into the rearview mirror at Germ bopping his head.

But Germ didn't answer. After the song finished, Germ reached up front and replayed it – he was officially gone.

"Pass dat weed, lil nigga!" Big-Rod barked, coming out of his slumber, the potent herbal jarring him out of his sleep.

The signs of a true pot head!

"Damn Unc, it's like dat? The smell of haze got you up?

182

Shit, I thought we were bad wit' it, but you on some Usher shit-you got it bad." Germ spat.

He was really clowning him though. Truth be told, he was a fiend also.

"Shut up, nigga, I been toting weed since I was eight years old. I'm a real weed-head, believe dat."

"I see."

They all laughed as the car began to fog up with the marijuana smoke. The caravan had been driving for hours, and was happy to finally see the big sign, 'Welcome to Alabama.' They smoked two more blunts before reaching the city of Birmingham. They called this part of the area 'Magic City,' where Germ and Pintz would go through a major transition – *From boyz to men!*

Chapter 33

New Beginnings

"*T*he 205, Magic City looked totally different, definitely nothing like back home,*"* Germ thought. There were lots of dirt roads. Trailer homes filled up empty lots and large open fields. As they continued down the road, Germ noticed there were several black oil drums openly burning in many of the open lots, also on the lawns of people's homes, which began to pique his curiosity. They also drove by many acres of woods, where he assumed plenty of skeletal remains had been buried.

"Damn, you could really kill a nigga and leave his body in there to rot; the perfect graveyard" Germ said to himself.

Lil Tone navigated the Chevy to the west side of Birmingham; a part of town that the Rivers controlled with an iron fist. Big-Rod had a reputation of a gangster around his hood, and Lil' Tone was by his side 24/7. Big-Rod was very well known throughout Magic City and had a large clique behind him. Big-Rod a.k.a. Rivers, was a Big Boy per se. From the way he carried himself, to the dope he moved, he had a swagger like a sea of water. So, most cats throughout Magic City referred to him as such. His level of respect was unmatched by any other boss or crew and had been for several years.

When the '77 Old School came to its final stop, Germ and Pintz were taken aback. Big-Rod had a southern style mini-mansion out in the Hoover section of Alabama, which rested on several acres. The boys grabbed what luggage they had, hopped out of the car, and went inside the huge fortress.

"Damn, cuz, dis place is hood," Germ mentioned to Pintz,

amazed at its interior design.

"Yeah, Unc is seeing some real scrilla, he definitely 'bout dat paper," Pintz countered, feeling the same way.

He had always looked up to him since he was a little boy. On many occasions, when down in Florida on mini vacations, Big-Rod would stop in on his sister, Bianca and his nephews. So, they had been in contact with each other a lot more than Germ had, only losing contact when she passed, leaving the boys to go stay in Connecticut.

"I tell you what, these niggas rock a lot of black, just like we do," Germ nodded in the directions of Big-Rods soldiers

He was obviously blind to life outside of Hartford, his misperception overriding any sense of rationalization. Germ was seeing first hand, that all hoods were basically the same – just in a different geographic landscape.

"Aye, there's two separate rooms upstairs. Y'all can kick it here or at the telly, it's up to you." Big-Rod told them.

He wanted to make his peoples feel as comfortable as possible under the circumstances.

"Nah, Unc, we hood right here," Germ confirmed, there wasn't no way in hell he was about to go stay at some bullshit motel when he had a palace at his disposal.

"Yeah, Unc, we straight right here," Pintz added, feeling the same way.

"Cool, I was hoping y'all felt that way. Well, I'm 'bout to go spark up the grill, y'all can shower and get some rest. When y'all wake up, we'll be out back," Big-Rod said. "Oh, here's some smoke to get y'alls mind right."

From Boyz To Men

He tossed them an ounce of Purple Haze and jetted out back to get the grill popping. Germ and Pintz took heed to their uncle's offer and did just that. After a hot shower and two more blunts, Germ and Pintz retired to their rooms. It wasn't until eleven-forty p.m., when they finally crashed the party going on in the rear of the expansion.

The outback of Big-Rod's house was open and very spacious. There were tall trees that led to a forest-like pasture, where he and his team rode their ATV's. To the far right, was a huge barn that twelve wild Hogs called their home. Of the twelve, there were eight females, which anyone from the south would know are the most dangerous of the bunch.

Under a large tent, were four oil barrels made into wood burning grills. On one of the grills was a fat pig roasting while the others held heavily sauced slabs of pork ribs and a variation of chicken. The real party was inside the huge netted gazebo just feet away.

Big-Rod and Lil' Tone was playing Bones (Dominoes) against two of his soldiers, while a heated game of spades was popping down just inches away. When Big-Rod looked up from the table, he noticed his nephews observing the festivities from afar.

"Yo, over here!" he yelled from inside the netted gazebo, then dominoed. "Let's get it nigga, count dat scrilla up," he spat loudly.

Big-Rod and Tone had a couple hundred on the game and were down a stack each, and from his energy, he was definitely anxious to get his paper back. It's not that he so much cared about the money. He was just a die-hard competitor.

"What's up Unc, Tone? Y'all really throwing down out here," Germ nodded, and then cringed some, still sore from the operations. He still had several stitches in his wounds, not to

186

J. Alexander

mention he was on a shit bag. So, he definitely wasn't feeling his normal 100%.

"Yeah neph, we does it real big out here err' day. You'll see. How you feeling though?" He noticed when Germ buckled some.

"I'm hood; it's this shitty ass bag that's got a nigga on pause. You know how hard it was letting my shawdy ride me with this thing on? Whew!" he sighed remembering the awkward sexual experience he endured with Melodie not many hours ago.

"Shit...I can see your little ass now, leaking shit all around the room," they all laughed.

Big-Rod could be a funny man at 11:00 a.m., and then turn into satin by 11:01 a.m. for no reason whatsoever. He was not to be taken lightly by no one.

"Go grab some grub, youngin'. Y'all know how to play bones, right?"

"Hell...yeah!" Pintz quickly answered. "We gots next." He said, definitely game to get in on the action.

"Dis here is a money game young," Lil Tone said counting his share of the winnings.

"Well we..." Big-Rod cut him off mid-sentence.

"Don't sweat it, playa, I left a couple stacks in your dresser drawers. I thought y'all would've found it, but seeing y'all down bleeding, that wasn't the case, huh?"

Big-Rod knew they were strapped for cash right now, and it was going to be his responsibility to bank them while in Magic City, so he blessed them both with ten-racks each.

"Nah, Unc, I ain't into snooping 'round nobody's crib, feel me?" Germ responded truthfully.

187

From Boyz To Men

He never even thought to look in the drawers. When they got up stairs, they smoked and crashed.

"I'm most definitely feeling the loyalty Germ, but it ain't snooping, young. We family and what's mines is now y'alls…you got dat? But damn, you should have seen it when y'all unpacked, which I can tell that y'all haven't yet." They both smiled because he was dead right. "Fuck all the small talk, go grab a few hunid, y'all gonna need it fucking with me and Lil' Tone," he confidently boasted.

They were the ones to beat around the mini mansion when it came to Dominoes. Germ and Pintz took off in search of their unknown allowance. Once upstairs, they parted ways in the direction of their rooms. Big-Rod wasn't bullshitting when he told them he had hit 'em off with a few stacks. They were stunned when they counted out ten-grand, all big faces. After grabbing a grand each, they went back to the shindig ready for some action.

"Come on, cuzzo, let's go show them fools how we do it up north," Germ said.

"After you, G'."

The four-man game had ensued, with Germ and Pintz, against Lil' Tone and Big-Rod. And before calling it a night, Lil' Tone and Big-Rod were surprised at how easily his nephews trimmed them out of fifteen hundred.

"Still think y'all the best in the mid-west?" Germ teased smiling.

"Fuck outta here, youngin…" Big-Rod spat then laughed with them.

"Don't worry 'bout it Unc, tomorrow is forever, just not promised," he stated, giving them some hope at winning back their paper on another day. "Holla at y'all in the A.M.," Germ

188

finished, and he and Pintz retired to their rooms.

Chapter 34

First Name Basis

Big-Rod woke his nephews up around 1 o'clock in the afternoon. He knew they needed some major rest with everything that had transpired over the last week or two. Nevertheless, they were in 'Magic City' now, and shit was about to get real crazy for them.

"Yo…yo, wake the fuck up, lil niggas," he shouted twice before either of them budged.

"Wassup Unc?" Pintz said in a groggy gruff.

"The world nigga!" he replied.

Big-Rod was about business, good smoke, bad bitches and murder! He had major plans for his nephews, and today would start off real hood.

"Y'all got thirty-minutes to be outback," he informed them and disappeared.

As Big-Rod bopped through his large crib, another thought hit him like a ton of bricks.

"Yo, what's up with Unc, P'; all this militant shit, he knows I'm still fucked up," Germ said, tossing the sheets off him. "I'm tired as…fuck," he claimed through a yawn.

"Beats me. But come on, let's get cleaned up. Unc probably just wants to win back dat scrilla," Pintz said, but Germ knew it was much more serious then that; his tone too defined.

"Nah, P', dis some gangsta shit popping off, trust!"

J. Alexander

"Shit...whatever it is, I'm game – bullshit ain't nothin'."

The two washed up then threw on some fatigue wear with some black Timberland Chukkas. Pintz laid his 360's down with some Sportin' Wave grease, and then covered them up with a black doo-rag. Germ pulled a black NY fitted low over his head, then put on his silver dog tags that said 'Corrupt Cunnuck'. Before heading down stairs, Pintz stuffed five grand in one of his pockets, he was the flashier of the two. Germ opted for the fifteen hundred he scraped up last night in the domino game. It was 1:35p.m. when they finally made their presence known outback.

"Look at this shit, Pintz, the party looks like it never ended."

It was early, but the grills were at full capacity with slabs of ribs, chicken and, of course, rotisserie pig. The only difference from yesterday was the hoes that were on deck today. In total, there were about five girls walking around in booty shorts and bikini tops. Germ immediately noticed the identical features on two of them.

"Yo, Pintz, check out those two right, there!" he pointed in their direction. "Twins," he nodded, feeling a sense of attraction to them.

"Man...You late as fuck! I saw 'em as soon as we stepped out the house. Gotdamn...they bad as shit! I'd love to fuck one of them," Pintz admitted, his lust dripping loosely.

Off to the side, Big-Rod and Lil' Tone was peeping how the Northerner's were lusting over the twins and laughed.

"Look at 'em, lil' young ass dicks probably rock-hard," Big-Rod said, and then came out of hiding. "Pick your damn lip up, nigga!" he said, slapping Pintz in the chest.

"Man, go 'head, Unc, they ain't all dat," he tried covering up the obvious, knowing he'd been caught in the midst of lust mode.

191

Big-Rod and Lil' Tone laughed it off, and then called the twins over. "Shai, Nai...come holla at me for a sec."

"What you think, niggas, scared of some pussy? I been hitting ass since I was nine," Pintz said, gripping the girth of his wood.

"That's what I like to hear, neph."

"Hey, Rivers," the twins never referred to him as Big-Rod, they chose his street name. "What's up? And who are these two fine ass niggas, we about to grill 'em, or what?" Shai questioned, popping on some gum.

"Nah, Rivers, we can't grill this one," she pointed at Germ, "He look like he know how pop dat tongue; turn a bitch-out!" Nai blatantly said.

She had a real mouthpiece on her. Shai and Nai were two red-bone twins who ran with the West Side Mob under Big-Rods wing. Shai was 5'7" with a very small waist that held her 30" ass. Nai was feisty, though lovely, but couldn't be trusted for shit unless it was Mob tied. She had D-cup titties and a mole at the end of her mouth, which gave her a sexy look. Nevertheless, they were Big-Rod's secret weapons when it came to getting at niggas. At the tender age of seventeen, the twins had eight bodies together; real killers they were.

"Chill Shai, these my nephews from up north; Connecticut. They're down here wit' me now. I just wanted to set y'all up, feel me. Show 'em a good time while they're around," he said looking at his nephews eyes.

He knew they were feeling what he'd just said.

"Here boys," Nai said, "Come on, you're mine!" she said with a sense of authority as she gripped Germ's shirt.

J. Alexander

As she dragged Germ away, you could hear him say, "You don't even know a nigga's name, ma!"

"I'll get it later," she responded.

If Big-Rod put him on, she knew he was hood.

"Sup shorty?" Pintz asked in his pimp like tone.

Shai smiled so hard, her dimples almost connected.

"You know how to roll up? I'm tryna get high," she stated and then pulled out an ounce of Magic City's best.

"Fuck you think, I'm some lame or something," he laughed, "I got a dick don't I?"

"I don't know, let me see!" Shai said with her hands on her hips, ready for a peep show.

Pintz looked at Big-Rod and Tone for a brief second. He was dazed by her remark.

"Go head lil nigga, whip dat shit out!" Lil' Tone urged, he didn't think Pintz had it in him.

Had it been him, his dick would have been doing the crip-walk for a chance to bed Shai. On many occasions, he tried to get Shai into his stable, but he was a man-hoe, not the type of dude she was into. Not to say Lil' Tone wasn't bout dat life, but Shai craved that thug-love, someone she could bear children with, without having to put a bullet in his head and then bury him as if it were nothing.

"I gotta stack dis nigga ain't bout dat porn life," he challenged, throwing a thousand-dollars onto the ground.

"A stack...? Dis fool don't know we gets it wavy in Cunnuck?" Germ countered, tossing his fifteen hundred onto   the ground, and with that, Pintz gained a little more confidence about whipping his manhood out.

"Well...?" Shai smiled, ready to see if it was really wavy up north or not.

With a nod from his Uncle, Pintz pulled his shit out; no shame – no game.

"You satisfied, ma?"

He stood in the open with his dick protruding from his grasp; his balls hanging low.

"Whoa...you can put my new friend away for my sista sees it. Fuck around and put some blood in your food – have you whipped!" she said honestly. "Come on, let's go get better acquainted. What's your name though?"

"Pintz."

"Sheiit...you mean gallon?" they all laughed.

Germ and Pintz were feeling at home. The southern hospitality was like no other. While burning some Hydro and sipping syrup, they got to know the entire West Side Mob. Big-Rod was puffing on something fat when he received a disturbing phone call.

"What...keep his ass right there!" he yelled into the receiver, then slammed his flip phone shut.

It was time to ride out.

Chapter 35

Time To Ryde Out

After seeing how pissed off Big-Rod was by that call, everyone in the backyard chambered a round in their straps. They all knew what it was hitting for. What was everyday life for the Westside Mob, was unfamiliar territory for Germ and Pintz. As Germ and Pintz looked at Big-Rod's soldiers assembling, they thought they were on the set of a real live gangster movie shit.

"Whaddid do Unc, everything hood?" Germ asked, he definitely wanted in on the action.

He felt it was time his trigger finger got some action. If he couldn't get the proper retribution for the death of his pops, then he would get it now.

"Nigga, do it look hood?" Lil' Tone replied, sucking his teeth.

He was itching for beef 24/7, but bringing it to young Germ wasn't such a good idea. He too was raw-heat and lived for this type of shit.

"Who...whoa playboy, you can miss me with dat tough talk. I ain't for that slick shit!" Germ responded with grimace and pulled his heat out and chambered a round.

Nai liked what she just observed, but the beef wasn't here, so she intervened before things got out of hand.

"Come on Germ, save it for these bitch ass niggas over Pratt

City," Nai said stepping in between them. *"Sexy,"* she thought.

Here Germ was walking around with a shit bag and was ready to catch a homi.

Wasting no time, Lil' Tone and Big-Rod hopped in the '77 Chevy, while Pintz and Germ took seats in a '05 black 'Vette driven by the twins. Nai and Shai were seeing a nice piece of change fucking with the Westside Mob and had stacked up some major chips over the years and celebrated their come ups with designer fashions and the latest vee's.

The main beef the Mob had was with the Pratt City Boys; a clique of rowdy niggas who slang a lot of work and dwelled at the Drift Track. Cheese was their leader. He was 32 years old. He stood 5'11 with a chubby gut, and there was no doubt his pretty boy looks and large stash, kept the ladies flocking. Some time ago, Cheese and Big-Rod used to sling dope together, but Cheese got greedy and stuck up their connect, which caused major beef with Big-Rod and the Koreans. One night, while seeking retribution against the Mob, the Koreans crept up on Avenue Z, where the Westside Mob had set up shop, and killed Big-Rod's younger cousin, Bull. Being the coward Cheese was, he quickly fled the scene and ran off with ten keys of girl (dope) and three hundred thousand dollars in cash, and they have been feuding ever since.

Big-Rod wasn't running nor backing down from anyone, let alone the Koreans. He held onto Avenue Z like a parent holding their child in an open storm, which he now had 'boy and girl' pumping 24/7. The block was wide open, a pure gold mine.

Making their way towards Pratt City, Shai thought it would be a good time to put Germ and Pintz on to their current situation not wanting them to be left in the dark.

"From what Farm said, Benny and two of his flunkies rode through the trap and let off some shots. They hit two of Rivers'

196

workers, but Farm clotheslined one of them as they tried to duck off."

"Who the fuck is Farm?" Germ asked, confused, not having the chance to meet the infamous yet.

"Oh my bad, dat's Rod's main worker, he controls Avenue Z for him. He's 'bout dat life, too," Shai informed.

"So, they got one of 'em right now?" Pintz asked checking the clip on his .50 cal he made the long journey with.

"Damn straight; but not for long," Nai said.

She held an AK-47 down by her feet. A bitch wasn't playing, she was ready to cut some shit up in a bad way. As the 'Vette turned corner after corner, Germ thought about how Angus was doing back home all alone. Before they passed out last night, Pintz informed Germ on the accounts of T-Kill and his two flunkies, also how Angus had hit granny up after they'd found Uncle Marv slumped in the basement.

"Word...I missed all dat?"

He was surprised they handled their business while he was laid up in I.C.U.

"Straight like dat, cuzzo!"

Germ figured Angus was dead broke, lonesome and hiding out from the cops. Through many attempts, they begged him to come out to Magic City with them where it would be safe for a while, but to no avail. Angus claimed Connecticut was his only home, and he'd be hood. Not to worry, he still had his strap. After a night of reminiscing, it was time to say goodbye. They promised to stay in touch and send some scrilla as soon they got their one's up, then closed the books on the first chapter of the M.H.B.'s. Looking out the car window, Germ wished his right hand was there riding shotgun like always.

Soon, the two cars full of armed West Side Mobbers, pulled up on the Avenue Z and though the police was non-existent, the yellow-tape was still visible. Along the Avenue's sidewalks stood a few nosy gawkers and fiends, waiting to see how things unfolded. They knew Big-Rod ruled Magic City with an iron fist, and shit was about to turn ugly for the captured man they saw clotheslined and drug away on his stomach.

"Yuck...look at all the skin and blood on the ground," someone blurted out, cringing at the crimson streaks bee-lining a direct trail to where his body could be found after the Mob was through torturing him.

The two car procession came to an abrupt halt in front of their trap house. When Big-Rod stepped out of his old school, his black Dickies sagged low on his ass, while his short-sleeve shirt hung loosely over a white a-shirt; his .45 Eagle nestled in the lining of his waistband. Over his eyes were some dark specs, concealing a portion of his current temperament, which frightened the two fiends he bumped when passing.

"Fuck out the way, hype!" his voice deep and deadly.

His entourage followed close behind, only Shai's wild side came out a little too early. She fed off the hype Big-Rod displayed, and then pistol-whipped them twice before catching up to the crowd.

"Dis bitch liver than most cats I know," Pintz mumbled.

He shook his head at her wildness and concluded that he was dealing with some strange, but vigilant pussy.

Now inside the trap, Big-Rod and Farm met face to face.

"What's on the menu, my dude?"

J. Alexander

Farm smiled devilishly, he lived for times like these.

"Something that used to be tough, dat's about to be shredded pork."

"You know how I like dat pork, baby..." Big-Rod sucked his teeth.

"No doubt, Rivers."

They dapped one another. Like the twins, Farm also used the moniker Rivers.

"Follow me boss-man, he's right down the hall," Farm suggested. "Check it, his bitch ass in there singing like he tryna get a fucking R&B deal," he had to laugh.

"Oh, yeah?" Rod replied. "Well, West Side Records ain't signing shit 'cept death certificates!"

At first sight, Farm paid the extras no mind, though that hadn't deterred him from inquiring, "What's up with the new help, Rivers?" Farm asked, staring at the boys.

"Slow your roll, Farm, this here family!" he said sternly. "Never mind that, what type of tracks ol' boy laying down?"

"Family, right," he quickly became submissive to Big-Rod's request. "He's talking about Cheese sent him through to dead some shit. Dat he's back to take over what's rightfully his."

"Is dat right?" Lil' Tone intervened. As second in command, he had often took charge of critical situations so Big-Rod could lay back. "Take dat shit out his fucking mouth," Lil' Tone ordered, "So you Cheese's little mouse now! You a gangsta now? You wanna shoot our shit up?" he chuckled. "This is West...Side, mufucka!" he barked, spit spewing from his mouth.

Lil' Tone retrieved his gangster meter and pistol-whipped

199

dude a few times to show that he was the one in charge of his destiny. However, it was Big-Rod who would make the final decision on whether he lived or died. Nevertheless, Tone was an opportunist and was going to take pride in torturing Cheese's do-boy. He was always trying to make an impression on Big-Rod and the rest of the Mob, solely because he didn't like playing second fiddle to Farm.

"Enough!" Rivers said calmly; he had other plans for dude.

He needed clarification, before he carried on any further. "Now, who gave you your orders again? I need to hear it from you."

"It...it, was Ben-Benny!" he struggled to say through his bloody mouth.

Benny was Cheese's right-hand man. Obviously mapping out some new scheme in his wicked mind, Big-Rod shook his head.

"Humph! Oh...so Benny wants to be a big boy now, huh? Okay, big...Benny. You got dat!" He directed his dialect towards no one in particular. "You Pratt City sissies never learn, but I'm gonna let you go back to your peoples with this message," he paused and stared the man in his pleading eyes.

With what Big-Rod just said about going back to his peeps, he knew his life would be spared this time, and he felt relieved.

"Aye neph," he nodded from Pintz to their hostage.

Pintz knew exactly what it meant. He pulled out his ratchet and dumped five shots into his face nearly severing it from his body. Blood and brain matter covered the nearing wall and floor. Happy with his nephew's first kill, Big-Rod smiled.

"Now dat's, how you air a nigga's shit out, baby-boy," Shai complimented impressed with Pintz gun game. "I think we can be a great team, Mr. Up North," she said, watching the smoke billow from the muzzle of his .50 Cal.

"A'ight, enough of the flirting, we're still on the clock. Y'all can take dat shit back to the compound. Listen closely, drop dude's body off by the Drift Track. I want that bitch ass nigga Benny to see the life he cut short tryna play a game made only for gangsta's. I'll see y'all back at the spot."

Tone and Farm followed Big-Rod, leaving the twins and his nephews to finish up there. When it got dark enough, they covered dude's riddled head and put him in the 'Vette. The top was down, so it would be easy to toss once they arrived at the Drift track. Once they hit Pratt City territory, they put the high beams on and sped down their strip blaring Biggie's hit single, *Life's A Bitch*, then flung his limp body to the curb. The 'Vette peeled out and headed back to the party.

"You know, I think I'ma like it down south, Germ," Pintz admitted after tongue kissing Shai deeply.

"Yeah, me too," Germ said while Nai caressed his rod as she steered the sports car back to the Westside of town.

Chapter 36

Watch Yo'self Nigga

When Big-Rod finally finished oiling his personal collection of handguns, he checked his watch; it was 4:30 a.m. He glanced at Jona, who had drifted off to sleep after pleasing him sexually. Jona was one of Rod's main whores he kept around for the sake of pleasure. She was 26 with a cute face. Her pinched nose made her southern accent extra risqué, she was definitely his maintenance woman. Big-Rod knew the beef with Pratt City would never die down, there was just too much bad blood lingering in the street sewers for that. Both crews had lost too many soldiers to count, but it was part of the game. He thirsted for the day he got his hands around Cheese's neck. His betrayal would find him in a bad situation very soon. However, his two flunkies were going to die a very slow, painful death once entrapped in the West Side's web. He wasn't into taking over Pratt City territory, he had his share of clientele and streets with Avenue Z. He also ran Avenue U. Avenue U was a well secured strip that ran in the U shaped loop. It was a strip where if you didn't know what you were doing or knew someone of hood significance, you could get your shit twisted back and was deemed one of Magic City's most dangerous blocks to date. Some of Big-Rod's most dangerous killer's plagued the U-loop. It was so bad, cruisers only breezed through during the wee hours of the morning like five, and six a.m., but even then, it was off the hook. Big-Rod had a young arrogant war-buff, by the name of Straw. He earned his moniker by his habit of keeping a plastic straw in his mouth and up to his nose. Don't let the raw thing confuse you, he had it very mucg under control. It was something he'd picked up in prison fucking with his white boy cellmate.

A sudden noise broke Big-Rod out of his trance. He   quickly spun around, Glock .40 in hand; ready to send a mufucka underground.

"Chill Unc, it's just me, Germ."

Big-Rod was a looney for real, and because so Germ wasn't taking no chances. He wasted no time raising his hands up high into the air, surrendering to Big-Rod's blunt actions. From there, all he could do was smile at his crazy uncle.

"Lil' Germ, you can't be sneaking up on a nigga like dat. I almost blew that little head of yours the fuck off," Big-Rod warned for Germ's sake. "Shhh...I don't want to wake Jona." She had fallen asleep right beside him. "What's up though?"

"Shit, just woke up and saw you out my room window."

"Yeah, I like to get my chill on around these hours, it's peaceful out here, feel me? You know, your big Unc has a lot on his plate, and sometimes needs dat space away from it all."

"Yeah I hear dat Unc, but you have so much. This big ass mansion, cars, hella cash, bitches, niggas that'll kill at will, and the key to the city...what is it that you need space from?" Germ was confused; Big-Rod had the life they had been chasing since entering into the streets.

They were playing the game in novice mode while Big-Rod seemed to be in expert, and he couldn't seem to understand what was really troubling his uncle.

"Listen young, what you see here is years of blood, sweat and tears. I built the West Side Mob from scratch. I lost a lot of soldiers due to greed and envy. Yeah, I can buy anything I desire, fuck a different chic every hour, drive the latest whips, and walk around my damn fortress ass naked if I choose, but there's really no true happiness once you accumulate a certain status, young. I'm telling you this because I lived it, I made it out the ghettoes of

From Boyz To Men

Alabama filthy rich, but with a conscience. Lemme ask you something, young."

"Shoot," Germ replied.

"Do you have any idea the percentage of murder we're responsible for in Magic City?"

Germ thought for a minute and then shrugged his shoulders. "Half?"

Big-Rod laughed at his nephew's answer.

"Close but no cigar, which reminds me." He dug into a black onyx humidifier that sat on a table to his left and pulled out a Havana Cigar. "Here, light dis up, young."

Germ did as told, and Big-Rod continued, "As I was saying, you were close, but it's deeper than what you think. We are murder! We control the murder, and can account for at least 75% of the homicides since the late 80's. The Rivers, your family, has controlled Magic City since the heroine epidemic took over back when. What I'm tryna say is, I'm tired, neph', I ain't got no kids, I ain't married and I have to look over my shoulder every minute, not to mention the help."

"The help? To me it looks like you have a squad that's pretty loyal."

Germ's visual perception was that everything was everything within the Mob, and that's just it; when you're looking from the outside in, you really don't know the half.

Big-Rod shook his head at his nephew's stupidity. He figured Germ had never dealt with the unconditional love and loyalty of others outside of family, which in his case was understandable because of his age and position in the streets.

J. Alexander

"Take heed to what I'm about to say…make sure you rewind this in your mental daily, it might just save your life one day." Germ nodded, and Big-Rod continued, "Germ, you're fam to me, and only family can get dat close to me, we gotta keep it tight and strong and never let what you think is loyalty cloud your judgment as I have in the past. The blood in the Rivers' veins will always be thicker than the water we drink!"

Big-Rod could tell that Germ was absorbing the information as he stood nodding with his arms folded across his chest. No more was needed to be said from this point on, Germ had been chasing a gangster's dream with no guidance, but now he had a major mentor that he would utilize until he was able to take it on the solo road.

"Before I forget, don't you go and let Nai get you whipped now – she's good like dat." He advised, changing the subject as Germ stood in his plaid boxers blowing smoke from his nostrils.

"You ain't never lied Unc. She sucked and fucked a nigga to sleep; even cleaned a nigga's shit bag!" he said surprised.

"This the south, neph, our women are much different than the chic's up top. It's dat southern hospitality. Just remember what I said about her!"

"Aye Unc, I would have slumped old boy, too, this shit bag don't control my trigger finger." Germ confirmed.

He would have gladly accepted the opportunity to put in some work, but he figured his uncle was going easy on him because he wasn't fully recovered yet.

"Oh, I know you's ready, neph, it just wasn't your turn at bat, it's coming though. Now go and wake dat pussy up," he laughed.

"Shut up Rod, leave him alone," Jona said, stirring out of her sleep, shoving him on the arm.

"Later Unc," Germ said and walked off taking heed to Rod's sexual idea.

When he got to the door something made him turn around, when he did, he saw Jona giving Rod some lustful head. Seeing that shit made him hustle upstairs and attack Nai. He was a little hungry, so he thought he'd return the favor by sucking on her clit for breakfast.

"Oooh...shit!" she moaned in a world of sexual bliss.

Nai thought she was dreaming until the explosion of her sweetness saturated the bed sheets and Germ's face, which Germ had no problems slopping up.

"Boy...you gonna have a sista fucked up with that tongue action you working wit'. C' mere, let me taste my pussy," she pulled him closer and licked her fluids from his lips.

"Ummm," she moaned again.

She then grabbed his stiffness and eased it into her wetness.

"Oooh yes, ummm Germ, you feel so good. Fuck me Germ, fuck me hard, and long," Nai begged.

Complying with her request, Germ served her just right until she had multiple orgasms, then they fell out for the   count.

Chapter 37

Is You Ready?

H ours later, Germ and Pintz dressed then stumbled into a foggy room where they saw Big-Rod, Lil' Tone, Farm and a few other cats that ran with the Mob conducting business. Lil' Tone had a phat blunt dangling from his mouth, while Farm was sticking what appeared to be a switchblade into a kilo of dope. They noticed him taste the white substance, then nod to Big-Rod. Whatever it was, it was hood. Germ was skeptical about bum rushing the room, so he called out Big-Rod's name.

"Oh, what's up, fellas? Come on in, stop standing in the doorway," Big-Rod said.

He was running a stack of paper through a money machine.

"You know we ain't wanna just barge in, peeps," Germ said, as they walked into the smoky room.

"So what's hood, Unc? I see you doing your thing," Pintz said gazing at the metal table stacked with grey-slabs maybe two-inches high.

He was doing some calculating in his head and knew there was some serious paper stacked up on the table being Big-Rod sold nothing but heroine.

"Yeah, we doing real good, some major shit, young!" he answered, referring to the West Side Mob's dealings in Magic City. "Y'all trying to get your hands dirty, or what? Y'all tryna see what it feels like to count so much paper it'll hurt your hands?" Rod questioned seriously.

For him, it would be good to get some money with his bloodline.

"All day long," Germ responded.

"Hell yeah, Unc!" Pintz said anxiously.

"What's up with your man Angus? Why dude ain't come down? I could really use a little brave heart like dude on my team."

He viewed Angus as a true soldier. A nigga who's for real about the game in all aspects and wouldn't hesitate to lay a nigga on his back. Sheeit...he knew firsthand, having almost become a victim of his treachery not five minutes off the freeway in Connecticut.

"We tried to get him to rollout wit' us, but Angus is pure Connecticut. If it ain't UConn football and basketball, it's New England Patriots. Dude is probably just afraid to leave the hood, Unc," Germ reasoned.

"He ain't lying, Unc. Angus is gangsta about his and stuck on the hood, so I don't see him crossing state lines," Pintz added.

"Everybody's got to leave the hood one day, neph'. Y'all gave him all the numbers down here right?" Big-Rod asked.

No matter what his nephews said, he was somehow going to induct Angus into his Mob.

"Yeah no doubt, but I doubt he'll ever use them; it's just him Unc," Germ answered.

For now Big-Rod dropped the Angus subject, he had things going on tonight and wanted his nephews on deck. On the metal table was Rod's last fifty joints, which was going to his two strips;

208

twenty-five apiece. The money he was running through the machine was half of the buy money for a new shipment of work. It was the way he and the Koreans worked out their dealings; half on demand and the rest on consignment.

Through Jin-Tow, he copped fifty bricks of dope at $15,000 each, so $750,000 was his price on delivery, the other $750,000 would be paid off in 30-days tops, or he'd owe an even $1,000,000. Although Cheese pulled that bull-shit stunt, making things iffy between the Koreans and the Mob, Big-Rod paid off the debt, and they started to do business again. At first, things were uneasy when dealing seeing Jin had killed some of Big-Rod's peeps in several drive-bys, but too much money was at stake, so they buried the hatchet and moved on.

"Listen, tonight I have a major buy going down, and I want you both there. Now, these fifty birds are going to Avenue Z and Avenue U, which later on you'll both be in charge of, but for tonight, I need you all on deck and ready to kill somethin' should I give the order."

"Say no more, Unc," they both said, cocking their heat.

This was what Pintz and Germ envisioned being a part of and were about to make their dreams a reality.

"Let's move," Big-Rod said.

Chapter 38

Game Tyme!

B
ig-Rod and Lil' Tone were seated in the old school Chevy, with the quarter-mill and a high-powered choppa on the back seat as some added insurance. He forever kept the reminder that their relationship with the Koreans could go south at any time, so be chose to be safe rather than sorry. The meet was set for nine-thirty p.m. on the south side of Magic City. Business with the Koreans would have been somewhat of a caution to the Mob had they been conducted on the north side, because that's where most of the federal police frequented, and the real stick-up kids lied. Therefore, the south side was a safe haven for the Mob. They Mob entered South Hampton, which Shai and Nai had on lock and key. It was another spot that produced a good portion of the Mob's cash flow. Lil' Tone was in the driver's seat leaned back with his hands creased in back of his head. He knew Jin wasn't due for another twenty minutes, so he let his high sort of marinate a bit. When Rod saw that Tone's eyes had been shut a little too long, he chambered a round in his Glock, making him jump up nervously.

"See nigga, you off guard all laid the fuck up. Fuck type time you on, Tone?" he barked.

"Huh?"

"Huh? Nigga I got nearly a milli in the car, and you snoozing off!"

"Hell nah Rod, you know a nigga just a little high. I'm hood though," he spoke now sitting up.

He knew he shouldn't have leaned back in the first place, but he knew they were heavily guarded, so he said fuck it. Big-Rod shook his head at Tone's parlayed state, but now wasn't the time or place to get into a heated debate about Tone's actions while on the clock. When he looked out the front windshield, he saw that the 'Vette was easing further down into the projects. *"Good job,"* he thought. Being it was his nephew's first run out, Big-Rod sent them along with the twins to drop the work off to the Ave's on purpose. He wanted to put Pintz and Germ to the test. However, that was simple, minimal danger; this part would tell everything. He had that much confidence in not folding during this test that he told Farm and Straw to remain on their strips, he had his nephews to cover for them.

The 'Vette pulled up directly behind the Chevy and deaded the lights, however, no one got out. Instead, Shai chirped Big-Rod on their Nextel 2-way's.

"Everything went as expected," Shai informed him about the two drops.

"Cool, keep your eyes open for the jakes, ya' heard," Big-Rod chirped back.

No sooner did they end their 2-way, did two silver S430's pull up across the street from them. Their headlights died, but you could hear the faint sound of an engine and its fan obviously cooling the motors engine. Then there were two ambient flashes from one of the Mercedes neon lights. It was a sign they used to proceed with the transaction.

Lil' Tone returned the signal, and then a total of twelve car doors opened almost simultaneously, Germ and Pintz thought this was a scene out of Black Rain with Michael Douglas, when he went to meet with some Japs to make a deal of a lifetime.

The projects were dark and quiet. The only light casting in the area was from a crooked street pole that was on its last limb. The city dared to come out and service the pole even with the countless number of homicides that occurred in this particular

211

section of South Hampton.

Big-Rod nodded at Jin-Tow, and he did the same. Then a stocky Korean appeared out of the darkness with two very large duffle bags the size of body bags. The trust issue wasn't on the Korean's side. It was Big-Rod who didn't trust a soul, meaning that once the stocky Korean delivered the bags to them, he'd then pass over the money, and only then. It all worked in Big-Rod's favor.

With a quick look inside the bags, Big-Rod nodded at Tone, he in-turn turned over the duffle bag full of money to the Korean, only it was much smaller. After thumbing through the bag, he okayed it, and Jin and Rod met midway in the street.

"My good friend, it's always a pleasure to do good business with you, and I see you've got two new body guards with you tonight."

"Yeah, I'm grooming them for something great. As a matter of fact, I'd like to introduce them to you." He nodded at Germ and Pintz, and they sauntered over in their gangster walk then flanked their Uncle on both sides. "I want y'all to meet my good friend and supplier, Jin-Tow."

"What's up Jin?" Germ spoke first.

"Sup?" was all Pintz said.

He was militant-made and wasn't about to appear too friendly in case he had to dead the flat-face where he stood.

"Nice to meet you two; I think I'll be seeing a lot more of you both in the future. As Big-Rod will tell you; money has only one color with me, and that is green; after that – it's all red!" Jin said in a philosophical way, but they read his warning.

It's either correct money or no money, and with no money

comes death.

"See you in thirty!" Jin ended and parted ways.

$$$$$

Back at the spot, Lil' Tone did his usual thing, only Bid-Rod instructed him to run Germ and Pintz through the routine. He wanted them to know every aspect of the game. They followed Lil' Tone into a room. Three steps through the doorway, their jaws dropped, seeing a hundred bricks of dope at once. However, their smiles were hidden by peculiar looks. They were eager to sit through dope class and then score an A-plus of the final review.

For the rest of the night, Lil' Tone, the twins and the boys broke down twenty of the kilos into ounces for South Hampton. They also put aside ten of the kilos for any weight sales. Since the boys were already twerking with the twins, Big-Rod felt they could get it popping in South Hampton with them. It wasn't on some watch dog type shit either, Big-Rod just felt it should go that way and whoever didn't agree, could rot in hell.

As the night ended, he told the twins not to be slipping on dick-time while they were in the projects and to make sure his peeps were okay.

"For sure, Rivers," Shai promised.

"Yeah, we got dis," Nai added.

Chapter 39

Stay 'n Your Lane Duke!

The money was flowing like water in the South Hampton PJ's. This was some shit they weren't used to, but they adjusted well. Big-Rod had good connections throughout Magic City and through Jona. He'd gotten both Germ and Pintz some Alabama driver's licenses. He couldn't risk them getting yoked by the Po-Po with a car full of dope or money. He also took them down to the dealership and told them to both pick out a whip of their choice. Pintz was from up north now but still loved his old schools, so he got him a Dunk on sixes. Germ wasn't for all that old, stretched out shit, nah – he had to have some up to date shit. He copped a 2005 Yukon Denali Sport with 22" chrome factories and dark tints. Although they lived with Big-Rod, they also had their own bachelor pad in the PJ's. Of course, the twins were there every night, so to get some fresh catch besides them, they would hit the Residence Inn off Route-250.

In the alley leading from the main street, Pintz stood, unnoticed by passersby, watching the movement up and down the street, while Germ was counting some dude's paper that came through for a quarter-key of boy. Elroy was an older cat who'd been checking Big-Rod since touching down from a lengthy state-bid for drug trafficking a few years back. Pintz heard Elroy's voice get a little too loud for his liking, and wasted no time stepping up behind him. The next thing Elroy felt was the muzzle to the back of his dome.

"Wassup cuz? Dis nigga outta pocket?" his voice full of grit.

"Fuck you mean, am I, outta pocket?" Elroy barked loudly.

He couldn't believe what he was hearing. Back when, he would've never let some young jitter bugs get down on him, nah, he was a low tolerant type of cat; shoot first, ask questions later. Elroy was that nigga to see if you wanted something took care of, you needed a stolen car, a busted check, to a hit. What he hadn't realized was that those days was no longer, West Side Mob was the ones to see if you were looking to get your bucks up or a for a free trip to hell.

"He ain't trying to die tonight," Germ said pulling out his .50 cal, "Is you?" he looked Elroy in the eyes and saw he was unfazed by the pistols threatening his life.

Germ knew he should've pulled out a little faster, being the older man was taller and brawnier. He underestimated Elroy for the sake of relationship with the Mob. He let a biggest part of the lesson he was given by Big-Rod go right out the window; *'never put trust in anything except blood.'* Although this was their first large hand-to-hand since taking reign over the P.J.'s, Germ treated it as if it been many, which could've cost him his life because so.

"Listen youngin' that tough shit doesn't scare me, and it's best you get that iron out my face!" he warned.

"Oh yeah...dat's how you feelin' duke? You wanna play dat OG roll now, like this young buck won't handle his?" Germ asked to make sure.

"Yea..."

Boom! Boom! Boom! Boom!

Bloc! Bloc...!

Before he could finish saying yeah, Germ put four hot ones in his upper torso, then Pintz added a couple also. They had him dancing doing the dead man's shake.

"Bitch nigga!" Germ spat. "Come on, let's get his old ass out of here."

215

Together they dragged his body to the end of the alley. After the alley ended, there was a path that led to an alligator infested swamp. Germ had plans for his O.G. ass.

"Yo cuzzo, this old bastard is heavy as shit!" Pintz said exhausted.

"What happened to Pintz wit' his t-shirt off on the block?"

"Fuck all dat, we can leave his ass stankin' right here!"

Germ had to laugh at his cousin's laziness.

"Did you even hear what you just said? Leave duke here, and we gon' hot the block up, feel me? Come on, it's only about three feet more."

Just as Germ said, the swamp was now within small steps. They lifted Elroy by his hands and feet, and with three good swings, he now lived with the murderous reptiles.

"Here's a late night snack, boys," Pintz shouted into the dark water.

As the duo walked off, they heard a big splash, which meant the gators were feeding.

"You think we should call Unc and fill him in?"

"Nah, if it's one thing I've learned about the game, it's dat a phone will always tell your fate with the courts. We'll tell him tonight, you got dat scrilla, right?" Germ was well disciplined with words and wanted to make sure Pintz had the buy money intact.

"No doubt," he answered, flashing Elroy's scrilla.

"Good."

"We need to get back to the spot, it's still early cuzzo," Pintz said leading the way. "Aye cuz, you ain't heard from Angus yet?"

"Fuck made you ask about Angus at a time like now?"

"To tell you the truth, cuz, he just popped into my head."

"Nah, but I'm glad you brought him up. I'm about to call back home to see if he's around the crib."

$$$$$

The phone rang in Angus' house three times before anyone picked up. When Germ heard a woman's voice, he knew it was Angus' step-moms.

"Hello?" she cordially answered.

Her voice was soft and calming, one he never got the chance to enjoy from a mother's perspective.

"Hey, – I mean hello, Mrs. Hamilton," Germ said, correcting his choice of words.

Yeah he was street with it, but Uncle Marv had taught him to always have respect for your elders.

"Is Angus around?"

"Hey chile, is this Germee?"

"Yes ma'am, it is," he smiled, hearing his full name being called by a woman.

"How's everything down south?"

"Everything's great, Mrs. Hamilton, I love it down here, just too many dirt roads."

"Well remember, Germee, you're in the bottoms now. It's

217

different from city life, but it's a place you can sit back and relax and start anew."

"You're right about that. I think I found the new me."

"So, are you guys working yet?"

"Yes Ma'am, Me and Pintz work for this big company making good money."

Germ didn't want Angus' mom to think they were still into the life down there mainly because they wanted her to let Angus come down there, so he lied. He just compared his position in the West Side Mob. Although he was a crack head, she was his mother and she cared.

"Well that's good, I hope Angus going down there with y'all. Take care, and he's in his room, I'll get him for you."

"Thank you and take care, Mrs. Hamilton. *Damn...*," he mumbled when she put the phone down to yell for her son.

"I will, and you do the same down there in the south."

She only knew of them because Angus had told her about them going to live with their uncle after the funeral. There was silence for a brief minute, then Germ could hear static and shuffling, which he knew was them exchanging the phone between each other.

"Wassup boyee?" Angus shouted cheerfully, happy to hear his man's voice again.

"What's up with you, my dude, and why you ain't hollered at a nigga yet?" Germ replied with much enthusiasm.

"Shit, man, you know me, Germ, I'm just trying to get in where I fit in. What's good wit' Pintz, y'all down there fucking some big booty hoes, huh?"

218

Germ laughed, but it was true. He loved the difference between the southern girls and the one's back home. They seemed to have like two and three asses on them.

"You already know, kiko. We fucking these twins, straight fire too! But fuck all dat, what's really hood?" Germ pressed.

"Just laying low. You know the streets is talking and shit, got all of us pegged for knocking off T-Kill and his peeps. So, I'm just chilling, doing me. Me and Asia been kicking it still, but that's really it."

"Oh yeah? What's hood with the rest of dem hoes?"

"Melodie finally bounced out of state to go to medical school, but Avonne and Courtnee still around the way. Oh yeah, I know I shouldn't be talking on the phone, but rumor has it that, that broad, Avonne, got old boy Dro and Dex from the Law to run up in the spot, so I'm thinking it was them who got at Uncle Marvin too!" Angus heard Germ's throat swallow even through the hundreds of miles that separated them.

"You sure?" Bothered by the news, Germ bowed his head, smashing the phone into his jaw.

"Not really, but it's out here like government cheese, and dat bitch has been rocking some fly new gear lately. She's definitely come into some money or some nigga's trap."

"Good looking 'Gus. Aye you straight on ends? 'Cause I can send you some fetti right now."

"A nigga hit up. It's too hot to do my thing, so I've been laid up in the crib since y'all fled the state."

Germ knew Angus must have felt like a fucking snail or a turtle trapped in a shell, because he was a live-wire, for real. If Angus didn't have, he'd stick up a crap game, run in a nigga's crib or whatever it took to come up, so he felt his pain.

"Yo check it, can you get to a Western Union anytime soon?"

"It's too hot for me to be walking around the hood, bruh, so nah,"

"Alright check it, call Amanda and have her dip you over there. I'll send you a couple of stacks a-sap. I got you my dude – we M.H.B.'s for life!"

"Good looking, kiko. Tell Pintz I said one-up too, and good lookin again, bruh. I love you, G." Angus was nearly in tears when Germ said M.H.B.'s for life.

"A'ight and call a nigga sometime, this is my cell number, write the shit down. One-up!"

"No doubt, one-up!"

The line went dead.

"So what's good with old boy?" Pintz asked, seeing the scowl on Germ's face.

"I'll fill you in later, but for now we gotta send 'Gus some change. Come on, let's jet. Go tell the girls we'll be back in an hour and to hold fort 'til we touch back."

Chapter 40

No Good Bitch

After sending Angus five-stacks, Germ and Pintz stopped at Green Acres, a soul food spot Big-Rod turned them onto a couple days after arriving in Alabama. While contemplating over what to order, Pintz could clearly see that Germ was still fucked up about the sudden news Angus revealed to him. He wasn't sure what to believe or what he should do, but murder was definitely on his mind and in a fucked up way.

Since Shai and Nai had the projects under control, Germ thought it would be a good idea to sit down and get their grub on. So much shit was flowing through his mind at the moment, he hadn't heard Pintz call out to him. It wasn't until Pintz nudged him, that he finally received his attention.

"Damn, wassup cuzzo, you was out of it. What's got you all twisted?"

Before answering, Germ looked around the small establishment, when he didn't notice any unwanted ears he broke down what Angus said to him over the phone.

"Yeah, so, I really don't know what to believe, feel me," Germ said, then sipped from the complimentary Tea, Green Acres offered to their customers upon entrance.

Now Pintz was in deep thought. His mind went back to that rainy day on Russ Street. He was in the Honda with Angus when they saw Avonne's trick-ass kicking rocks with Dro and Dex, and now it all made sense. *"Dat stank hoe, Avonne, tried to get back at me for smacking fire outta her silly ass. But damn, did they have to kill Uncle Marv in the process?"* He thought to himself.

"Yo cuz, I think it's true," he began, "because the next

morning after you were shot, I saw dat bitch hitting the pavement with them headed towards the Law. Angus was about to blast on them, but the light turned green. What do you wanna to do?" Pintz asked.

He was down for whatever. If it meant heading back to Connecticut to slump something, he was down.

"Real talk cuzzo, I want to be one-hundred on this, because if they did, they're gonna pay!" he swore. "Come on, let's get back to the trap, I lost my appetite."

After paying for their orders, they hopped back into their ride and sped off.

$$$$$

Back in Connecticut, Angus was collecting the stacks Germ had sent him via Weston Union. He was definitely thrown off by the amount they wired. He was only expecting like $500. Nevertheless, $5,000 would definitely hold him down for a minute. The first thing he did was have Amanda shoot to Wal-Mart, so he could cop a pre-paid Boost Mobile phone, figuring he would need it to holler back and forth with his boys. Knowing that it would be too dangerous to go inside himself, he sent Amanda in with a crisp hundred. He advised her to get any model phone, but it had to be Boost for some odd reason; preferably the cheapest one and to spend the rest on minutes.

While Amanda went in the giant store, he tuned into the radio station.

"Damn, if it ain't Soulja Boy, it's Gucci Mane," he cursed. "The East Coast really needs to step our game up with this music shit."

After further surfing the radio stations, he found Dj QT of 88.9 Cute FM banging some new Young Spaid shit. The young fourteen-year old was tearing the mix tape game down in Connecticut. Angus tried his damnedest to spit alongside with him, but the young vet was too nice, not to mention the music was new to him.

After fifteen minutes of loneliness, Amanda returned to the car.

"Here you go," she said and tossed him the sky blue bag with his new mobile device.

"Good lookin' girl. Where's my change?" He made sure to ask.

Angus was always leery about bitches and money, and he didn't trust anything when either was involved.

"Damn Gus, it's in the bag. You know I don't get down like that," she said honestly. "Oh the phone was $39.50 and it got a $50 monthly unlimited plan, so you're free to do you. All you have to do is call and activate it before you can use it."

Angus examined the petite phone for a minute, and then inserted the sim card and battery. He hit power on the phone, but it only stayed on for about five seconds.

"Fuck! I gotta charge this stupid thing up, too!" he shouted and threw it on the floor.

"Chill out 'Gus, you need some serious counseling. Look in the bag. I bought a car-charger for you."

When Angus further inspected the plastic bag, there it was; a car adapter as she said. "You're the best." He praised her. "I got you too!"

"I know, I'm the shit," she mocked playfully.

"Matter fact, since you're the shit, come give me some

223

head," he said then leaned all the way back in his seat ready to
feel her warm mouth around the thickness of his dick.

There was no shame in Amanda's game. She reached over
and unfastened his pants and pulled his limp penis out, then put it
in her mouth and gave him what he desired. It had been three days
since Angus had any type of sex, so each time he was about to
nut, he'd pull her head back. About ten wet minutes later, he
nutted long and hard in her mouth. He had to admit, even though
Amanda got high, she had some A-1 head, and excellent pussy.

Seeing that the phone had gained a little bit of charging time,
Amanda did him the favor of calling it in. The phone was
activated within five-minutes. Thereafter, he called Germ and let
him know he had gotten the scrilla and thanked him. He also gave
him his new number and said to stay in touch. Angus wanted to
continue the party with Amanda, but wasn't with all that smoking
rock shit around him, so he went and copped an ounce of Purple
Haze from one of them Connecticut Cartel niggas, also a quarter
of coke for Amanda to snort, then they went and rented a room at
the Red Roof Inn in the Meadows. Angus had plans to lay low for
a good while, so Amanda used her ID and paid cash to rent a
room at a monthly rate. She was white and still looked like she
was into things other than drugs and the streets, so it was cool
with the night manager. After accepting two key cards to her
room, Amanda walked back to the Honda and passed Angus one
of them.

"Here boo, you can go inside if you want, I'm gonna hit the
store real quick ok? Do you need me to get you anything?"

"Yeah, get me some plastic ma, I'm tryna knock them walls
down tonight."

"I got you," she told him and bounced.

While Angus ducked off inside the room, Amanda hit the
Mobil Gas station and got two bags of snacks along with a couple

boxes of Magnums. Next, she ran through the McDonald's drive-through. Unsure of what Angus liked to eat, she ordered one of everything off the value meal, and then went back to the room.

Using her key card, she entered into the room. After putting all of the stuff down onto a round table, she stripped butt-naked and watched as Angus' eyes blew up with lust.

"I'll be right back baby, I'ma go and wash this pussy for you, 'kay."

For the rest of the night, Amanda fucked and sucked his dick every which way but loose. She even snorted lines of coke off his large dick, which he was thankful for.

"Damn ma', you's a cold-freak."

"I know."

Chapter 41

Careless Whispers

After about a week's time, Angus had run through the ounce of haze. Surprisingly, Amanda got him to try some coke; something he thought he'd never do, but pussy had tricked his normal train of thought into indulging in a disastrous world he'd probably enjoy, love and possibly exit from.

Together, they sat in the dimness of the hotel room gazing at nothing, practically geeking for a hit. Amanda knew she needed something, but she was seasoned, meaning she knew how to control the urges and cravings a lot better than a new person entering into the coke cosmo did. It was too late for Angus. He was too far gone to back down now.

"Yo…come on, we 'bout to roll out," Angus said in a groggy voice; his eyes glassy and wide.

"You sure 'Gus? I can call someone to come through, if you want."

She saw what he was going through. He wanted that feeling haze could never provide him again.

"You're not thinking rationally," she concluded. "We can just lay low and have it delivered," she further insisted because of his state of mind at the moment.

"Bitch, fuck did I say!" he barked angrily, pulling Eastwood out, which startled her to a frantic point.

Amanda had no choice but to give in for fear that he would harm her; all for the love of the drug.

226

Although she was terrified and nervous, she yelled, "Okay…let's go then."

If she could only get a hold of his cell phone to call Germ, she would put him on blast. Unfortunately, that was not about to happen, he had already cuffed it in his pocket, so for now she would just have to roll with the punches.

$$$$$

The white Honda cruised the blood stained streets of Hartford at a snail's pace in search of Amanda's backup supplier when the M.H.B.'s didn't have any work. Amanda brought the Honda to Brook St., and slowly road the bumpy tarmac. At the corner of Mather and Brook St., she noticed CoCo, a known dealer, and then pulled over.

As the window rolled down, she said, "Hey Co, you holding anything?"

Coco was about six feet, 250 lbs, on the chubby side, with long Iverson styled braids. He slowly looked into the Honda and was skeptical, seeing a young hood looking nigga riding shotgun with a fiend. Just for his own safety, CoCo repositioned his gat in a way where he could draw quick if need be.

"Yeah, what you want some, girl?"

"Uh huh. Give me a half ounce in powder?" she asked nervously.

She did not want to send the wrong message to him, so she added a seductive smile to help secure the deal.

"Yeah, and only because you paying four hundred. Hol' up a sec, I'll be right back," he said, then dipped into a brick building where he kept is stash at.

It took five minutes before he came back to the car. He opened the rear door and hopped in back.

"Listen, drive around the block, it ain't safe right now. Somebody got murked a few hours ago, and the deeze's still riding through. Yo dat paper right?" he put forth with the quickness.

Hearing that, Angus turned around and passed him a fat knot.

"Here you go, my dude."

Coco accepted the knot and eagerly shuffled through it making sure it was '12:00' then passed the coke to Angus.

"Fourteen grams, right?" Angus asked in a skeptical tone.

He might be getting high now, but he was still him. If it was not fourteen grams as promised, he planned to swing back through, only this time he wasn't coming to purchase, he was coming to loan CoCo some hot-ones.

"No doubt, I'm about my B.I.," CoCo answered unfazed by Angus' tone. "Let me out, right here and holla if you need more."

"Fo' sure," Angus replied.

Just around the corner was Garden St. a.k.a. G-Street, which was a major Purple Haze and Dust spot. Once Amanda parked the Honda, Angus hopped out with a bottle of Remy V.S., and walked into the driveway where the hustlers usually grouped up doing them. As he sipped from the bottle, he noticed a tag on the brick wall that read *R.I.P. Lenny (Toss)*, and poured out the remainder of his Remy.

"One love Thunni!" He said, paying homage to one of G-Streets greats.

Just as Angus chucked the empty bottle to the grass, a light-

228

skinned dude with waves and a low taper approached him.

"Yo, what's hood, homeboy?"

"You got some bud and dust?"

"Yeah, what you need?"

"An ounce of bud and a coupla bundles of wet if its right." Angus replied, he wasn't around for that late night bullshit the youngins tried slinging when the real hustlers were off in the clubs or sleep trying to get their ones up.

"Hol' up a minute." He then turned around and yelled out, "Yoop, yo Cakes?"

Normally that was the call for the jakes, but nowadays, the young niggas in the hood changed up their codes like boxers. A short brown-skinned cat ran up with a paper bag and asked what was good.

"Yo, who's this dude, Dove?"

"He's cool – he M.H.B., you know them little nigga's from the south end dat stay coming through for oz's," Dove said in his defense.

He'd served them enough to remember just by hearing their voices in the dark.

"Yeah, yeah – you talking about young Germ and them. Yeah what you got playboy?"

"Four-eighty, I'm hood wit' dat?" Angus asked counting out his scrilla.

In the process of watching him count out his money, they also saw Eastwood's head poking out from his waistline.

From Boyz To Men

"Matter fact, kiko, just see me with four-fiddy. Be careful leaving the block, the Feds circling the hood type heavy," Cakes advised him; with the heavy flow of drugs and the murder last night, the block was hot.

"Good look. I'll probably come through in a few days. By the way, they call me Angus – one up! Oh here, dis is for the wet." He passed them another $150.

"A'ight playboy, be easy," they both said, as Angus got ghost. "Yo, dude ain't playing no games running around strapped up like he got hella beef out here. I thought he was on some stick up shit for real," Dove said truthfully.

He was a magnet for money, not drama.

"Sheeit...I had something for his ass though," Cakes stated and lifted his black tee, revealing a fully-auto Mac-11.

Dove smiled, and they went back to doing them; getting money.

Climbing back into the car, Amanda asked, "Is everything good 'Gus?"

"Yeah, drive and let me see some of that yae (coke)."

She passed him the whole pack after pulling it out from her panties.

"Smells good!" he said with a huge smile.

"I know it do, boy, I'm keep the coochie clean!" Amanda responded, a little offended by his remark.

He laughed, knowing he had struck a nerve.

"I wasn't talking about your pussy, girl – I meant the coke," he laughed again, and she joined in. "You're one crazy ass white

230

girl."

Amanda was cool with snorting coke, because the crack had her geeked out and chasing right now. She could control herself on just powder and weed, plus some good dick.

The Red Roof Inn was far from their destination. They had been circling the hood for over an hour getting high as a kite, when Angus' alter ego started whispering to him. *"Kill! Kill! Kill! – Murda! Murda! Murda!"* The voice that always sprung him into the same old devious type shit he couldn't seem to control once coming out.

"Yo pull over, I wanna drive while you suck me off!" he demanded, it was the bags of dust he had been smoking that had him tripping and aggressive right now.

Amanda had no problems either because now she could get her snort on, smoke a little, plus she enjoyed having a fat dick in her mouth whenever she got high. Respecting Angus' wishes, she pulled over at the Shell Gas station on Albany Avenue and hopped out. Angus watched as her thickness shook with each step. Her ass was fat and loose, and her small waist only helped to accentuate her curves perfectly. For a woman who got high every day, Amanda still had what her momma gave her.

Angus slid over the armrest when she got out. He grabbed a Vanilla Dutch out the cup holder and dumped the guts onto the ground. After breaking up some haze, he wrapped a fat piece, and then pulled out of the parking lot. By the time he hit Sigourney Street, Amanda had everything but his ass in her mouth, caressing his length with great perfection.

After passing through a few red lights, the Honda was on Broad Street in the South End of town.

"Uhhh," he moaned, as he turned right onto Lawrence St.

231

From Boyz To Men

Though he was in Heaven, he was very aware of his surroundings. While Amanda slurped and jerked on his dick, he slowly eased Eastwood from out of the door pocket. His lights were already off and had been since Broad St. His eyes were like miniature night vision beams for human targets. *"Murda! Murda! Murda! Kill! Kill! Kill!"* his ego continued to whisper to him.

As the car slowly crept down Lawrence Street, Angus dropped the window, and a gust of chilled air brushed over Amanda's bronze hair. She figured he needed some air and let the window down, so she kept up her fellatio act.

"There – there," his ego spoke, identifying a group of Snackz' workers, then just like that, Eastwood came to life.

Blam! Blam! Blam! Blam! Blam! Blam!

Six shots fired out of the Honda's window before Angus knifed away from the scene.

Blocc, Blocc, Bloc, Bloc... Boom, Boom, Boom! Pow!

The sound of three different guns letting off echoed into the still night. Angus swerved down the one-way street all the while pressing Amanda's head down on his shaft. He was in mad-mode. The high of the dust, coke, haze, drive-by and Amanda's head had him at full-length. Hearing the loud shots in her ear caused her to panic, but Angus ignored her muffled cries to let her up, forcing her to continuing blowing him.

With one hand, Angus stirred the Honda onto Grand St., then bent a right onto Babcock and floored the engine. As he got halfway down the block, two shadows appeared in the middle of the street and began firing into the hood and windshield of the Honda. He managed to swerve around the shower of bullets and struck both gunmen in doing so. He laughed as their bodies went about twenty feet into the air, then landed somewhere on the street, now prime candidates for the graveyard.

"Ahhh...what are you doing, Angus. You've fucking lost it. Call Germ – please call Germ!" she cried hysterically finally getting some relief for his dick.

"Good idea, boo," he replied and dialed the 205 area code once he felt they were out of danger.

$$$$$

Pintz and Germ had just shut down shop and were now riding in the 'Vette with the twins about to hit the strip club, when Germ recognized Angus' cell number flash across his screen. He thought it was odd when he checked the dash and saw the time, but they were nighttime vultures, so he quickly hit ok on his phone.

"Wassup Gus?" he spoke into the receiver.

"I'm out here, wassup witchu playboy?" he yelled with much excitement; almost hostile. Never giving Germ a chance to reply, Angus continued. "Whaddid do, Germ, I just blazed the 'Law' up for Uncle Marv. I know I dropped at least one body – yeah boyee!" He was in a crazed state, which really threw Germ for a loop.

For starters, Angus was yelling some dumb shit through the wire, and some murder shit at that. Even though Germ was pissed, he was concerned for his right hand.

"Yo, 'Gus, what the fuck did you do – who you with 'Gus?"

"Man I was on some gang...sta shit, G'. Mo' Body was slobbing me down while I shot up the 'Law'. They were all out there too, bruh; LateNiteSnackz, Dro, Dex, Blaze and dat bitch nigga Slim. I know I domed one of them, peeps!" His speech was slurred and irate.

"Put Amanda on the phone 'Gus!" he insisted in a heated

tone. "Dis nigga don' went crazy, P'," he said to Pintz.

"What's hood, cuzzo?" Pintz asked, hearing just a little of what Angus said, being they were sharing the earpiece.

"Hold up cuzzo, let me holla at Amanda real quick. Shit sounds fucked up for our Angus."

"Hello – Germ, he's gone fucking crazy. He shot up the whole street, and then ran two of them down. He's lost it Germ. Please talk to him," she begged and began to cry.

Angus snatched the phone away from Amanda.

"Yo, Germ, tell me how to get down there, I'm coming to kick it with my family – M.H.B.'s for life," he slurred as he jumped on the highway.

"Yo 'Gus, listen. Pull over and let Amanda drive a'ight. Tell her to take I-95 South straight to Alabama. Get a room and holla back at me a-sap. Yo, be easy and don't do nothin' stupid down I-95, them Staties ain't playing. You got dat?" Germ yelled, he was distraught and didn't see a good ending to this, however, his mans had went all out for his Pops, so he was going to aide him at all cost, even if it meant aiding and abetting a fugitive for murder.

"I got you, bruh, see you soon. Tell Pintz I love 'em too– it's M.H.B. for life!"

The phone went dead, leaving Germ feeling fucked up. His head doing an unknowing shake.

Chapter 42

We Live To Die

From the corner of Lawrence Street to Russ and Babcock, Crown Vitoria's, Detectives, Blue and Whites, and a couple of ambulances flooded the area like rushing waters from an open fire hydrant. Even Chief P. Roberts was on the scene tonight. The Homicide Unit was up to their necks in murders in this area of Hartford and was determined to put an end to it all.

The news trucks had more than likely been eavesdropping on the scanner when the call went over the wire about the heinous act of murder. As usual, the noisy gawkers were outside in their night apparel, trying to get a fix on tonight's melee.

"They should have killed the bunch of you!" one angry elderly man shouted while standing on the curb.

"Yeah…we want our streets back!" a young woman with two kids yelled.

Just the other day a stray bullet missed her youngest child by inches, tearing off several twists in her hair.

"Go back into your homes, please," a detective yelled into his bullhorn.

"This doesn't look too good, Chris," a female detective named Linda said to her team leader.

"Yeah I see, we've got two dead here and two on Babcock. He was packing some heavy fire power too." He held up a fully loaded .50 caliber handgun with an extended clip. "This is the type of weapon that'll put a nice size hole in someone from a

distance. Where are these young kids getting these guns from?"
He shook his head in a disturbing manner.

"You know…the out of towners," Linda responded. "This is
a real mess. I just got a good look at the two people he ran over;
pure recklessness. Doesn't surprise me that they all had weapons
on their persons, too. I'm sure it was a drive-by. And it appears
they ran through those back yards to try and cut whoever was
driving the car off to gain some retribution, but got rundown in
the process. I mean a leg here, an arm there. This guy wasn't
playing around," Linda stated.

"Any make or model on the getaway vehicle?" Chris
inquired.

"Yes, an elderly woman claims she witnessed the whole
thing. Guess what?

"What's that?"

"I'm not sure how she did it at this time of night, but
somehow got the plate number for us. Says the car slowed down
after sending these two into the air. Get this…she claims she has
seen too many cop shows to know it was a drive-by of some sort."

"Thank God for the nosiness of the elderly on this block.
Okay, get a brief statement and put out an A.P.B. on that vehicle.
I want this son of a bitch in lock-up by the end of shift!" Chris
demanded.

$$$$$

Inside the 'Vette, Shai turned down the music as asked. Pintz
wanted a full rundown of the phone call from Angus. He knew
how extreme and dangerous he could be, so it was more than
likely it was *Hell on Earth* back home for a few people. What
really took him to a heightened level of uneasiness was the mere
fact of knowing if Yak weren't on lockdown, he'd definitely be

236

entangled in Angus' mess, and he did not want him mixed up with any of it.

"So, what's really hood, Germ?" Pintz asked out of frustration, never mind the twins were in the car, he knew they were beyond thorough and would never breathe one word of what about to be discussed.

"Yo, shit is fucked up back home for 'Gus. Dude went off the handle with dis one," he paused for a second, "'Gus done shot up the 'Law' and probably killed a couple of Snackz' people in the process." The look on Pintz face was full of surprise. "Amanda said his crazy ass ran two of them over, too. When I spoke to him, dude sounded a little strange too, high, but strange."

"Word?" Pintz laughed, hearing the news about Angus' tirade. "Sounds type serious bruh, but fuck them bitch ass niggas, Germ, they killed Uncle Marv!" he reasoned with Angus' action.

To him it was justified retribution.

"No doubt, I feel da same way. They should be on 95 headed our way now. Hopefully Amanda can get him here in one piece, you know how crazy he can get," he laughed reliving the scene Amanda had vividly described to him.

$$$$$

Linda successfully noted the woman's account of what transpired that night and put an All-Points Bulletin out on a white, late model, 4-door, Honda Accord, with very dark tinted windows. Chief P. Roberts had half of the shift out in pursuit of this vehicle. He was not going to be the Mayor's pincushion come daybreak.

Linda shook her head at the grotesque sight of the hit and run victims while taking some more notes, then out of nowhere, a voice squawked loudly over the police radio.

"Attention; Attention; we have a definite match on the identified drive-by, hit and run vehicle headed south on I-95. State Police are in pursuit. I repeat...State Police are in pursuit!" the dispatcher relayed.

"Now, that's what I needed to hear," Chris mumbled.

He knew tonight would get him and Linda some fruitful leniency from the higher ups. Chris picked Linda up from Babcock Street in his unmarked car and wasted no time jumping on I-95 South, anxious to join in on the pursuit.

$$$$$

Angus was running off the rush of adrenaline from the murderous situation just 15 minutes ago. Feeling as though he could make the long journey down south, he was reluctant to hand over the wheel to Amanda. Every so often Amanda would steal a worried glance in his direction. She had calmed down after doing three lines of coke and was fogging the interior of the sedan as they sped down the highway. She felt much better seeing how relaxed and content Angus was as he blew rings of smoke through his nose.

"Gimme a line Mo'," Angus demanded after passing the blunt off to her.

"I think…"

"Don't think," he stopped her. "Just get me dat line and play with my dick, dumb ass," he urged.

Out of fear, Amanda complied. She did not want the evil side of him to return, especially while on the highway. After passing him a line on a dollar bill, she took his penis out, massaged its length with her hand, and then took him into her mouth.

"See how easy dat was? Ummm," he moaned, enjoying the

238

softness of her mouth against his stiffness.

$$$$$

It was with determination and great speed that Chris and Linda had miraculously caught up to the group of Crown Vic's trailing the suspected vehicle.

Angus was too inebriated to see the caravan of State Troopers in his rear view mirror. He was in such a world of profound gratification that he had not noticed the car on the side of him until the red and blue light on top of its roof twirled in a bright kaleidoscope.

"Oh yeah," he uttered, as it suddenly dawned on him what was taking place.

Thereafter, he looked into his mirrors and noticed an entire caravan of cars with matching hats and colorful toys eager to get to know him better. While Amanda excused his outburst for a symbol of pleasure, Angus found Eastwood and pulled back on the hammer. He was going out straight hood style, in a pine box; 8x10's were just too cramped for his style of living. Although the sky was pitch dark, the vibrant halogen-lights from the many cop cars and a Police helicopter illuminated the Honda like a stage play after a two hour show. Over the thunderous bullhorn, the command to stop and pull over echoed loudly into the night. Amanda heard the demand, but the coke induced high tricked her mind into believing it was just a song on the radio, so she kept doing her.

"Pull over and shut your engine off!" a troopers voice blared out of the loudspeaker box.

"Fuck you pig!" Angus retorted out the driver's window.

He and Eastwood took orders from no one. The chase had now ensued for over ten miles and many city limits. The authorities knew how this could end and didn't want to harm any innocent motorists, so the lead car tried a police tactic most favored all over the country.

As the interceptor slammed into the rear bumper of the Honda, Angus dropped the window all the way down. He was hoping to get a shot off and kill him a pig, but the trooper swerved away seeing the chrome long nose barrel on his .44 magnum. Even though the Honda swerved, he recovered just fine and floored the pedal.

"Angus...what's going on?" Amanda attempted to stop and look up, but he pushed her head back down causing her to gag.

"Shut up and suck – I got dis!"

He successfully maneuvered through the first one, but the trooper's next attempt proved to be immaculate. The Honda fishtailed out of Angus' control and flipped over several times, then smacked into the guardrail. Luckily for Angus, the Honda landed on all fours.

The parade of cars stopped and bunched up in a staggered flank. The crash site was now a misty white area of steam from the radiator. Anti-freeze leaked rapidly on the undercarriage of the car. The police held their distance cautiously, as they noticed a small gas leak forming at the rear of the vehicle.

"Come out with your hands up. We've got you surrounded – there's no way out!" the command was repeated several times, but to no avail.

Inside the Honda, the movements were labored, almost non-existent. Amanda's head was nearly crushed by the impact of the dashboard. Blood oozed out of her ears and mouth. However, Angus was luckier than Amanda was. She had given him enough cover with her body along with the air bag, so he slowly gained his train of thought and found Eastwood on the floor and slowly prepared for war.

"This is your last chance to come out, or we'll start shooting!" the voice boomed loudly through the bullhorn.

It was a scene out of an America's Most Wanted episode, back when John Walsh first began. Nowadays, it had a watered down affect and made for T.V. Angus looked at Amanda, there was no movement from her; no moan, no cry, no breathing. And she sure was not slobbing him anymore, so yeah, she was Audi 5000! With Eastwood in one hand and Amanda's head in the other, he took heed to their warning, backing slowly out of the car.

"Don't shoot, I'm coming out!" he informed them through a yell. "I've gotta hostage!"

"Fuck!" Chris yelled, slamming his fist down onto the hood of his car.

The many troopers in attendance kneeled down in perfect positions, guns drawn, ready to shoot, even kill if necessary.

"No one shoot. I repeat, no one shoot!" A trooper shouted loudly.

He saw how the situation was possibly going to end. Angus was now fully out of the car with Amanda's dead carcass shielding a great portion of his body.

"Don't shoot or I swear...I'll murk dis bitch!" From out of his peripheral, Angus saw someone move. "Don't get it twisted fool. As I see this, I only have two options outta here, in one of your cars or a body bag, it's your choice. Move again, and I'll kill dis bitch. I want a cruiser right now, or I'ma blow this bitch's brains all over dis fucking highway!" Angus swore slobbing at the mouth.

He could tell Law Enforcement was unsure of what to do, being they hadn't made a move just yet.

"Sorry, but we can't do that. Just drop the weapon and let the woman go," one of them urged.

"Fuck you, Pig! Y'all think I'm playing huh? Trust me...I'm not the one to be testing."

As Angus warned the swarm of officers, he was slowly inching towards the side of the road. From where he now stood, he could see a clear path to some woods and thought he could get ghost in the dark night. He reasoned that there was no way some old ass men in plastic and hard bottom shoes would catch his young athletic body in a chase through the rugged terrain; not to mention Amanda was going to ensure his safe passage to the woods.

"There's no way you're going make out of here alive! Now, let the woman go!" the warning blared through the bullhorn.

"Suck uh dick and stay the fuck back. I see you, Pig," he shouted and nudged Amanda in the head with the barrel of his gun to let them know he wasn't fucking around.

On the opposite side of traffic, an 18-wheeler blew its loud horn, which startled Angus and gave a heroic trooper enough time to sneak down the grassy hill where Angus intended on making his getaway. However, when Angus whipped his head back around, he saw the trooper's hat and let Eastwood bark.

Blooow...Blooow...Blooow...

The first two shots entered into Amanda's skull, the next one sailed into the trooper's neck. Angus was by far an expert shooter, but tonight his sighting was precise.

"I said get back!" he barked.

242

J. Alexander

The Lieutenant on scene knew he had to do something immediately before any more shots were fired, so he attempted to talk over the horn. Too late, Angus had started shooting again. After dropping Amanda's body onto the ground, he hauled ass, headed for the tall bush. In the pursuit of freedom, the bullets from the many service weapons followed his body like heat seeking missiles riddling his immature body with over forty rounds of lead projectiles.

For a moment, the area became silent. No man expects to go out like such, and no young man ever believes he will ever die by the hand of a cop. They might say during his eulogy: *That Angus might have been deprived of his youth; an opportunity to prevail in life, but as a man, as a human – we all have a choice of which road we'd like to hike. Therefore, when we mourn a young man such as Angus, we must also remember, uncontrolled violence is a vast fault of our youth, and we all live to die!*

Chapter 43

Have You Ever Lost A Loved One

B ack on the west side of Magic City, Big-Rod, Lil' Tone and two females, one being Jona, were kicking it while captivated by a re-run of a Lakers' Play-off game. They were passing around blunts and sipping on some Surp.

"Shit, we might just go all the way," Lil' Tone blurted out rooting for the Lakers.

"Nigga, bet a stack!" Big-Rod challenged, he was skeptical about them going all the way this year.

He wanted to see LeBron get his first ring.

"Bet it," he hoped the Cav's made it past the playoffs, so they could really put some money up on the finals.

"Hand me the remote, Jona," Big-Rod said, he wanted to turn the volume up.

Jona leaned up off his lap and fumbled for the large all-in-one remote; her finger accidently changing the channel.

"Oops, I'm sorry fellas," she apologized, and then tried to scan back to ESPN.

"Hold it right there Jo'!" Big-Rod said as he caught a glimpse of something interesting on C.N.N.

The caption read as followed: *Fleeing drive-by, hit and run murder suspect, gunned down on Connecticut Interstate.* Then they highlighted the mangled car and an undersized photo of the victim's riddled corpse.

"Damn…dat's some wild shit. Them up north Cats don't be fucking around!" Lil' Tone said then took a huge gulp of his Surp.

The familiar clank in the hollowness of the floorboard made the room turn about to focus on who had caused the sound.

As the twins and Big-Rod's nephews walked in, Jona said, "Damn Germ, y'all really got some live-wires back home I see."

"What you mean by dat, Jona?" Germ inquired, wondering where that came from.

"Y'all grandstanding on C.N.N., check it out. It's serious too," she replied.

He quickly took heed to Jona's words and fixated his attention to the Plasma Screen.

"Yo Germ, dat's Amanda's Honda! Fuck happened?" his voice echoed throughout the room.

"Ah nah…" Germ spat in defeat.

He read the caption and knew his crimey had gone out in a blaze. He ran out back in a crazed state and tried to murder anything possible in the sky as his .50 caliber shot into the night. He kept pulling on the trigger, but nothing came out.

"Nooo…" he cried. "Why Angus – why'd you go out like dis?" he questioned.

He and Angus were like day and night; music and singers; apples and oranges, and now he would never get to live lavishly with his righty.

Nai was concerned and attempted to go to his aide, but Big-Rod stopped her.

"Let 'im be for a while. He needs to man this one alone for now. Just give it a few."

Big-Rod wasn't worried about the thunderous ruckus Germ caused out back with his cannon mainly because there weren't any neighbors for over three miles away.

"Damn..." Pintz cursed.

Even though they were not as tight as he and Germ, he still had mad love for his mans. He knew what it felt like to lose a loved one long ago; so grieving would be easy for him. Nevertheless, it didn't mean he wasn't fucked up over the situation. After an hour of peace to himself, Germ walked inside the room, his .50 Cal protruding from the lining of his waist.

"You cool, neph?" Big-Rod asked.

"Yeah, I'm hood Unc, I just had to get some rage out of my system, feel me?"

"All day, Playa. Here toke on some of dis shit." Big-Rod tossed him a blunt to help ease the tension.

Big-Rod had been in the game far too long and had experienced death too many times. So, he knew what his nephew was going through.

Germ and Pintz shared a brotherly hug for a minute, and then Nai gently wrapped her arms around his waist and began pecking at his dark lips.

"You okay, boo?" she whispered into his ear.

As the weeks passed, Nai took a huge liking to Germ; falling head over heels for the northerner. He displayed all the qualities she desired in a man. Mind you, their age difference didn't mean anything. In her eyes it was just a number. Nai planned to   mourn his lose and walk down that painful road hand and hand with Germ until he got better. Before answering, Germ took her into his grasp, hugging her tightly letting her know that her affection was indeed appreciated.

"Yeah, I'm good sexy, thanks for asking. Aye, I'm about to retire for the night if y'all don't mind."

"Nah, y'all go do y'all...ya heard." Big-Rod responded.

"I'll holla in the A.M. Unc," Germ said, and then excused themselves from the party.

They retired upstairs for a night of ecstasy. They started off making love, which soon turned into some rough animalistic sex that lasted into the wee hours of the morning.

Chapter 44

Handle That

Benny, Cheese's Lieutenant, had just gotten word that four of his main workers on the Drift Track had been gunned down and robbed for 18-kilos of dope by Straw and a clique. Now Cheese had the unpleasant task of relaying the message back to Mr. Todd, his key supplier.

Old-Man Todd was fifty-eight and filthy, no stanky-rich. He had never so much as had a parking ticket in his life. Old-Man Todd had major ties to a cartel out of Mexico and supplied whomever Big-Rod did not. He controlled the east and west sides of Magic City. The two knew of each other and cursed the blood that ran through one another's veins. Mr. Todd was a man of his own rules and refused to play fair by the D-Boy rules of the game. He often chose to lower his prices at an unmatchable price, which lessened Big-Rod's pockets at times, and for this, Big-Rod wanted his head and all the arms that linked to him. Mr. Todd was getting old, but he possessed a thirty year old's features and wit. He stood a towering 6'4. His hair was slicked back in a single ponytail similar to Ice T's. He also wore a vast amount of rose-gold jewelry that went out of style months ago. A lame nigga, he was considered by most throughout Magic City.

Mr. Todd and Rajay were discussing the details and specifics about what transpired on the Drift Track. Rajay was his underling – his Capo. At twenty-five, Rajay held a fierce temperament. He had a low tolerance for excuses and bitch ass niggas. He was Mr. Todd's hammer and earned his keep by the pint - blood that is.

"You sure, Mr. Todd?" Rajay asked a second time.

He wanted to be sure that the orders he had been given were exactly what he wanted carried out.

"One hunid," he assured.

Cheese knew something such as this would have to be said in person. A phone call wouldn't be suitable and could be very dangerous for them both if overheard by the wrong people. Therefore, Cheese drove out to Hoover, a place where the ballers and major figures resided once they hit the last step on the rich ladder of success. None of his soldiers knew of this place, so Cheese rode out alone, but not before cuffing a .9 milli in his waist.

Fifteen minutes later, he was parked on Mr. Todd's smoothly paved driveway. He quickly noticed that there were three armed guards patrolling the grounds as he walked to the front door. Cheese rang the bell and waited for a response. He was met by Rajay and ushered inside the large estate. Cheese anticipated something going wrong, which is why he had chambered a round in his ratchet before exiting his car.

"Inside," Rajay mouthed sternly, which practically made his assumptions complete about today's visit.

Following orders, Cheese walked inside. He found Mr. Todd relaxed in a large burgundy robe puffing on a thick Cuban cigar. With nothin to fear, Mr. Todd kept his back turned away from the entryway as he gazed out into the serenity of his green acreage.

"Have a seat, Cheese. You know I hate when people stand behind me while I'm seated."

"My bad, Mr. Todd," Cheese nervously apologized.

"So, I hear you let those West Side Mob pussies take my work – is this true?"

"Um…" Cheese uttered, he was stuck and really didn't want to answer.

Truthfully, it wasn't his fault, all he did was put up the buy money for his shipping and then distribute his work to his blocks.

"No 'um's' Cheese, it's yes or no – plain and simple!" His voice calm – too calm for Cheese's taste.

"Yes sir, but I wasn't…"

Boom! Boom! Boom! Boom!

"Fucking coward!" Mr. Todd yelled, as Rajay's gun left a smoking trail from the barrel of his cannon. "Get him out of here. Bury his useless body out back somewhere, and then go drop twenty joints to Benny. Tell him he's in charge from now on, and he'd better handle those Westside pussies accordingly, or he's next!"

Chapter 45

Lock'd Up

"**M**ail call!" a burly, male Correction Officer yelled throughout J-Pod.

The hustle and bustle of the youthful offenders in J-Pod assimilated a normal day in Times Square, N.Y. They wasted no time crowding C.O. Cooper; who was the second shift officer.

"Jones; Williams; Trent; Walker; Alverez; White; Rivers; and Mack, pick up your mail," Cooper blared loudly, calling out the names of the men who had correspondence to pick-up.

All of the names called to pick up their correspondence showed up to the bubble as expected. One of the young men standing in line had grown by two and a half inches. His body had filled out from the thousand plus reps of push-ups and dips he'd been doing on a daily basis. His body now replicated one of a diligent body builder; rips and cuts everywhere.

"You got some mail for me, Coop'?" the young man questioned.

"Yeah, where's your ID?" C.O. Cooper replied.

It was policy to view the inmates ID before handing over any form of correspondence. It was a felony when it came down to issuing out mail of any kind and it went to the wrong person.

"Come on Coop', why we gotta go through dis shit every day? You know who we are. I get mail all week, and you're the one passing it out, so what's the dilly?" he challenged.

"Because, it'll be my ass on the line if y'all of a sudden feel you want to file some frivolous claim on me about missing   mail, or it went to the wrong inmate!" C.O. Cooper replied in his defense.

"Whoa Coop', I ain't in here for ratting, and I don't do claims!" he shot back sternly.

"This is the last time. Here, and you better have your shit together tomorrow Ya'Velle, or no mail – I mean that!" C.O. Cooper warned, he was getting tired of the inmates taking his kindness for a weakness.

"Good look, Coop'!" Yak said, as he walked off with a stack of mail.

In the pile, there were three magazines; F.E.D.S.; AS IS; and the latest edition of Don Diva. His men's health wasn't in there, and he wondered why. He had a yearly subscription to every known magazine currently out. There were two letters amongst the stack, also four colored envelopes, which he knew were his birthday cards.

The birthday cards were from his peeps down in Magic City and one from a chic he met while behind bars. Her name was Secret Shanelle. She was fifteen and very beautiful. *'Prison Pen Pals'* was a great way to meet people, and he was very thankful for them, being he'd finally met a female of his liking. He admired how her cards and letters always came with a vibrant smell from different fragrances. He made sure to put them up in a safe place where he could pull them out and reread whenever he felt the need to hear her voice. Yak knew his birthday card from Secret would depict a vivid sexual scene in its writings, so he planned to cuff it a for late night reading, especially since he had no cellmate at the time. Instead, he decided to read one of the letters that was from Pintz and Germ. It read:

Dear Yak,

What's hood Kiko? I hope this letter finds you in the best   of

J. Alexander

health and mental state. We know it's hard for you inside the "belly-of-the-beast" and you may often feel lonely, but you're not bruh. We're only a call or letter away, so drop a dime or stamp whenever. Oh yeah, Happy birthday bruh! Fifteen now huh – you still got lil' nuts, boyee! Listen, things is going really good down here in Magic City for us, so you already know when you touch-d, we got chu. You ain't gonna believe how caked da fuck up nigga's is now. You know we don't send photo's inside – never know who's watching or duplicating 'em, but here's some xxx photos of some big booty hoe's! Oh I just dropped 5 stacks on your books, too. Call when you run out of bread too Kik! Love You Bruh-One up, "M.H.B's for 'Life"!

Pintz and Germ! 2005.

What Pintz neglected to leave out was the death of Angus, he didn't want him bugging out in there. Unbeknownst to them, he had seen it on C.N.N. just as they had.

"Damn, my peeps really doing them, five stacks. Sheeit...I don't need no more change for the rest of my bid. This'll last a nigga till I touch-d," Yak said as he sat on his bunk contemplating how life down south was for his peoples right now.

He wanted to read his letters from Secret, but it was way too early to be killing his future babies. Next, he glanced over the pictures they'd sent from down South. There were several photos of nude women with their legs spread eagle. The explicit photos were allowed in prison as long as there wasn't any penetration of any kind.

"I don't know, Secret; this bitch is giving you a run for your money," he smiled wondering what Secret's goodies looked and smelled like in the flesh.

Thereafter, he grabbed a tube of Fresh Mint toothpaste and pasted the photos along the wall and under the top bunk, so he'd be able to lie in bed and jerk-off at night. After putting his mail

253

away, he showered then put on a fresh white tee, brown khakis and a fresh pair of uptowns (Air Force ones). Yak stayed fresh to def' on the daily. Having more than enough money to play with, Yak popped more tags than a nigga on the outside. It was very common for him to splurge on commissary weekly as if he needed anything. He had more than enough food and cosmetics for one inmate.

Yak now stood 5'11 and weighed a 163 rock solid. His first year inside taught him the rules of jail. He fought almost every day. There was always some less fortunate cat who wanted some easy wreck, and being new to the Pod, Yak became a fish in shark infested waters. J-Pod was a high-leveled Pod and full of your most hardened criminals on a youthful plane.

He wasn't placed in J-Pod for his crimes. He was placed there for his attitude and trail of violence he participated in during his entry to the facility. There were a few cats from around the way up there, but New Haven, Stamford, and the Bridgeport cats outnumbered Hartford by 60% on average. However, Yak would never back down from a fight – he loved putting in work, something he adopted from Angus.

Yak had befriended a young cat named Trevor. He was two inches shorter than Yak and a shade darker. Trevor had only been in for six months after selling a gun to an undercover vice detective. Even at 15 years old, Trevor was heavy into guns. Tyquan was another youngin' they ran with. He was equal in height with Trevor but far more dangerous. On the streets, Tyquan hung with all the older Gee's, sold drugs and toted guns as if he was a sworn-in Officer of the law. Now that the three of them had formed an allegiance, they terrorized anything or anyone who opposed them. They knew it was Yak's B-day, so they whipped up some Nacho bowls and had some weed on deck. Trevor copped some Pruno (jailhouse wine) from Hicks, the Juice man, and they partied all night long. When it was time to lock down, they all gave each other a One Up (dap) and went their separate

254

ways. Finally, inside his cell, Yak pulled out Secret's card and letter, then grabbed his Fee-Fee (a handmade pussy), Palmer's Lotion and went to work; it was going to be a long tedious night, with several baby killings in the honor of his pen pal Secret.

Chapter 46

Fun n Da Sun

Over the past year, the beef with Pratt City and the West Side Mob was above minimal, and that's because the Feds were out and trying to lock everyone up on conspiracy charges, to the RICO Act, so they minimized war to stay safe. Nevertheless, that did not mean certain plans were not being implemented, because Big-Rod and the Mob had something real nice in the makings for Mr. Todd. At the moment, only South Hampton was moving work. Avenue U had been shut down two months ago when Straw bodied two cats on some stick-up shit. Shit, everybody throughout Magic City knew that Avenue U was the last block to try and hit. Nevertheless, the example was made, and Straw was out of dodge in Arizona hiding out until shit died down. Although Avenue Z produced major stacks, Big-Rod knew he had to step back for a minute, so he redirected all of the traffic to South Hampton. Farm was a little upset with his decision, but he had no other choice but to comply, or he could join the other corpses out back; the graveyard of too many of the West Side Mob's adversaries. In the meantime, Farm went to assist the twins and Big-Rod's nephew in the PJ's to help circulate the flow of money.

$$$$$

Today was Saturday, the weather was hot and sticky, but it would never deter the mounds of fun that went on in George Wood Park. Everyone and their momma would come out to George Wood to get their grill on. Today the Park was flooded with women of all sorts; tall, fat, skinny, thick, pretty, and very ugly, dressed down in skimpy designer wear, looking to catch a baller, a jump-off for the night or even a baby daddy.

This was the perfect time for the city's dope-boys to come out and flaunt their rides, motorcycles, and old school cars. For

256

them, it was a major event; something someone at the entrance could have sold tickets too and gee'd up crazy. You had crews from all over Magic City hovered in small to large packs, doing them. Moreover, even though you might bump into your archenemy, George Wood was off limits; a place of truce. Every crew pledged their name on it, so to say an all-out shoot-out would not transpire today would be correct. But we all know how niggas act when it gets hot out; not to mention with some Surp, Haze, Hydro and beer included into the equation, you could have a small world war on your hands, especially with Straw back out of his crawl space. There was no way he was going to miss the today.

The West Side Mob had a secluded section of the park with four large open tents and two more that were enclosed by strong netting. Big-Rods older brother, Wes, was controlling the four grills, while the twins and Jona set up all the fixin's and condiments. There were large Tupperware bowls full of potato salad, macaroni salad, coleslaw, baked beans, tuna salad, shrimp, deviled eggs, and fresh corn-on-the-cob.

Off to the side, in the shade, was two Rubbermaid trashcans filled with wine coolers and personal bottles of Rose Moet. The other held all top shelf pints of Henny, Remy V.S.O.P, Jamaican Rum and Kahlua for the not so hard women.

Nai and Shai were engaged in small chit-chat, smoking a blunt, while Lil' Tone and Big-Rod were at it with Farm and Straw in a heated game of Spades. They had a stack a man on the game, and Straw called Lil' Tone on some bullshit.

"Nigga you reneged!" he shouted loudly, spit spraying everywhere.

"Fuck you stupid nigga, I ain't renege, you wasted!" Lil' Tone barked back, matching his tone.

Rod was in tears, he knew Lil' Tone played a diamond on the

From Boyz To Men

spade play, but he loved drama, so he let them argue.

"Say something, Rivers, you know what time it is," Farm said.

He caught it too, and he knew Big-Rod did as well. Farm and Straw might couldn't hold their own in Bones (dominoes), but Spades were their thing.

"Man, I ain't saying shit!" Big-Rod said through laughter. "Y'all handle it," he continued laughing nearly tipping out of his chair.

In the midst of their squabbling, Pintz and Germ rode up on two GSXR 1100's, fresh off the lot. Germ had an all-black and chrome one, with matching leather Ed Hardy wear on, complete with boots and goggles. Pintz had a fireball red and chrome one with the matching attire. They pulled right up to the tent, hopped off their new toys, and joined the loud ruckus.

"Wassup y'all?" Germ asked giving them all some dap.

"Shit, these two fools arguing over Lil' Tone's reneging ass," Big-Rod answered, lighting some Dro up.

"Sounds about right, Straw," Pintz butted in. "You good for pulling some bullshit during a game, Lil' Tone."

"Fuck you nigga, what you and your mans tryna do?" Lil' Tone stood up and fanned through a huge knot.

He could care less about spades and was ready to switch the game to Dominoes.

Pintz laughed. "You know you ain't tryna to see us, Lil' Tone, so let it go fo' I take your scrilla," Pintz said through the open slit of his helmet.

"Matter of fact, here   Lil' Tone," Straw tossed him two

258

stacks for him and Big-Rod to get their Domino game on, his thing was Spades, so he was going to take pleasure in seeing them handle the youngsters like children.

"Let's get it poppin' y'all!" Lil' Tone stood up and grabbed the small black box containing the dominoes. "What it's hitting fo'?" tired of losing to them, he questioned ready for some get back.

"You call it, the number's open for all I care," Pintz answered with no emotion for the challenge.

He had a pocket full of money and was ready to add to it.

"Put two stacks up fool, what up?" With that, Lil' Tone began setting the table.

He placed a large cover over the table, so that the bones could move with ease when it came time to mix them around for each player to grab their seven.

"Better yet, let's get it poppin' foreal... Five stacks a head," Germ intervened with authority. "Now what's up? Our shit is on another level, so you can miss us with all dat little bank talk, homey."

Everyone paused and looked at Germ as he held two bundles of cash in his hands ready to rumble.

"I'ma love taking your money champ, let's do it!" Lil' Tone finally answered.

For Big-Rod, it was always a pleasure watching the four of them battle it out in spades, but in the war of Domino's, he and Lil' Tone would claim victor.

Knowing the stakes were high and tempers could flare at any second, the twins came over to caress and cheer the boys on. Shai stood behind Pintz rubbing his shoulders, while Jona did the same for Big-Rod. Nai stood to the side of Germ rolling up some Hydro for them all to enjoy. When you had weed by the pounds, there was no sharing blunts at all. After she completed rolling the sixth one, she passed them out with a personal bottle of Rose Moet, and then stood behind Germ for moral support.

Normally one game would take anywhere's from ten-minutes to thirty, but Germ and Pintz were in assassin mode.

"Copy Coo, nigga!" Pintz shouted, gaining a hundred points, plus the second prize of fifty more points.

They were down three games and were trying to come back like cooked-crack. The score was 300 Lil' Tone's way and 250 Pintz' way with one prize of 25 left.

Slowly Germ and Pintz started to get the edge on the game, earning the last prize and another Copy Coo worth 100 points; they now had 375 for the lead. Big-Rod had control of the bone and locked the game gaining 70 more points. Tthey now had 370 and were down by a mere 5 points.

$$$$$

While the West Side Mob was entertaining themselves, the Pratt City boys were in a football like huddle. Mr. Todd was in the center of the huddle playing quarter back. After issuing out his play selection, his starters quickly took to the field ready for some two-hand-touch action.

The Pratt City boys were high off pills, Remy V.S., and hella weed. Mr. Todd didn't take the notion of sharing time nor space in the large park with Bid-Rod and his mob affiliates. He knew the day would come when Big-Rod would let his guard down, and he planned to capitalize on the opportunity. *"Did he really think the park truce would save his ass forever; if so, he was very wrong,"* he displayed a devilish frown just thinking about the

J. Alexander

Mob's future in hell.

Chapter 47

Fuck uh Truce!

The Domino game was in full swing, and the dead Presidents were switching hands like the NFL draft pick. Lil' Tone was really feeling himself, as well as the effects of the potent Hydro. Whenever Pintz started to play off his emotions, it would cost him and Germ big time, and Lil' Tone knew this, which is why he always taunted him throughout the game.

"Sup lil' nigga, you can't hold your own?" he boasted full of energy.

"Shut da fuck up and play Bones, nigga!" Pintz fired back, his voice loud and boisterous.

Shai gripped his shoulders and told him to relax.

"Fuck dat ma', dis nigga can't play wit' out talking – old soft ass nigga!" Pintz gritted his teeth as he spoke, despising the competitiveness of Lil' Tone.

"Fuck you call me?" Lil' Tone asked. "You know what I was doing when I was seventeen youngin'?" he shouted at a higher octave.

He couldn't stand Pintz' disrespectful mouth. The only reason Lil' Tone had not bucked, was solely due to Big-Rod. Had they not been kinfolk, he would've slumped Pintz a long time ago.

"Sheeit…ain't nothing I ain't done or doing – fuck you think I'm some hoe ass nigga? I bust my gun 24-7-365! Matter of fact, chuchaso! Gimme my points, nigga!"

Pintz went out with the double blank, which gave them a hundred points, plus what points was left on the board.

"See, baby, relax," Shai urged, massaging his broad shoulders.

She knew from previous actions that he was ill-tempered and wouldn't hesitate to bring it to Lil' Tone with the hands or the gun.

"I know babe, I got dis chump. Now, wash those dishes, nig...ga!"

Now it was Pintz who was doing the taunting. Germ and Big-Rod were in tears. Pintz and Lil' Tone always went at it about something. However, it never escalated into anything serious. As Tone washed the Bones for a new play, he noticed a small group of niggas on big-boy scooters approaching at a fast pace. All of them wore large white towels over their heads, so it was very hard to see their faces. Knowing the truce was in effect, he set his attention back to the game. He assumed they were just some youngsters enjoying their day. He would have felt a threat had they been on 1100's and Ducati's, because that's what all the big-boys rode around Magic City.

The scooters did a quick ride by around the area where the The Mob was doing them, and then detoured back the way they came, which really calmed Tone's suspicions. The next hand had begun, and Lil' Tone started his usual taunting. By the time the play got around to Big-Rod, the scooters were on their way back towards them, and because they assumed they were just kids, no one paid them any attention.

As the first scooter closed the distance between them and the West Side Mob, the driver pulled out a .9mm Taurus and aimed it at the Mob; the others following suit.

Plow...! Plow...! Plow...! Plow...!

263

Following Mr. Todd's orders, their shots fired without precision; just flat out dumping, looking to cease all life existing within the Mob.

"Yo, it's a hit!" Big-Rod yelled. "Everybody get down!" he yelled again before being struck in the thigh, causing him to tumble over in his seat. From the ground, he could see Lil' Tone took one in the left shoulder.

Straw quickly took cover behind a tree and began dumping back at the scooters with his .40Cal. dropping one of the shooters. He was amazed to see him get back on his scooter and ride off.

"Fuck!"

Shai was 38-hot at the violation. Her killer instinct made her retrieve the choppa from under the picnic table and without a thought; she began spraying anything not affiliated with the Mob. It didn't matter your age, color, creed or gender, some unlucky soul was going to be the recipient of the choppa's deadly reign.

Brrattt...! Brrattt...! Brrattt...!

Shai hit two of them and happily watched as they crashed into one another. Empting the whole clip, Shai pulled out a nickel-plated Desert Eagle from her Dooney and Burke tote and walked up to the two she dropped and ripped their towels away from their heads.

"Fucking cowards," she spat angrily, and then hot-combed both of their heads with two more shots.

Germ and Pintz was trying to get their .50's out as they lay in the dirt ducking the flying shells. Finally, Germ got his cannon out and started clapping back, but the scooters were now in retreat mode.

"Nah, fuck-boys, dis shit is far from over!" he cursed. "Come on Pintz, it's time to put in some work."

The park was in a world of pandemonium; women and children screaming at high octaves, people running for safety, praying they didn't become a victim to the senseless travesty of war.

As Shai and Nai started to run towards their Corvette, they passed a family laying low on the ground, scared out of their wits.

"Please don't kill us, please don't!" a male, cowering with his hands up begged with much compassion.

"He can't be your man, boo, ol' hoe ass nigga!" Nai spat and continued to their vehicle.

The twins shook their heads in disgust at his cowardice actions, and then fishtailed across the park in pursuit of the four remaining scooters. Being they lost sighting on Pintz and Germ as they hunted the pack of scooters, they were unaware of their destination.

"Nai, you know those were Pratt City Boys back there right, so Mr. Todd had to sanction the hit on us. They broke the park truce, and now it's on!" Shai growled as she drove through Magic City headed towards the Drift Track, home of the PCB's. "Fuck uh truce!"

Chapter 48

You Done Fucked Up Now

When the smoke cleared, Big-Rod and Lil' Tone had been shot, but in minor fashions. Both of their bullets went straight through. They used some hand towels as a source of bandage and tourniquet to slow the loss of blood. When Big-Rod looked around to make sure all of his people were ok, he received the shock of his life. Wes, Big-Rod's oldest brother, had been hit multiple times and was dead by the grills where he'd been preparing food all day. Upon further observation, he was saddened to see that Jona had taken a dome shot to the head and was done.

"What the fuck?" he barked in a state of rage.

Unsure of which body he should cradle and mourn, he chose blood over water and stayed by Wes' side until the bus would arrive to transport his body to the morgue.

"Damn Rod, this is fucked up. I saw those fucking toy bikes approaching, but their faces were covered. Dat fucking Mr. Todd has over stepped his boundaries with dis one," Lil' Tone shouted, which went unheard.

Big-Rod was grieving for another one of his brothers due to the game, however, this one hurt the most. Wes' head was cradled in his little brother's arms for comfort. He wiped away all of the dirt that was caked up and mixed with blood off of Wes' face. While continuing to shake his head in disbelief, not a single tear escaped his ducts; he was all cried out. Having been down this road too many times, not to mention just earlier this year with Marvin, death seemed to no longer affect him.

"Get all the guns out of here before the folks come around," he ordered Lil' Tone.

J. Alexander

"You gonna be straight peeps?" Lil' Tone asked out of concern for his boss.

He in no way wanted to leave him there alone, but he knew Big-Rod was correct. If the authorities hit the scene and found their weapons, they'd be in a cell for centuries and then some.

"I said...get!" Big-Rod shouted loudly, as spit particles spewed from his mouth about.

It was then that Lil' Tone did as told. Lil' Tone sympathized with Big-Rod, but he was right, so he collected all of the guns and kicked rocks in fear of the boys arriving at the scene and them being caught dead-to-rights.

$$$$$

On the other side of town, the Kawasakis' roaring engines caught up to the scooters on a one-way street. Germ and Pintz could tell that they had just pulled up. From a distance, where they couldn't be seen, they observed as the scooters parked in front of a yellowish-brown house. Pintz and Germ cut their boisterous engines off and rode the pavement steadily, so not to be noticed by their enemies.

The four gunmen weren't paying attention to their surroundings. No, they were too busy giggling and high-fiving each other, knowing Mr. Todd would be pleased by their actions back at the park. They were hoping for the bonus he put on the table for the death of his adversaries.

Covertly creeping up to them, Germ and Pintz noticed how young the shooters appeared to be. He and Pintz were maybe two to three years their senior. It didn't matter at this point. Remorse had flown out of the window in George Wood Park.

Since the young shooters were careless and heavily consumed with their achievements from the park, they hadn't noticed when their death, clad in leather bike wear, appeared out of nowhere until it was a too late.

"Aye…" Pintz whispered in their direction.

Hearing the low chatter and crunch of broken glass, one of them turned around only to meet face-to-face with the barrel of Pintz' ratchet.

Boom…!

The first shot from Pintz' cannon blew half the kids jaw clear across the street.

Boom…! Boom…!

Germ's .50 Cal, hit the taller one dead in the eye, making his socket four sizes bigger, his body withered slowly to the ground. Caught off guard, the last gunman took off running for his life, but was immediately cut down by several shots to his back and head, leaving several gaping holes throughout his body that now leaked a mass of blood.

"Come on cuzzo, let's get ghost," Pintz urged.

He noticed Germ was stuck and barely moving.

"Come on cuzzo…we gotta bounce! I hear sirens coming this way!" he shouted this time.

After putting two more shells into the body closest to him did he finally comply, "A'ight."

In their hasty getaway, two police cruisers bent the corner, however, Germ and Pintz made a smooth getaway.

$$$$$

Shai could tell the cats at the Drift Track had no   knowledge

J. Alexander

of what just transpired at George Wood Park, so it was going to be easy for them to maneuver their way down the block undetected.

"Let me out right here, Shai, I got something for their asses!" Nai said deviously.

As told, Shai pulled over and let Nai out of the 'Vette. Nai didn't care if someone recognized her, because she hadn't come on some friendly shit. She was playing off the fact that they would be too busy checking out her goodies instead of the Mac-90 cuffed in her Speedy.

Nai had on some tight shorts that highlighted her elephant's foot and a light colored bikini top, with some pink air max 90's. Her thick thighs were blemish free and sturdy. Before getting any closer, she made sure to hike her shorts up some to entice her prey, while adding a little more passion to her step.

On the stoop of a brick building was a group of Pratt City Boys parlaying. The girls that were keeping them company frowned as Nai walked up and asked if they had any smoke for sale.

"You need something, pretty lady?" Benny asked, beating the others to the punch.

He saw Nai as a potential jump for the night.

"Yeah handsome, y'all got quarters of dat good shit?" Nai asked, and then batted her long eyelashes at him.

"Fo' sure ma', we keep dat good shit 'round Pratt City," he responded arrogantly.

Benny reached into a large zip lock bag full of weed and pulled out a quarter of Hydro.

269

From Boyz To Men

"Here you go, pretty lady. You're not from 'round here, where you be at ma'?"

He let his attraction for her cloud his better judgment as he made an inquiry into her history.

"Nah, I'm not from 'round here," she replied digging into her bag for the money. "I'm West Side Mob – faggots!" she proclaimed, then sprayed the Mac-90 through her purse hitting everything on the porch.

Happy with her foolery, Nai bucked her head and spat on their dead corpses. When the shooting ceased, Shai eased up in the 'Vette, and Nai quickly hopped inside, leaving over six bodies slumped next to and on top of each other in a large pile of blood.

"Nice work, sis," Shai congratulated.

Chapter 49

Stupid Ass, Nigga!

The George Wood Park incident had the whole city in an uproar. Certain truce amongst crews was severed, all on Mr. Todd's account. Two months had gone by, and not one family had come to the green pastures of George Wood Park to grill, play sports, drink, or socialize. They were too afraid some drug-gang would shoot it up again.

Bodies started to pop up all over Magic City and best believe Straw, the twins, Germ and Pintz had a lot to do with it. Big-Rod had sanctioned the hits on every crew they had beef with or had owed the Mob some scrilla. They assumed that the Feds had fled the city, or so they thought, *'because when the Feds watching – you'll never know'*.

Jin-Tow, Big-Rod's connect, had fallen back from serving anyone around Magic City, he was too scared of the repercussions of their senseless murders. Nevertheless, there were always others who loved to take up the slack of supplying dope in the city.

$$$$$

Tonight was baller night – big pimping at its best. The line to get in to *'Bell Bottoms'* was a quarter-mile long and wrapped around the front entrance of the club all the way to the back. *'Bell Bottoms'* was an upscale type of environment where an acquired mixture of people would gather for a night of pleasure. A club where very few fights ensued. You had your Italians, Koreans, Blacks, et cetera, and each group had an abundance of drugs and money to last them a lifetime. Big-Rod had fully recovered from his bullet wound and was out in the club's VIP tonight with Farm right by his side. Lil' Tone had received word that his mother had lost her seven-year battle with cancer, so Big-Rod thought it was only right that he fly out to Arizona to his peep's house to mourn her death. Unfortunately, Straw had been caught up in a hotel with two freak-ass hoes. The manager of the hotel recognized his picture from a recent news clipping and reported his whereabouts to the authorities. A heavily armed tactical team was quickly assembled and raided the hotel where Straw was held up. The door was kicked in, catching him in the midst of a steamy ménage trios, leaving him no time to react to their intrusion. As the many red laser beams outlined his person, the girls began screaming at the top of their lungs.

"Ahhh… What the fuck is going on?" one of them yelled, attempting to cover her nakedness from the police.

Straw thought about going for his gun that sat on the table only inches away, but was halted by the by a harsh warning.

"I don't think that would be a good idea, my friend. I suggest you slowly ease off the bed with your hands up. I promise you there will be a good chance you might just make it to court in the morning," said the man in charge.

Straw saw no way out of his predicament and surrendered without incident. He now faced a rack of 1st degree murders and would more than likely die in an Alabama State Pen!

"Wassup Unc, you gonna holla at ol' boy tonight?" Germ questioned his uncle on his plans to get with Tran, another major dope dealer in Alabama.

"Fo' sure. I need you and Pintz to watch my back for any funny shit, so stay on point ya' heard."

"No doubt, what about the twins?"

"They're in place already," Big-Rod concluded. "If this Tran fuck doesn't speak my type of language, dead his ass!"

J. Alexander

Big-Rod wasn't taking any shorts whatsoever these days. Losing his two brothers had put him in a dark place, an unforgiving place where only murderous acts of retribution were feasible. He had so much respect and juice in Magic City. It was nothing for the Mob to get in any club with their weapons, he just hoped the rest of tonight's patrons had the same respect, for their sakes.

While most of the West Side Mob congregated in VIP, the twins mixed in with the crowd of partygoers taking their perspective places awaiting the unknown to show its true color. They were stunningly dressed and vivacious as always, modeling black-sequenced dresses by Chanel and matching black leather thigh-high boots. Large Marilyn Monroe style Chanel shades with diamonds, shielded their eyes.

"So, sis, how the hell we gonna get next to Mr. Todd and watch Tran at the same time? For one, Mr. Todd knows us. Now, Tran is a different story." Nai said confused.

"Duh…we got on large shades and wigs, not to mention it's not that often we get dressed up like this. Sheeit… Pintz and Germ didn't even recognize us at the bar! And from where we'll be seated, I'll have a direct line on that fuck Tran should he blink wrong." Shai patted her purse letting Nai know that she had her silencer and beam intact tonight.

"I guess you're right, sis, we'll red dot his ass!" Nai agreed.

Seeing their mark from a distance, the twins came out of hiding to set things off. Mr. Todd was a sucker for pretty women and thick thighs, so it was nothing for the twins to join his entourage.

"Hey O.G., you mind if we tag along with you and your crew in V.I.P. tonight?" Shai asked in a sexy tone.

From Boyz To Men

Mr. Todd did a quick once over the twins; his lustful eyes bulging out of their sockets.

With thoughts of sexing them tonight, he said, "Y'all can spend the rest of your natural born lives with me, come on."

Shai immediately clung to Mr. Todd's right arm and Nai to his left. On the opposite side of the club was another V.I.P. that was within eyesight from the one Big-Rod and the Mob was in.

"So, what are y'all drinking tonight?" He asked, ready to get them wasted, hoping that if they were drunk, he would have a better chance at sampling their goodies.

"It's whatever, if you're buying, big-daddy. I've never tried dat Ace of Spades though," Shai cooed.

"How about you, sexy?" he looked directly into Nai's lenses, hoping to get a glimpse of her eyes, but with the dark lighting in the club and her glasses, it was impossible.

"I'd like some Rose Moet if your pockets can stand it," Nai rubbed his thigh, and then whispered something into his ear.

It must have been something to his sexual likings, because it made him blush. He returned a geedy smile and made one of his hired goons fetch several buckets of champagne. In the meantime, they lit up some Dro and popped a couple of E-pills. When he offered them some pills, they had no problems accepting; they were seasoned vets.

$$$$$

Back in V.I.P., Big-Rod and Tran had come to a lucrative agreement, with Tran promising the delivery of a vast amount of kilos per month at a high price. It wasn't what Big-Rod was hoping for, but he really needed some work bad, so he went along

J. Alexander

with it, for the sake of staying paid.

Every so often, Big-Rod would steal a glance over where the Pratt City Boys were chilling. Being the lighting was dim, it was straining to the eye, though he smiled as he noticed the extra baggage lingering around him like two groupies. So, to say things were hood on his end was correct. Tran would live to see another day, but he couldn't say the same for Mr. Todd.

$$$$$

"Hey daddy, give me a shotgun," Shai said in a seductive voice that made Mr. Todd's groin inflate.

He took the blunt stuffed with Dro and blew through its butt and into Shai's mouth.

"Damn…that thing gets wide, ma'. You can swallow a whole one huh?" Mr. Todd said, fantasizing about stuffing his dick down Shai's throat.

"You ain't seen nothin' yet. Why don't we slip off to the restroom, and we'll really show you a good time, Daddy," Shai said seductively.

Mr. Todd's eyes widened with lust. And with every pulse of his penis, his guard withered away. After downing his glass of Henny, he took the blunt from one of his stooges.

"Come on ladies!" he said, happy as a clam.

Following him through the mob of drunken dancers, they ended up in the club's bathroom. On the way in, they passed two women who turned their noses up at the twins, assuming they knew what was about to take place.

Shai responded with a middle finger and said, "Fuck off

275

before you find yourselves in a bad situation."

Inside the bathroom, Mr. Todd chose the larger stall made for handicaps for obvious reasons, and then, took a seat on the toilet. In a seductive manner, Nai walked up to him and hiked her dress above her D-cups; her nipples dark and erect. Shai had no problem doing the same. Only she stuck two fingers inside her warm oven and moaned softly. Mr. Todd's eyes were wide as a deer stuck in a bright light.

"Let Daddy Todd taste your sweet nectar, sexy!" he begged Shai.

Shai did as he asked and stuck the same two fingers in his mouth, it wasn't what he ordered, he wanted to taste her pussy.

"Umm, you're sweet, and you taste like strawberries."

He pulled Shai in closer and dug into her shaved mound tongue first while fingering Nai with rapid strokes. The twins were panting like female dogs in heat. Although they had some wreck to catch, they were going to enjoy some lustrous satisfaction first. After they both climaxed, they selfishly pulled their dresses back down. They heard a repetition of small chatter mixed with giggles coming from outside of the stall, but didn't care who heard the explicit affair.

"Come on Daddy, we wanna show you how we really get down. This cramped bathroom isn't cutting it!" Shai suggested with much sex appeal; a temptation no straight man could resist.

"Lead the way!" he responded, thinking with his little head, of course.

From the bathroom to the parking lot, they fondled each other. And once outside, Shai suggested he jumped into Big-Rod's Nissan Titan pickup truck with them.

"Come on, it'll be fun. We can come back in the morning for your car."

After gladly accepted their offer, Nai took the wheel, while Shai and Mr. Todd played in the backseat. Kissing and ravenous fondling was all that was heard from the front cab. Shai pulled Todd's wrinkled dick out and massaged its length. Shai thought he was well strapped, but he wasn't rocking up, and putting him in her mouth wouldn't be happening in this lifetime.

Driving for several miles, they finally arrived at a massive estate. Mr. Todd was so caught up in the moment, that he had not paid attention to where Nai was driving, nor where he would now become a hostage. Out of the corner of her eye, Shai realized they were home, and it was party time and added a little more ummph in her hand job.

In the peak of her thigh boot laid a sharp 8-inch survival knife. She covertly pulled it out while continuing to jerk him off. She held him by the base of his shaft tightly pulling it out to its full length, the sliced it clean off.

"Ahhhh..." he screamed, and then, bellied over on the gray seating in sheer agony. It wasn't long before he passed out cold.

Chapter 50

Wild Kingdom

Throughout his entire life, Mr. Todd held a tenacious character. He gave nothing away. He expected everything to go accordingly to the way he designed it, or else nothing occurred at all. He was very pigheaded and led a coursed wild life, so the Mob was going to ensure that he died wildlife style. When Mr. Todd finally woke up, he was tied upside, ass naked 4-feet off the ground by a large black hook connected to a mechanical pulley that was attached to a wooden beam 12" thick.

While Big-Rod was still in Bell Bottoms, they beat Mr. Todd's aged body with two-by-fours for over an hour. His limbs were shattered into miniature fractions. All of his ribs were broken, and he sustained a nasty gash across his wrinkled forehead. They definitely took pleasure in beating him into a concussion. Underneath Todd were Big-Rod's wild hogs, and by the sign of the females, they were famished. The trickling of his serum made the hogs anxious, causing them run around the small pit. Shai was getting quite bored as they awaited the Mob's return, so she decided to have some fun.

"Wake up Mr.!" She jerked the hook a few times by pressing the green go button.

"Hummph, ahhh?" he moaned in a state of dementia.

He had no recollection of where or how he had gotten in this predicament. Suddenly, Todd's eyes refocused, and he glanced at the rowdy pigs just below him; his blood quenching their thirst as it continued to trickle downwards.

"Mr. Todd," Shai called out once again, "you won't be needing this will you?"

J. Alexander

She held out his severed penis for him to see for the last time. He struggled to look upward, but when he did, he let out a sickening howl. Shai tossed his sexual tool into the pit of hogs as a festive treat. As the wild life fought over his third leg, the rest of the Mob strolled in the barn.

"Aye...," Germ said with a grotesque look on his face, "Damn y'all got dude strung up butt naked, and y'all cut dudes dick off, too? Y'all are something treacherous. How you gonna cut a niggas dick off?"

"Yeah, dat's some fucked up shit. How he supposed to have children now?" Pintz questioned.

"Sheeit...he ain't gonna need it where he's going," Shai answered, with a huge grin.

"So Todd," Rod now intervened, making sure he showed him nothing but disrespect by not applying the Mr. before his name. "You broke truce; killed my brother and my bottom bitch; not to mention all the bullshit you've done over the years. You got some last words? You know a last wish, rite; a request for a certain meal?" Rod continued to patronize him. "You do realize you've been tried in the West Side Mob court, and the verdict came back in the death penalty?"

"Yeah, fuck you and your faggot ass brother. Yeah, Big-Rod, you ain't known old Wes was a cum-drinking faggot, did you? Well he sucked my dick more times than I can remember; pretty damn good, too!"

Hearing that practically had steam spurting from Big-Rod's ears. The thought of Wes being a fag sickened him to the core. However, he'd already known since kids that Wes was going to suck some dick later on in life, but being Mr. Todd put him on blast in front of his cohorts sent him over the edge.

"I think it's time for chow," Big-Rod concluded. "Lemme

see dat control real quick, Shai."

"Here you go, boss."

Seeing his temperament had sky rocketed, Shai tossed Big-Rod the controller with the quickness.

"See you in hell, pussy!"

He then let Mr. Todd's head linger in the musty snouts of his female hogs. They wasted no time ravaging his head taking huge chunks of flesh and meat off with every bite. You could hear his skull fracture in the hollowed barn-home of the wild. In two days, there would be no sign or trace that Mr. Todd visited the West Side Mob's compound, nor Wild Kingdom.

The Mob walked away in a gangster fashion, happy to have ridded themselves of the Pratt City boss.

Chapter 51

Fame, Fortune and Family History

Three years later, after uncle Marv and Wes' deaths, Big-Rod's temper and chaotic actions seemed to simmer down a bit. He had Pintz and Germ, his real family right there to help him cope with the everyday hardships of their deaths. He had also graduated to a more sophisticated woman. Her name was Fiona – Fiona Wilkins.

Fiona was half Korean and half Black. Her foreign ancestry proved to be extremely dominating in her facial features. She was petite and slender, though her C-cup titties were perky and sizeable enough to stuff in his largemouth during intercourse. Fiona didn't have the biggest nor roundest ass, but every time Rod got the chance, he stuffed his thick rod deep in it in attempts to fluff it up some. As most Asian's, Fiona's eyes were slit like two almonds with aqua-blue centers. Rod often teased her that she had such a large triangular shaped nose that sometimes got in the way of a lustful kiss – overall he was in love.

When Fiona hit the scene, Big-Rod calmed down and concentrated on his empire's fortune and destiny. The Mob now controlled seventy percent of all the drugs in Magic City through Tran. Farm still had control over Avenue Z, which now moved grams of Boy, and boy, did it bump to the point he had to run the strip in shifts it generated so much currency. After Straw's misfortune with the authorities, he received a sentence to die, and now resided on the death row quarters of the Alabama State Penitentiary, thereafter leaving a position wide open for ruling within the Mob. Avenue U had been handed down to the Mob's newest addition, Fat Cat. Fat Cat was just as it sounded. He was fat in the face and had cat features and endured hours of jokes, until one day he split a nigga's shit to the white meat for cutting on him. And since then, he was never teased again. Big-Rod offered him a place within the Mob, and he never looked back.

The sound of a baby cooing joyously in her crib could be

heard over the Graco room monitor. Pintz and Germ were playing NBA Live on the Play Station 3, while blowing some Dro. Germ cursed the selection of weed in the Magic City. He thought Hydro was over-rated and not as potent as Kush or Purple Haze and missed back home intensely.

"Ooh-oooh oo oo!" the joyous sounds persisted from within the crib.

"Man what's got Lil' Paisley all cracked up in there?" Germ asked. "Let me go check on my Lil' niece!" he said and started to the baby's room.

"She's always happy and laughing, cuzzo. I sometimes wonder if my little girl is seeing people – you know like a drop dead Fred?" Pintz laughed, and then followed closely behind Germ.

When they entered the dimly lit room, there she was, just as happy as a person who found out their cancer was in remission, or a not guilty plea was handed down in a murder case.

"What you so happy about, 'Pae?" Uncle Germ said as he reached into the walnut colored crib and picked her up.

She wasn't in the talking stages quite yet, though she was a charismatic smiler.

"Why da baby so happy?" he used his best baby voice when speaking.

"I told you, cuzzo, she's always perked up, like she high and shit," Pintz laughed. "It's probably all that damn weed we smoked during Shai's pregnancy."

"Dat's definitely what it was, because Paisley won't quit smiling," Germ added, tickling her in the tummy.

"Daddy-daddy, I gotta go pee!" Lil' Marvin shouted, holding onto his wee-wee.

"Tell Uncle Pintz to take you, and make sure you wash your hands, too!" Germ said to his three-year-old son.

It was the next best thing that had happened in his life besides meeting Nai. After losing his Pops, Nai sort of took his place; consoled him in a way a mother would have, only it was sexual and explosive. Nai helped Germ get over his loss and gave him life – life with a beautiful son.

"Come on, Lil' nigga, run!" Pintz told Lil' Marvin.

It was only fair Germ named him after his Pops – his tribute to a great upbringing. Tonight the boys – well men, decided to sit home with the kids while the twins handled the business concerning South Hampton, then Shai and Nai were planning on having a girl's night out with Fiona and the rest of their female entourage. The fellas hadn't minded much, because they knew how women such as Shai and Nai could get without any excitement in their lives. You would have thought that their offspring's would've slowed them down some or even changed their choice of profession, but it didn't – they seemed to go much harder now with the obligation of raising children.

The West Side Mob's net was worth a good thirty million right now. Big-Rod was very smart and thorough when venturing into the business world. He made sure to put all of his establishments in his folk's name. They had been natives of Birmingham, Alabama since the 1930's and had enough land, franchised Eateries and fundamental commercial enterprises that when and if audited, the Mob's trail would be untraceable. The Rivers were literally flowing green. They had several businesses all over Magic City; from Barbershops and Salons, to Car Washes, Laundry Mats, Clothing Stores, to Night Clubs, and even a small Real Estate firm. You name it, and the West Side Mob had it. Furthermore, to keep the IRS at bay, he had crooked Politians, Lawyers and Bankers to assist them in their cleaning of their drug money. Over the past three years, they had lost more than enough soldiers and loved ones to violence in Magic City. Escaping the few raids and minor arrests by the local police unscathed, they

283

had yet to go toe to toe with the likes of the DEA, ATF, or FBI. Nevertheless, there was always a blank indictment ready to be handed down for Conspiracy, RICO, and C.C.E., so they played the game cautiously.

The next morning everyone met up at the mansion in Hoover. Just for kicks, Big-Rod was out back shooting his AR-15 at a 30" tree trunk, it was something he did often to relax his mind a bit. Farm and Fat Kat was behind the black grills hoisting a fat pig over the hot coals. The two unwedded couples walked into the backyard where everyone was assembled and set their things down. Shai opened up a Graco Play-Pen set and placed Paisley inside with some of her favorite toys, while Pintz and Germ accompanied their uncle.

"Look at this fool, Germ. Ain't nobody left in Magic City to kill, so he wanna kill ol' Treesy," they all laughed, knowing he was right.

Big-Rod was now like a spoiled little kid with nothing to do except rip the heads off their toys and beg for new ones.

"What you say, lil nuts, you know I love to bust my guns back here. Dis bitch won't die fo' shit. The more I poke holes in her fuckin' ass, she just gets stronger and grows back," Big-Rod responded, and let off some more rounds – Brrattt…!

"That's because you need to pull out a chainsaw, Unc," Pintz added with a golden smile, his gold-teeth gleaming with the sun.

They loved busting their uncle's chops, and would do so any chance given.

"Nah, I don't do saws unless it's on a nigga's body. So, what did y'all wanna talk about fellas?"

Germ had mentioned that he needed to holler at him once they finished up on business later on, however, he was giving them the floor ahead of time, thinking that it would be much more suitable to the outlook on today's get together.

J. Alexander

"Yeah right," Germ answered quickly. "Well for starters, you know Ya'Velle is being released next week, and we want to be at those Iron Gates as soon as he steps out, feel me?"

"I don't see it no other way, neph. Is dat all, because that's nothing we have to discuss. Family sticks by family no matter what state you're in, ya heard."

"Well, we kinda wanna chill back home for a minute. It's been three years since I've seen my hood, and a nigga is a little homesick," Germ said truthfully.

Germ was born and raised on Babcock Street – the South End of Hartford was all he had known, except for the Magic City, and he was desperately seeking that city life again. Big-Rod broke into a hearty chuckle, and then pulled the trigger on his AR-15. The automatic assault rifle spit out twenty casings so fast, you couldn't see anything but shards of wooden chips soaring about the surrounding area.

"Now, Germ, let's put things into its proper perspective," he paused and loaded another extended clip into the rifles belly, "you left Connecticut dead broke, came to Magic City and experienced a luxurious life filled with sultry women. You had a kid of your own, and you now sitting on millions of tax-free dollars. Be honest neph', y'all trying go home and floss, show them mufucka's back home that y'all done came up *'from boys to men'* with long paper! Am I right?" He held a tight face never letting on his true feelings.

"Yeah…I guess dat sums it up Unc – you got me," Germ shrugged, he was busted.

He just hoped that his big Uncle approved of his request. He definitely did not want him to feel like they used him to get rich and was now abandoning him, because that really was not the case at all. No, their plans were bigger than that.

"Well, if that's what y'all really want, I'm not gonna stop you's. Go show them mufucka's how we do it down south in   the
285

Magic City," he said, giving them his blessings to move on as the men they had grown to be.

With that, the three of them shared a group hug and discussed a few things concerning the Mob, and then went to join the others.

Germ's plans to head back North for a minute really put a damper on Big-Rod's scheme. He was getting old and bored. The Rivers' legacy would always continue on, but not from his human creation. He wanted some kids of his own before his sperm count dwindled away to nothing but sour milk. Luckily for him, he now had Fiona, who was expecting his child eight-months from now, and he was ecstatic inside. Therefore, he planned to move away to the Bahamas and was leaving the Mob to his nephews. However, with their sudden news of traveling back home, he had to halt everything he'd foreseen for the future of the Mob until he was sure what and where they'd spend their nights and days.

"Well, we plan to leave on Wednesday night, so we'll have things in place for Ya'velle when he gets out that following Monday," Germ informed him.

He already had a few things he planned to do and get for his little cousin, now that they were millionaires.

"So, what did the twins say about this, 'cause if I know them they're 38-hot!" He knew firsthand how they thought and reacted when they felt threatened.

"They weren't too happy about it, but it is what it is Unc'. I'm taking Lil' Marvin with me since he's much older. Paisley's staying behind with Shai, you know she wasn't having Pintz thousands of miles away with her baby girl all up in bitches faces and shit." They laughed.

"Well, I guess it's settled then," He nodded very proud of his nephews for making the big step and decision on their own. "Just make sure to stay in touch. A fella's getting' old, plus you know y'all bout to have a lil' cousin runnin' 'round here soon, and I might need some help."

Big-Rod cut it short, he was afraid of showing any further emotions, fearing it would make him look weak in their eyes. Inside he was broken up. He was going to miss them immensely, but even he knew this day would come, and it had.

"You know it Unc, and thanks for everything you've done for us!" Germ was grateful and felt indebted to Big-Rod for his mentoring after his pops passed.

"Thanks Unc, I love you," Pintz admitted teary eyed.

He had really made two men – rich men, out of two broke boys! Big-Rod had heard and said enough, so it was time to move on and enjoy the remainder of their stay in Magic City.

"A'ight, come on let's eat!" he said as Lil' Marv attacked his leg with a bear hug.

He wanted to play with the big gun.

"Please, Uncle Rod, please, can I shoot it?"

"Boy…if you don't get your tail back over there with your mama…" Germ threatened playfully smacking him on the butt.

"Yeah neph, you're gonna have your hands full with this lil' fella here," Big-Rod swore.

"Looks that way don't it?"

"Sure does," Big-Rod ended and took one last look at his peoples with admiration. He had witnessed them transforming from boys to men, in a matter of three years. They all laughed and enjoyed the rest of their time together.

www.ingramcontent.com/pod-product-compliance
Lightning Source LLC
Chambersburg PA
CBHW071949040426
42447CB00009B/1293